BIGGER SECRETS

Books by William Poundstone

Big Secrets
The Recursive Universe
Bigger Secrets

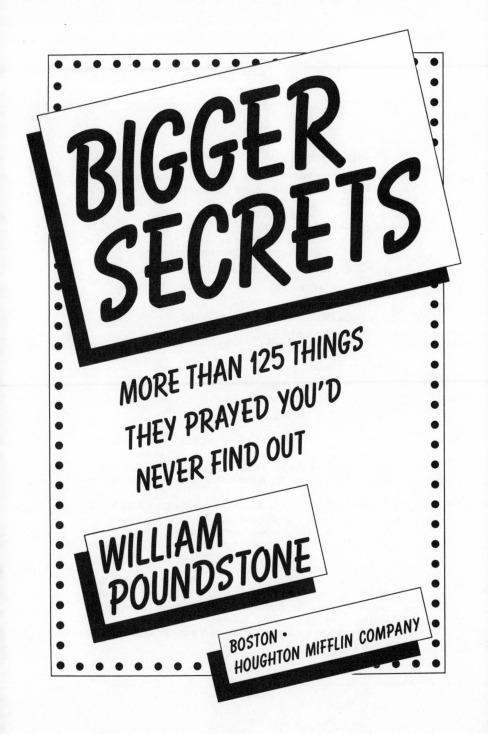

BIGGER SECRETS

MORE THAN 125 THINGS THEY PRAYED YOU'D NEVER FIND OUT

WILLIAM POUNDSTONE

BOSTON · HOUGHTON MIFFLIN COMPANY

Library of Congress Cataloging-in-Publication Data

Poundstone, William.
  Bigger secrets.

  1. United States — Popular culture — History — 20th century — Miscellanea. 2. United States — Social life and customs — 1971–   — Miscellanea. 3. Secrecy — Miscellanea. I. Title.
E169.12.P68   1986   973.91   86-7505
ISBN 0-395-38477-X
ISBN 0-395-45397-6 (pbk.)

Printed in the United States of America

Q 10 9 8 7 6 5 4 3 2 1

The drawings from the Children's Apperception Test on pages 89–95 are copyright 1949 by Leopold Bellak; the two from the CAT Supplement, on pages 94–95, are copyright 1952 by Leopold Bellak. They are printed with the permission of C.P.S., Inc., P.O. Box 83, Larchmont, NY 10538.

The Menninger Word Association Test is copyright © 1986 by The Menninger Foundation. Permission to reproduce this material has been obtained from The Menninger Foundation.

The Dr. Bronner's Pure-Castile-Soap label on page 171 is copyright © 1973 by Soapmaker Dr. E. H. Bronner, Rabbi of All-One-God-Faith, and is reproduced with his permission.

The Porteus maze test on page 97 is reproduced by permission from the *Porteus Maze Extension*, copyright © 1955 by S. D. Porteus, and from *Porteus, the Maze Test and Clinical Psychology*, copyright © 1959 by Stanley D. Porteus. All rights reserved.

The illustrations on pages 188, 204, 205 and 213 were drawn by ANCO/Boston.

To Terry Fonville

ACKNOWLEDGMENTS

A project like this draws on the cooperation of many individuals. Many readers of my earlier book, *Big Secrets: The Uncensored Truth About All Sorts of Stuff You Are Never Supposed to Know* (William Morrow, 1983), wrote with helpful advice for new areas for research. Thanks to David Tilles, Andy Hertzfeld, Dave Ingram, K4TWJ, Steve Silverstein, Chris Isley, Lana Spraker, Mark Tomorsky, Michael J. Hockinson, T. A. Egan, Paul Selwyn, Inas Elattar, Anthony J. Caristi, Ben Redner, Stanley Easton, Keith Tanaka, Arthur S. Merrill, William Emanuel, Sarah Scoville, Mark P. Scully, R. Tucker Abbott, Esther Gross, Barbara Ely, Ty Osborn, Laurie Tucker, Larry Hussar, David Epstein, Mark Rubin, Arthur Stark, Tom Iannucci, Sherry Noone, Earl Black, Nick Ingram, Dan Gutman, Correy Avner, Steve Nam, Kathy Downs, Barry Routh, Dora Enright, Philip Chien, Jean Ulrich, Nadine Rust, Lee Schaub, Robert Ives, Gerard Van der Leun, Luis Estevez, Max Weiss, Barbara Rosenbloom, David and Diane Isaacs, Nicole Tow, William English, Randi Patterson, Ron Udall, Genevieve Blair, Steven Levy, Erik Ivans, Brad Sherman, John Hult, Russell Erwin, Peter Rydell, Scot Morris, Jim Bradbury, Charlie Kadau, Linda Litchfield, Gerry Kroll, Karen Kroll-Zeldin, and Dr. Alfred Haunold.

CONTENTS

FOOD

CLUBS

POWER

COMPETITION

COMMERCE

ILLUSION

ENTERTAINMENT

· 1 ·

OYSTERS ROCKEFELLER

Antoine's is the premier restaurant in the inbred, decadent tradition of New Orleans. The front door is always locked, the shades always drawn. On specified days, service is restricted to certain Mardi Gras krewes. The ambiance is like that of a country club, not necessarily of this decade, and the attitude is as thick as the sauces. The menu is entirely in French; the address is "Nouvelle Orléans."

Antoine's is the home of what is arguably the most jealously guarded secret recipe in the world of gourmet dining. The term "secret recipe" is often used freely and disingenuously. Many a "secret" recipe was published in the food section of the local paper a few years back after an editor asked for it nicely. Let it be said, then, that Antoine's takes the secrecy of its recipe for *huîtres en coquille à la Rockefeller* — Oysters Rockefeller — dead seriously.

Antoine's invented Oysters Rockefeller; as far as it is concerned, the dish has never been prepared outside its kitchens. That does not prevent your ordering an alleged Oysters Rockefeller at virtually any seafood restaurant that takes American Express. Dozens of imitation Oysters Rockefeller recipes are to be found in cookbooks, and many a New Orleans clan claims to have developed an Oysters Rockefeller that is a dead ringer for the original. But these are pirated versions of the one and only true Oysters Rockefeller.

Antoine's Oysters Rockefeller has an ambrosial, vegetal perfume and just enough tanginess to round out the blandness of the oysters. It is a dish of non sequiturs. Fleeting suggestions of cut hay, of licorice, of smoke, enliven the aroma. The genuine Oysters Rockefeller is appealing even to many who are not particularly fond of oysters.

Duck à l'Orange, Eggs Benedict, Beef Wellington — each was the product of a single chef or restaurant at one time. Yet these dishes were soon duplicated faithfully in restaurants worldwide. What makes Oysters Rockefeller different is that even the basic ingredients (other than oysters) are open to conjecture. Oysters on the half shell are topped with a rich emerald-green sauce, broiled, and served on a bed of hot rock salt. Green vegetables predominate in the sauce, but what vegetables are a mystery. The ingredients are so finely minced that they cannot be identified. No single flavor overpowers the others.

Many restaurants imitate Antoine's presentation, up to and including the rock salt. But anyone who has tasted Antoine's Oysters Rockefeller will affirm that imitators' sauces rarely succeed in duplicating anything more than the color of the original. Some aren't even close. For nearly a century, food critics have speculated about Antoine's recipe, and they have reached no consensus. *Bigger Secrets* sneaked a sample of Antoine's Oysters Rockefeller to a food chemist for analysis.

History

Oysters Rockefeller was invented in 1899 by Jules Alciatore (1865–1934), son of the restaurant's namesake. He was motivated by an escargot shortage, for Snails Bourguignonne, a popular dish at Antoine's, required the imported mollusks. Alciatore needed a similar appetizer, using the local oysters, to push as a substitute. At the time, cooked oysters were almost unheard of. Oysters were expected to be served raw, on crushed ice. Alciatore served his cooked oyster creation on a snowbank as synthetic as a shopping mall's Santa's Village — a bed of hot rock salt.

No Rockefeller ever had anything to do with the dish. The Alciatore family just liked to name dishes after people. (In France, patriarch Antoine once whipped up a rare beef dish for Talleyrand. When the minister asked what it was called, Alciatore dubbed it *"Boeuf Robes-pierre"* on the spot because the meat was bloody, like the French Revolution.) Oysters Rockefeller, green as a fresh hundred-dollar bill, was said to be so rich that it was fit for the richest man in the country.

As the reputation of Antoine's increased over the years, it came to be known for the secrecy of its dishes as much as their quality. Recipes were passed from father to son to grandson. Talented New Orleans chefs tended to work their way up to Antoine's and remain there for the rest of their careers. Defections to other restaurants were few. In recent years, the restaurant has been run by Roy F. Guste, Jr., a great-great-grandson of Antoine.

In 1980 Guste dropped a bomb when he published *Antoine's Restaurant Cookbook,* a collection of recipes from Antoine's kitchen. "This book is a statement of my own feelings," he writes in the introduction. "This statement is that there is no value to 'secrets' in cuisine. Most likely in past times there *was* some value in protecting one's own ideas and creations, but today, the value lies in quality of production."

Guste came to the very brink of revealing the secret of Oysters Rockefeller. Then a familial ghost stayed his hand: "Oysters Rockefeller! — the one important recipe that I have not included in this volume. I have not omitted this to retain the secret of the original recipe created by great-grandfather Jules. I quite simply feel that it is not mine to give. It is as though it is part of the physical structure which cannot be removed. . . ."

He concludes: "The original recipe is still a secret that I will not divulge. As many times as I have seen recipes printed in books and articles, I can honestly say that I have never found the original recipe outside of Antoine's. If you care to concoct your version, I would tell you only that the sauce is basically a puree of a number of green vegetables other than spinach. Bonne Chance!"

Guste's exclusion of spinach is a taunt. Spinach is the *main* ingredient in most cookbook recipes for Oysters Rockefeller sauce. A purée of spinach is about the color of Antoine's sauce.

Except for the use of spinach, outside recipes vary considerably. *Redbook* of October 1970 describes a modernistic Oysters Rockefeller using frozen spinach and margarine. *Talk About Good!,* a cookbook published in 1969 by the Junior League of Lafayette, Louisiana, reports rumors that mashed bell peppers and squash are the secret ingredients in some New Orleans restaurants' Oysters Rockefeller. There is a genre of Oysters Rockefeller recipes emphasizing flour or breadcrumbs and cheese, a hearty combination more in the tradition of the Big Mac than Antoine's dish. There are sauces that seem little more than stewed spinach as well as doughy productions you could stuff a turkey with. Some sauces aren't even green. A few recipes use ketchup and end up a mousy brown. Craig Claiborne once apologized, "As far as our extended research is concerned there is no such thing as a 'classic' or definitive recipe for Oysters Rockefeller." Antoine's management cringes at that kind of talk.

Is There Absinthe in Oysters Rockefeller?

Deirdre Stanforth, author of *The New Orleans Restaurant Cookbook,* pried the Oysters Rockefeller recipes from two of Antoine's competitors in the French Quarter. Galatoire's version of Oysters Rockefeller is made from two kinds of celery, spinach, shallots, anise, parsley, butter, Lea & Perrins sauce, absinthe, salt, pepper, cayenne pepper, and oysters. The Commander's Palace uses a recipe calling for bacon, garlic, butter, shallots, spinach, parsley, celery salt, cayenne pepper, oyster liquid, absinthe, salt, breadcrumbs, and oysters.

Absinthe? Absinthe is illegal. It is a 136-proof apéritif invented in Switzerland and once popular in France. Absinthe was green and smelled like licorice. It was popular in New Orleans — more so there than in the rest of the United States — and was also a favorite of John D. Rockefeller's. One of absinthe's ingredients, wormwood, was found to be toxic, and in 1916 it was outlawed.

Absinthe is or was in Antoine's recipe. In another cookbook, *Restaurants of New Orleans,* Guste states that the Oysters Rockefeller recipe had eighteen ingredients, and one of them was (past tense) absinthe. Guste leaves you hanging as to whether it is still an ingredient.

It is legal to sell apéritifs very similar to absinthe that do not contain wormwood. Herbsaint, produced by the Legendre Company of New Orleans, is a yellow, 90-proof anise-flavored liquor that is widely used as a substitute for absinthe in local mixed drinks and recipes. The recipe for the Sauzerac cocktail in Guste's *Antoine's Restaurant Cookbook* uses Herbsaint in place of the traditional absinthe.

Eighteen Ingredients

You'd think that a recipe that's been around almost a century would leak out. Between chefs, waiters, busboys, dishwashers, and the people who deliver the produce, there would have been dozens of people who knew the recipe or were in a good position to learn it. These people would have spouses, children, and friends to whom they might reveal the secret — especially in New Orleans, where food is the main topic of conversation anyway.

I took out a display ad offering a reward for the "secret recipe for Oysters Rockefeller" in the *New Orleans Times-Picayune*. About twenty people responded. Practically all the recipes called for spinach and were clearly taken from magazines or cookbooks.

Only one respondent claimed any direct connection to Antoine's. As the hostess of a daily cooking show in the 1950s, she had managed to get the recipe for Oysters Bienville out of Antoine's chef. Oysters Bienville is a different dish, with a cheese topping. According to this woman, "The employees were threatened with death, worse if they gave out the recipe." But Antoine's Oysters Bienville recipe was revealed in the 1980 cookbook.

I also searched for old newspaper and magazine articles about Antoine's to see if anyone, at any time in the dish's long history, might have coaxed some clues out of the Antoine's staff. The closest thing to a revelation was in a recipe booklet long out of print. In 1948 proprietor Roy Alciatore — he's the great-uncle of Roy F. Guste, Jr. — consented to reveal the recipes for ten dishes. These appeared in *Recipes from Antoine's Kitchen*, a "service booklet" edited by Clementine Paddleford and published by *This Week*, a syndicated newspaper magazine. "Next to going to heaven to dine on ambrosia is going to New Orleans to eat at Antoine's," the booklet smarms. "Nowhere else in the world is eating so surrounded by mystery, by legend; restaurant of a thousand dishes and each a guarded secret — that is, until now."

Alciatore chose ten of Antoine's recipes that he believed might be duplicated by the average American housewife. The introduction gently chides envious 1940s homemakers for their culinary ambitions: "A majority of the Antoine's specialties require a ritual too involved to be practical for home use. Home cooks lack the necessary seasonings, stock pots and sauces to produce the masterpieces. 'How many women would want to make Sauce Marchand de Vin?' Mr. Alciatore asked. 'Not one,' we agreed when we heard the step-by-step procedure that takes a full day. . . ."

Alciatore did not divulge the recipe for Oysters Rockefeller, of course. The booklet includes only a spinach-based imitation recipe "for the fun you will have in trying to imitate a dish kept secret since the 1890's." More interesting are some tantalizing hints about the real recipe. The booklet's editor had dinner at Antoine's and, reading between the lines, tried to worm the recipe out of Alciatore. She didn't get it. But she did get Alciatore to reveal a few ingredients that his great-nephew doesn't talk about.

"Mr. Jules added to the dish's prestige by making a mystery of its recipe, knowing the world loves a secret it can never guess," says the booklet. "This much is told: the sauce is made with 18 ingredients, including chopped celery, minced shallots, minced fresh chervil, minced fresh tarragon leaves, crumbs of dry bread, a dash of Tabasco, a dash of herbsaint — in lieu of the illegal absinthe. . . . The ingredients are pounded together in a mortar for blending. Then the mixture is forced through a sieve and one tablespoonful placed on each pair of oysters, resting two by two à la half shell, cradled in their own juices, the shells bedded on rock salt, which is filled into pie tins, six half shells for each serving."

Welcome to Nouvelle Orléans

Antoine's maître d's do not have enlightened views about dress codes. When I showed up at Antoine's for a seven o'clock dinner reservation, a casually dressed couple was at the door, puzzling why it was locked. "They must lock the door when they're full," the man said. In a few moments a maître d' opened the door and let me in. He did not so much as make eye contact with the man in the sports shirt, clearly a talent refined by years of practice. Inside, the restaurant was almost empty.

You may eat in any of fourteen dining rooms, each decorated according to a different theme. There is the Mystery Room, the Dungeon Room, the Rex Room, the 1840 Room, and the Proteus Room. (The Mystery Room is lined with portraits of U.S. presidents who dined there. The mystery, you find, is that one of the paintings disappeared "mysteriously." In other words, someone stole a picture.) Beneath it all is Antoine's cavernous wine cellar, stocked with 25,000 bottles. That's enough to throw a wine-tasting party for the entire population of Monaco and have plenty of leftovers.

I dined in the main dining room. I suspect it must be Siberia to the habitués of the Rex Room, but it is a large, tasteful, dimly lighted dining area. The walls are covered with autographed pictures of old celebrities, the inscriptions addressed to assorted patriarchs of the Alciatore dynasty.

Baroque ritual accompanies some dishes. Periodically the lights dim as in a prison movie. This means someone has ordered Crêpes Suzettes or Café Brûlot and the waiter is about to ignite it. "What could be more sublime than to taste the delights of heaven while beholding the terrors of hell?" the Antoine's people quote John Ringling as having said of one incendiary dish.

At one time Antoine's labeled each order of Oysters Rockefeller with a card bearing a serial number. They got this idea from Paris's Tour d'Argent, which numbers its pressed duck. Perhaps this frill has been discontinued; my order was not numbered. In the 1980 cookbook, Guste estimated that they had served over 3½ million orders of Oysters Rockefeller.

At some restaurants, Oysters Rockefeller is a meal in itself. Antoine's portions more befit the dish's billing as an appetizer. Six smallish oysters, the shells selected to be of approximately the same size and shape, are arranged on a plate of heated rock salt.

The sauce is a green slurry flecked with darker green. Broiling produces a delicate crust. It is pleasantly rich but not greasy. The oyster taste is prominent in the sauce. There are no visible stems or leaves, no crouton-sized breadcrumbs.

In aroma and flavor, one ingredient stands out: parsley. There is also a hot taste, as in chili pepper.

While no waiters were looking, I spooned a sample of the Oysters Rockefeller sauce into an emply plastic-lined cigarette case. This was taken to Associated Analytical Laboratories, a New York City firm specializing in food analysis.

I asked the lab to do a qualitative analysis. They were to determine, as well as possible, what ingredients were in the sauce. If they could get an idea of the proportions, so much the better. I prepared a list of possible ingredients from other recipes to give the lab an idea of what might be present.

This sort of analysis is done by painstakingly separating the sauce into its respective components under a microscope. The fragments of vegetables, herbs, and spices can then be identified by trained individuals. I was advised that some of the liquid ingredients that might be in the recipe — Herbsaint or Tabasco sauce, for instance — would probably not be identifiable, for these volatile ingredients evaporate in cooking.

Lab Results

The findings were surprising. None of Antoine's imitators was even close. Associated Analytical's chemists identified eleven ingredients in the sample. They were (in rough order of decreasing amounts) olive oil, parsley, capers, green onions, lemon juice, chili pepper, celery (green), salt, black pepper, tarragon, and smoked oyster stock. True to Guste's word, the lab found no spinach.

Among the vegetable and herb ingredients, the capers and tarragon were the big surprises; as far as I can tell, no one had suspected they were ingredients in Oysters Rockefeller. The analysis was exacting enough to tell that the capers had been pickled in vinegar — the kind you buy in a jar in a gourmet food store.

The lab report states that the "green onions" may be chives. Chives are the same genus as onions and are almost impossible to distinguish when finely minced. But we can all but rule out chives. Roy Alciatore conceded that scallions were an ingredient in 1948, and "scallion" is synonymous with "green onion." The lab must have found Alciatore's scallions.

The olive oil is another surprise. Every recipe I have seen assumes that butter or margarine is the fat. I found just one recipe that used lemon juice. Notably absent from the lab findings were cheese, cream, and flour, sometime ingredients of pirated recipes.

If *Antoine's Restaurant Cookbook* is any indication, the people at Antoine's have a white pepper fixation. Virtually all the recipes calling for pepper in the cookbook insist on white pepper. Black pepper and white pepper come from the same plant. The skins are removed from the white pepper and the berries are picked a little later. The main difference is that white pepper is slightly milder. (The ordinary ground pepper that you buy in a supermarket is usually a blend of black and white pepper.) I asked Associated Analytical if the "black pepper" might actually be white. They said it might be. What they found were fragments of peppercorns from the regular *Piper nigrum* pepper plant. That finding is consistent with either black or white pepper or a mixture thereof. But based on the circumstantial evidence of the cookbook, I suspect that they use white pepper only in Oysters Rockefeller.

Similarly, the chemists said their finding of "chili pepper" was consistent with finely minced chili pepper pods, or cayenne pepper, the commercial powdered seasoning made from one type of chili pepper. Since cayenne pepper is used quite liberally in Antoine's published recipes, I suspect that the chili pepper found was cayenne.

Three of the ingredients mentioned in the 1948 booklet (celery, shallots/green onions, and tarragon) were found. Roy Alciatore did not mention parsley and capers, which seem to be the most important vegetable ingredients.

The booklet mentions four ingredients that were not found, though. Herbsaint and Tabasco sauce are volatile and would probably not be detected in this sort of analysis. Only "a dash" of each is used, anyway, according to the booklet. Chervil and breadcrumbs were not found, either. But the sample supplied was small — about a tablespoon. If the sauce was not mixed perfectly, a particular dab might lack some minor ingredients. On the strength of Alciatore's admission, I'm inclined to think that small amounts of chervil, breadcrumbs, Tabasco sauce, and Herbsaint must be in the official recipe even though they weren't detected in the analysis.

Adding those four ingredients to the eleven detected gives fifteen. The oysters make sixteen. For all I know, they may count the rock salt and shells as ingredients, too. That just about accounts for the claimed eighteen ingredients.

Oyster stock is itself a composite. Antoine's may number the stock ingredients in the eighteen. (Of course, Tabasco sauce, Herbsaint, and capers in vinegar are composites, too. But they're not made on the premises, as the oyster stock surely is.) *Antoine's Restaurant Cookbook* gives recipes for fish, chicken, and beef stocks. All contain meat, poultry, or fish scraps, water, onions (regular white), celery, parsley, salt, and bay leaves.

It therefore seems safe to assume that Antoine's oyster stock is made from oysters, water, onions, celery, parsley, salt, and bay leaves. Some of these have already been counted as ingredients, but the water, regular onions, and bay leaves are new. If you prefer, scratch the water, but count the rock salt. That gives you a list of exactly eighteen ingredients: oysters, rock salt, olive oil, parsley, capers, green onions, lemon juice, cayenne pepper, celery, salt, white pepper, tarragon, white onions, bay leaves, chervil, breadcrumbs, Tabasco sauce, and Herbsaint. I wouldn't swear that that's their list of eighteen right on the nose, but it can't be far off.

A lab report does not give cooking methods. The description in *Recipes from Antoine's Kitchen* and the other baked oyster recipes in *Antoine's Restaurant Cookbook* fill in most of the details, though. Even the cooking temperature can be guessed with confidence: Antoine's recipes for Oysters Bienville, Oysters Thermidor, and Oysters Bonne Femme *all* prescribe an oven temperature of 400° F. Here's an educated guess:

OYSTERS ROCKEFELLER

INGREDIENTS

Oysters: Antoine's zealously preserved secret recipe starts with Gulf oysters, detached and served on the more concave half shell.

Olive Oil: Olive oil — not butter, as most thought — is the basis of Oysters Rockefeller's mellow richness.

Parsley: The predominant green ingredient. Nearly all Antoine's imitators are wrong: there is no spinach in Oysters Rockefeller.

Capers: A secret ingredient no one guessed. It has a smoldering olive-nutty flavor, with an aftertaste strangely like steak. Capers are the green flower buds of a Mediterranean shrub, plucked in the morning and kept in a dark place for several hours before being pickled in vinegar. Our lab analysis even detected the vinegar.

Green Onions: A.k.a. scallions. Many restaurants trying to duplicate the recipe correctly guessed this ingredient.

Lemon Juice: Piquant element to cut the high fat content.

Cayenne Pepper: Adds zest to oysters.

Celery: Minced, crushed in a mortar, and pressed through a sieve to prevent telltale strings.

Salt.

White Pepper: Looks less like a flyspeck in light-colored foods. Antoine's has a white pepper fetish, and probably uses it exclusively.

Tarragon: A licorice-camphor flavor with grassy notes; ingredient in tartar and béarnaise sauces, *nouvelle cuisine* vinegars. The unexpected licorice nuance is echoed in the chervil and Herbsaint.

Oyster Stock: The Creole tradition eschews water in favor of stocks for cooking. Our lab analysis found it smoked. If it is similar to Antoine's fish stock, it is seasoned with onions, celery, bay leaves, parsley, and salt.

Chervil: The "gourmet's parsley," revealed as an ingredient in a 1948 booklet, has a flowery aroma with anise-pepper zest. Used in French *fines herbes* mixes. This and the following are minor ingredients.

Breadcrumbs: Revealed as an ingredient by Roy Alciatore, breadcrumbs are used sparingly; they were not found in our lab analysis.

Tabasco Sauce: A Cajun table condiment capable of raising blisters on a cow's hide. "I have watched it being made," said James Beard, "so I know there are no secret ingredients, simply Tabasco peppers, salt, and good vinegar." It's brewed by the McIlhenny Company of New Iberia, Louisiana, and aged three years in white oak.

Herbsaint: A depraved yellow apéritif made only in New Orleans; 90-proof, alleged aphrodisiac. Oysters Rockefeller contained absinthe until it was outlawed in 1916 for causing shocking public behavior.

Rock Salt: Trompe l'oeil backdrop for oysters. Supposed to look like crushed ice while conserving oven heat (400° F).

Shuck 4 dozen oysters (6 per serving). Leave the oysters in the more concave half shells. Prepare oyster stock by boiling the oyster liquid, scraps, and discarded shells with ½ onion and ½ stalk celery minced, a small sprig of parsley, and a bay leaf in 2 cups water salted to taste for four hours. Skim periodically; strain when done.

Mince 2 large bunches parsley, 1/2 cup capers, 1 bunch green onions, 1/2 bunch celery, 1 bunch tarragon, and a few chervil leaves finely. Sauté lightly in olive oil (about 1/2 cup). Do not overcook; the mixture should be bright green. Place the greens and oil in a mortar and crush with a pestle. Add 1/2 cup of oyster stock and lemon juice, salt, cayenne and white pepper, breadcrumbs, Tabasco sauce, and Herbsaint to taste. Mix well; discard excess liquid. Strain the mixture through a sieve, taking care to avoid celery strings in the strained sauce. Arrange the oysters on the half shell in metal pie pans filled with coarse rock salt, 6 oysters to the pan. Do not let rock salt get into the oyster shells. Spoon a tablespoon of sauce over each oyster.

Cook about ten minutes at 400° F, until the oysters and sauce are hot. Serve immediately. Yields 8 servings.

· 2 ·

JUNK FOOD TRASHED

*T*here's no free lunch in the food business. Convenience food companies seem all sweetness and light, but the minute you turn your back, they're selling hot dogs in packs of ten and buns in packs of eight. Simple, wholesome ingredients just aren't a paying proposition for mass-produced food. Not when companies can make chemical gunk taste so good. Stop eating and read this unless you *want* to end up like those people in the supermarket with carts full of doughnuts and upper arms bigger than Arnold Schwarzenegger's. Here are the chemical-laden secret formulas for some of America's most loved-hated foods.

Is There Suet in Twinkies?

Hostess Twinkies are the creation of James A. Dewar, who scarfed three a day and lived to be eighty-eight. "Twinkies was about the best darn-tootin' idea I ever had," he said. It makes you wonder about his bad ideas. Dewar noticed that bakers sold a lot of shortcake during strawberry season but couldn't give it away the rest of the year. He figured that stuffing some sort of quasi-cream filling in the shortcake would make it palatable even without fruit. The first Twinkies were "creamed up" in Chicago in 1930 and were successful from day one.

"Dewar says its formula is a little bit of a secret," reported the 1976 edition of the *Snack Food Year Book*. "He always refers to it as a cream*ed* filling, emphasizing the need to add the 'ed.' " Get the hint? It isn't fine Devonshire cream in there.

Contrary to popular belief, Twinkies do not have the shelf life of gravel. The modern Twinkie is baked in 190-foot-long ovens operating around the clock. The Continental Baking Company forecasts sales and delivers only a few days' supply. (Demand is remarkably stable. If you've got a Twinkies monkey on your back, he's on a short leash.) Twinkies are discarded if they don't sell in four days.

Food labeling laws allow a certain amount of equivocation. The Twinkies label reads: "partially hydrogenated vegetable and/or animal shortening (contains one or more of the following: soybean oil, cottonseed oil, palm oil, beef fat, lard)." *Beef fat*? Well, they don't really concede that beef fat is in there. They just bury it in a list of *possible* ingredients.

I contacted Continental Baking and asked if beef fat and lard are used. D. F. Owen, Ph.D., Continental's director of Nutrition & Consumer Affairs, said only that the label's parenthetical list "describes those shortenings that we might use at any particular time. Their selection is based on availability and price." I think that means he's admitting that they use beef fat in Twinkies, but only if they can't find something cheaper.

The *Food Products Formulary,* the bible of the junk food business, gives a formula for Twinkies-like cream filling. Basically, it is almost half sugar and another 30% or so is shortening. Much or all of the sugar is in the form of corn or sucrose syrup. You might count air as an ingredient, too, since they whip it up. The label's unspecified "natural and artificial flavors" surely include vanilla and probably a synthetic butter flavor as well.

TWINKIES CREAMED FILLING

INGREDIENTS

Air: Whipped into the white stuff to make it frothy.

Sugar and Corn Syrup: The filling is about 42% sugar by dry weight. Needed for quick energy, diminished-capacity legal defenses, etc.

Hydrogenated Vegetable Oil: On a scale of nutrition, this rates some-where between Teflon and an air embolism. Twinkies' chemists bubble hydrogen through vegetable oil, turning it into a soaplike solid.

Lard: The label hints at "vegetable and/or animal" shortening. Twinkies are not kosher.

Beef Fat: Major gross-out ingredient. The fats used vary with commodity prices. Total shortening content: about 28%.

Skim Milk: A modest source of protein. About 7%, measured as weight of milk solids per total ingredient weight. No one at Continental Baking tries to promote Twinkies as a health food (they save that talk for Wonder Bread), but one executive claimed that a Los Angeles man lived for seven years on a diet of Twinkies and Cutty Sark. This isn't recommended.

Salt: About 0.25%.

Vanilla: Gooey nuance in the Twinkies bouquet. Continental Baking experimented with banana- and strawberry-flavored fillings, but they never approached the popularity of plain vanilla.

Butter Flavoring: Needed to make beef suet taste like whipped cream straight from the can. Probably synthetic.

Lecithin: In everything and probably a Commie plot. They *say* it's an emulsifier.

White Castle Hamburgers

White Castle burgers are a recurrent motif in bulimic tall tales. High school kids like to bet on who can eat the most without throwing up. Twenty-five is good. One Larry Iorizzo, who weighed 410 pounds, had fifty White Castle burgers in a single meal. Yet a lot of people are ready to believe that there are unsavory additives in White Castle hamburg-ers, hence the nickname "roachburger." Some outlets post a defensive sign saying that the burgers are made from "only 100% all-American beef." This would rule out your basic wormburger stories, but would seem to allow just about any part of the cow's anatomy they cared to grind up and fry. Liver is often mentioned as a possible ingredient.

Not that the burger's unusual taste is all bad. Some say White Castle burgers are an acquired taste, like fine Scotch. People who move from White Castle's home turf (the Midwest east to Long Island)

17

have a propensity for ordering massive amounts of the frozen burgers by air.

Each White Castle restaurant is a tacky castle simulacrum that looks like it belongs on a miniature golf course. They are said to be popular with winos. The chain was founded circa 1921, a good three decades before McDonald's. The very concept of ground meat was suspect back then, and the company had to combat stories of unwholesome additives from its inception.

A White Castle burger is more of a canapé than a sandwich meal. It is dwarfed by the plain old hamburger at McDonald's. Both bun and patty are square. A three-by-three block of nine postage stamps just covers the patty (I tried it). White Castle's "Surf and Turf" is the regular hamburger with a fish stick on it.

The burgers are greasier than most, and there is a oniony note to the flavor. The texture of the burgers is quite unlike that found anywhere else: there is no "chew" to them, and the burger almost melts into the bread. When you try to peel it apart, part of the bread sticks to the burger and part of the burger sticks to the bread. I scraped a few patties from the buns and found a few small bits of grilled onion underneath.

Gloria Pitzer of St. Clair, Michigan, publisher of a newsletter called *The Secret Recipe Report,* tried to match the White Castle recipe in 1981. Pitzer specializes in devising recipes that duplicate junk foods. She works by trial and error in her own kitchen and does not claim any special knowledge of the actual recipes. Her recipe for near–White Castle burgers uses onion powder in the patties and requires that you fry freshly chopped onion in the grease to be used for the hamburgers. The recipe calls for ground beef liver: one part liver to four parts ground round. She allows liverwurst as a substitution.

In response to my inquiry, however, the White Castle company firmly denied that beef liver is used. It's just regular beef, they insisted.

The real secret, as extorted from White Castle employees, is in the cooking method. A mixture of water and dehydrated onion flakes is ladled onto a griddle. The meat patties — supplied by the corporation and containing 25% to 27% fat — are slapped onto the griddle to *boil* in this onion soup. The buns go on top of the patties. Exactly five holes punched in the patties allow steam to heat the buns.

How Do They Salt Peanuts in the Shell?

Ballpark peanuts, the kind salted in the shell, are one of the great family secrets of the food business. At one point, it was claimed that only one person knew exactly how it was done. However, the U.S. Department of Agriculture and allied agencies are in the business of promoting peanuts generally. The Georgia Experiment Station has tried to surmise the secret and has come up with a successful method.

It's like pressure cooking in reverse and is done with detergent and a vacuum. Sort the peanuts, discarding those with cracks. Immerse in a warm (100° F) detergent solution. The Georgia Experiment Station recommends 1.3 ounces of Calgon water softener per gallon. Stir for five minutes and rinse with water.

Then soak the peanuts in 100° F brine (3 pounds salt per gallon of water) under a vacuum of 15–20 inches. Release the vacuum suddenly. Repeat this soak-and-release process several times. The more times the vacuum is applied and released, the more salt seeps into the peanuts.

After that, rinse the nuts in plain water to remove salt from the outside of the shells. Centrifuge to drain off water and air dry at about 120° F — the same steps, basically, as laundry spin and dry cycles. There is but a trace of Calgon in properly prepared nuts.

Counterfeit Pimientos

Those red things in olives aren't pimientos. They're red mush.

Stuffing *real* pimientos into olives is about as lucrative as bending wire into paper clips at Bob and Ray's Great Lakes Paper Clip Factory. The stuffer must extract the pit, whittle a plug of pimiento (a sweet red bell pepper) exactly to size, and insert it gingerly. Tear the olive, and it goes into the reject bin. Successful attempts are packed in a glass jar, pimiento facing outward. It's just too hard to do, and it's not worth it. In 1985 the *Wall Street Journal* reported, incredibly, that a typical pimiento stuffer averages *eighteen* olives an hour and has an average income of about $100 a month. The few remaining genuine pimiento stuffers are in Portugal.

The rest of the world's olives are stuffed by machines that can throughput 1,800 olives an hour. The problem is, no one has been able to design a machine that will stuff real pimiento strips into olives. So it's good-bye pimientos, hello pimientoids. About 97% of the olives now sold sport ersatz pimientos.

I examined the "pimientos" in some popular brands of olives and found them all to be fakes. The label on Krasdale's olives says in fine print: "Stuffed with minced pimientos." Actually, the synthetic pimientos are reported to be made by mixing minced pimiento with an undisclosed white powder.

Each fake pimiento is a rectangular translucent strip folded in the middle so that it fits, doubled over, into the olive cavity. Under a magnifying glass, it appears almost like a pale red jelly containing tiny flecks of darker red. The latter, apparently, are the bits of real pimiento.

Extracted "pimientos" taste like pasta — or like what you'd imagine pasta to taste like if it was cooked in olive brine.

Oreos

Oreos are far and away the best-selling cookie in the world. Nabisco whips up enough Oreo filling to fill a small football stadium each year. Both Oreo and Sunshine Biscuits' Hydrox have their own secret recipes, which they guard mostly from each other; Hydrox is the older brand. Old ads boasted that "Hydrox is totally unlike any other bakery product made in America or Europe" and "The recipe originated with us and it is guarded like a priceless treasure." Nabisco lost little time in coming up with a very similar cookie. Some find Oreos a little sweeter.

There is an almost universal conviction that Crisco is the filling in Oreos, or at least the main ingredient. The thought of sugared Crisco is enough to kill most people's appetites, and perhaps for that reason Nabisco has preferred to keep the matter of the filling ingredients quiet. In 1975 *Esquire* magazine sent a journalist to an Oreo factory, and he was barred from the floor where they make the white stuff.

Nabisco obviously does not buy Crisco, a Procter & Gamble consumer product, for use in its cookies. It might use a shortening *like*

Crisco. Crisco is not lard. It is a mixture of soybean and palm oil that is hydrogenated to form a white solid. A few mono- and diglycerides are thrown in as well.

Oreos' ingredient panel resorts to the same multiple-choice doubletalk as the Twinkies label. Nabisco claims "animal and/or vegetable shortening" on some Oreo packages and "vegetable and animal shortening" on others. This is followed by a parenthetical list that includes lard but not beef fat.

As you might expect, the Oreo filling has been thoroughly analyzed by food chemists. An essay on "Sandwich creme fillings" in Volume 2 of the *Food Products Formulary* pronounces these fillings to be a sugar-shortening mixture. "Almost all available forms of shortening, including lard, are being used,' the *Formulary* says, with hydrogenated coconut oil being most popular.

According to the *Formulary*, "sandwich creme" is compounded of sugar, shortening, vanillin, salt, and lecithin. Twinkies' filling and Oreos' middle have pretty much the same ingredients and differ mainly in the proportions. There is water in Twinkies' filling: sugar syrup is used, whereas dry sugar is used in Oreos. Twinkies' filling has more shortening, less sugar. The sugar to fat ratio (based on dry weight of sugar) is about 1.55 to 1 in Twinkies' filling, about 2.38 to 1 in Oreos' middle.

The Hydrox creme — universally preferred by anyone who is really into this kind of stuff — is wetter. Hydroxes are made with vegetable shortening only.

The rococo surface design of Oreos is the work of Nabisco's William A. Turnier. The pattern includes 12 four-petaled flowers, the Oreo name in a spacey logo, 12 arcs and dots, 90 radial ticks on the outside, and assorted curlicues. As it happens, 90 does not divide into 12 evenly; there are 7½ ticks for each flower or arc. So what is the numerological significance of 90? No one presently at Nabisco claims to know. Hydroxes have 72 ticks. Turnier, whose oeuvre also includes Animal Crackers, was given the original Oreo die, encased in Lucite, upon his retirement in 1973.

Mystic Mints

Oreos are the secret ingredient in another cookie. Nabisco's Mystic Mint Sandwich Cookies are mint-flavored and chocolate-covered — rather, they have a "rich cocoa coating," which is Nabisco's way of telling you that some federal spoilsport wouldn't let them call it chocolate. Mystic Mints cost more than Oreos — about $1.99 for 11.5 ounces versus $1.89 for a pound of Oreos. The label pictures them being served on fine china. Two Mystic Mint cookies, one of them demurely bitten into, rest on a saucer next to a cup of coffee. You wouldn't serve Oreos on the good china, would you?

But if you lick the chocolate coating off a Mystic Mint, you find an Oreo, a standard-issue Oreo, complete with the Oreo name and Turnier design. Mystic Mints are retread Oreos. Somewhere the Oreo flow chart forks, they dip a few Oreos in mint-flavored chocolate, mark them up 50%, and sell them as Mystic Mints. The chocolate coating is just thick enough to glaze the Oreo insignia.

Once I was put on to this, I began to look askance at other Nabisco products. They make something called Chit Chat Bars, which are described as a "fudge cream wafer." Lick the coating off it, and you find what appears to be a Nabisco Sugar Wafer. This is the cookie that has a Styrofoam texture with a stamped motif of Nabisco trademarks. They slice a Sugar Wafer in two and stack the halves on top of each other to throw suspicious consumers off the track.

Moon Pies

The Moon Pie white stuff is in a class by itself. It has the appearance and the elasticity of the stretchy white rubber used to hang posters. It's foamy — you can hear the bubbles burst as you chew it — and has a more marshmallowy flavor than the Twinkie or Oreo white stuff. The label admits the presence of gelatin, a common component of marshmallows.

I wrote to the company, saying I wanted to use their filling recipe in a cake. I got back a courteous letter explaining how impossible it would be for the layman to make Moon Pie white stuff at home. Executive Vice President John A. Kosik seemed to think this would be like making a cruise missile at home. He wrote: "Some of the ingredients used in making marshmallow involve liquid sugars such as cane sugar and/or corn sugar. These particular ingredients would only be available to you in a 350 lb. drum or a railroad tank car."

According to experts, the Moon Pie filling is a rather adhesive marshmallow similar to that used in Nabisco Mallomars. It is probably made from sugar (about 39% by weight), invert syrup (about 24%), water (about 20%), corn syrup (about 16%), and gelatin (about 2%).

Girl Scout Mint Cookies

The only researcher in the country with the guts to take on the Girl Scouts of America is Gloria Pitzer of *The Secret Recipe Report*. Her recipe for knockoff Girl Scout Mint Cookies calls for devil's food cake mix, eggs, water, cooking oil, Postum powder (a fake coffee mix made from grain), peppermint extract, cocoa, chocolate, and, uh, paraffin wax. For those puttering at home, Pitzer recommends melting some colorless birthday candles right into the chocolate.

Famous Amos Chocolate Chip Cookies

"Not until 1970, when Wally Amos started to bake his secret recipe, has any chocolate chip cookie been so thoroughly authentic and delicious at the same time," extols the Famous Amos bag. But three inches below that, the ingredient list seems to tell the whole story: "Enriched Bleached Flour, Chocolate Chips, Margarine (partially Hydrogenated Vegetable Oil), White and Brown Sugar, Pecans, Eggs, Coconut, Vanilla Extract, Baking Soda, Salt and Water." The salient feature of Amos's original recipe is coconut. They don't even use butter rather than margarine (for cookies that sell for $7 a pound yet). Only the price lends any credence to the silly and utterly untrue rumors claiming hashish as a secret ingredient.

The disparity between the cookie pictured on the Famous Amos label and the cookie in the bag can only be compared to that existing between Sea Monkey ads and the actual product. The label shows a

platonic ideal, the nuts and chips artfully arranged and faintly glis-
tening with butterfat. The real cookies are lumps. They're kind of hard
and kind of dry. The nuts and chips are mostly buried in the dough.
A disclaimer on the label says: "enclosed Cookies are smaller and their
surface appearance is different from the illustration."

Red Velvet Cake

Red Velvet Cake is a blood-red confection with pink or white icing
that is said to derive from a secret recipe of the Waldorf-Astoria Hotel
in New York. It is a dessert in the grand 1950s Jell-O-and-miniature-
marshmallow tradition, and recipes for it turn up in women's magazines and newspaper food columns from time to time.

The story behind the cake, often mentioned in recipes, is that a
woman was dining at the Waldorf-Astoria and liked the cake so much
that she asked the chef for the recipe. Shortly thereafter the woman
received the recipe in the mail along with a bill for $300. Outraged,
she went to her lawyer. She was advised that since she had taken
possession of the recipe and had not asked about price, she had no
choice but to pay. The woman was so angry that she started a vendetta.
She publicized the secret recipe at every turn — sending it to newspapers, including it in her Christmas letter, and so on. Which explains
how this "secret" recipe turns up in magazines.

Out of curiosity, I wrote to the Waldorf-Astoria and asked for its Red
Velvet Cake recipe. In response, I got a very nice letter from its executive chef, Kurt Ermann, and a photocopy of the recipe. Ermann
said, "Please use this in all good health," which may have something
to do with the fact that the cake contains 1/4 cup of red food coloring.

Ermann's letter said nothing of the woman and her $300. The recipe
notwithstanding, Red Velvet Cake seems to be a hoax. In 1963 folk-
lorist Jan Harold Brunvand analyzed the story in the *Oregon Folklore
Bulletin*. He wrote to the Waldorf-Astoria, inquiring about the recipe,
and got an entirely different response. The hotel said it had clippings
of accounts of the cake (with prices ranging from $5 to $1,000) and
that it had investigated the matter and found it to be completely base-
less. Nothing like that had ever happened; it couldn't have because
there was never any such cake served at the Waldorf. The recipe *I* got

must have been something they now send out to satisfy cranks who write in.

The recipe is fairly consistent from version to version. You can follow it and get an edible red cake if that appeals to you. (The batter looks like nail gloss.) The Waldorf's recipe goes like this:

WALDORF RED VELVET CAKE

½ cup butter	1 cup buttermilk
1½ cups sugar	1 teaspoon soda
2 eggs	2¼ cups cake flour
1 pinch salt	1 tablespoon vinegar
¼ cup red color	

Cream butter and sugar till fluffy. Add eggs and beat well. Add salt and soda, half of the flour followed by the buttermilk, and then the red color, vinegar, and remaining flour.

Bake in two 9-inch layer pans at 350° F for 20 to 25 minutes.

ICING

1 cup milk and 5 tablespoons flour. Cook till thick and add: ¼ lb. butter, 1 cup powdered sugar, 1 teaspoon vanilla, and red color to suit. Beat until thick.

Skate Scallops

A skate is an ugly little critter that fouls fishing nets and usually qualifies for the epithet of "trash fish." Long-standing rumor claims that seafood restaurants and supermarkets sell plugs of skate meat as scallops. Or sometimes it's parts of sharks, rays, or other marine oddities that get served up as scallops. Even fish paste has been claimed as a scallop substitute. It may be claimed that much or most of the "scallops" sold in this country are skate.

This is one of the most epistemological of food substitution tales. Wouldn't anyone taste the difference between scallops and skate? Well, sure — *unless* the "scallops" one has learned to recognize have been skate all along.

Skate is perfectly edible and probably has loads of protein. Craig Claiborne once sampled poached skate with black butter and wrote that it was "pure delight."

I contacted two mollusk experts, R. Tucker Abbott, formerly of the Smithsonian Institution and Delaware's Museum of Natural History, and Arthur S. Merrill of Harvard's Museum of Comparative Zoology, to see what they thought of "skate scallops." Abbott recalls hearing the same rumors as a boy in Boston in the 1920s. He suspects that if there is a germ of truth to the stories, it may have been set off by an incident or two in the 1890s. But an "old-time government inspector in New York" once told Abbott that he had never come across a genuine case of another seafood being sold as scallops.

According to both Abbott and Merrill, there is a simple way of authenticating scallops. Picture the alleged scallop as a flat cylinder, like a can of tuna. In a true scallop, the grain runs up and down. In a plug cut from the fin of a skate or ray, the grain runs parallel to the flat round surfaces. You couldn't cut plugs of skate or ray so the grain would run the "right" way because the layer of meat is too thin. And in Japanese *surimi*, processed fish paste, there's no grain at all.

The true scallop muscle is composed of a large round part loosely attached to a small oval part. The small part is tougher, and good chefs remove it. So if you find scallops with the small muscle attached, they are genuine — but the lack of the small muscle does not mean the scallops are fake.

I checked the grain on a sample of Mrs. Paul's frozen French Fried Scallops. Mrs. Paul's scallops look like Tater-Tots. If anybody's scallops were fake, you'd think these would be. The label lists forty-some ingredients, but "select scallops" is at the head of the list. Some of the scallops were so small or misshapen that it was hard to tell just which way the grain ran. An examination of the less teratological morsels revealed that the grain did run up and down as it should. The clincher was one specimen found with the quick muscle still attached.

I also inspected the grain on some supermarket and restaurant scallops. Not one fake scallop was found.

Scallops aren't the only seafood subject to questioning. It is said that some restaurants offering "swordfish" on their menus actually serve you mako shark. Mako shark appears on some seafood menus, and lots of people like it. Supposedly, the two fish taste similar, though swordfish is described as moister. The tip-off is a dark spot found only in mako shark. This is actually a dark stripe running through the flesh, seen in cross section in a mako shark steak.

A widespread story about Arthur Treacher's Fish and Chips claims that they use shark meat for the fish. In England, at least, a kind of shark called dogfish is often the "fish" in fish and chips. It is claimed that Treacher's secret recipe calls for soaking the fillets in buttermilk and then club soda, a ritual that is supposed to exorcise the shark taste. I was assured by a Treacher's franchisee that shark meat was not used in her restaurant.

That's not to say that shark is the zircon of seafoods. There are cases of other fish being sold as shark. Shark fins, used in the Chinese soup, fetch about $60 a pound. But the Japanese sell a counterfeit shark fin. It is almost impossible to detect this substitution because the genuine article is nearly tasteless.

Eggs in Wine

There are eggs in some cheap wines. Also gelatin, sulfur dioxide, casein, potassium sorbate, and isinglass (a jelly made from fish air bladders). These additives were revealed in 1981, when the Bureau of Alcohol, Tobacco and Firearms was contemplating a comprehensive ingredient-labeling law for wine. What's this stuff doing in there? The eggs (both whites and yolks) and other gelatinous ingredients precipitate *fines* and clarify the wine; the sulfur dioxide and potassium sorbate are preservatives. The wine lobby convinced lawmakers that what goes into modern wine is too unappetizing to list right on the label — so these additives remain secret ingredients.

Revolting Condiments

Government nutrition consultant Robert Choate once claimed that there is more protein in the *insects* in some breakfast cereals than in the cereals themselves. He was probably kidding. But it's still a jungle out there. Lest anyone get too cozy about the hygienic standards of American food, the Food and Drug Administration periodically updates a list of allowed contamination in processed food. FDA technical bulletins inform packers of such fine points as distinguishing a rat hair from a squirrel hair. ("Indoor squirrel traffic would be indicative of the laxest sort of sanitation," says FDA Technical Bulletin No. 1, *Principles of Food Analysis for Filth, Decomposition, and Foreign Matter.*)

Some of the highlights of the current regulations:

• As many as 10% of the beans in a sample of coffee can be infested or damaged by insects.

• 250 milliliters (about a cup) of orange juice is allowed to contain ten fruit fly eggs, but only two maggots.

• Apple butter can have 5 insects per 100 grams (about 25 in a 16-ounce jar), but little insects like mites, aphids, thrips, and scale insects don't count toward the limit. Generally speaking, the cleanest apples are sold whole, and the wormy ones are made into apple butter.

• Wheat can average "9 milligrams rodent excreta pellets and/or pellet fragments/kilogram."

• Peanut butter can have 50 insect fragments per 100 grams (as many as 620 in the 40-ounce jar of Skippy's Super Chunk) or one rodent hair per 100 grams.

• Curry powder can contain 100 insect fragments per 25 grams. Most spices are rife with insects before they reach the market; the FDA acknowledges there isn't much that American spice importers can do about the matter. (But "no live insects are permitted," an American Spice Trade Association spokesman insisted.)

• 100 grams of tomato juice can contain two *Drosophila* maggots, five eggs and one maggot, or ten eggs and no maggot at all.

• Frozen Brussels sprouts can have 40 aphids or thrips per 100 grams. That amounts to about 200 vermin in a 1-pound package.

The catch-all term "foreign matter" opens another can of worms, so to speak. It is not generally appreciated how much *metal* gets into processed food. There is enough for there to be a market for metal detectors expressly designed for food production lines. Once the detector finds a hot macaroon, say, it either drops markers to identify it or automatically flicks it into a reject bin. The reject bin can be studied to find where the metal is coming from. Lead shot is often found in raisins, the result of hunters traipsing through vineyards.

· 3 ·

THE ROSICRUCIANS

*T*he Ancient and Mystical Order Rosae Crucis (AMORC) spends over a half a million dollars a year advertising for members. You've seen its typographically naive come-on ads in publications ranging from supermarket tabloids to the *New York Times Book Review*. The Rosicrucians are a mail order fraternal lodge with secret initiations, passwords, and symbols. They reveal mysteries to folks who cut out the coupons and send a $20 fee. I did just that.

The Rosicrucians have a muddled history that their publications do little to clarify. Their literature blandly asserts that they go back to the Eighteenth Dynasty of ancient Egypt (about 1350 B.C.). And they claim that Jesus, Benjamin Franklin, Isaac Newton, René Descartes, Leibnitz, Plato, Balzac, Francis Bacon, St. Thomas Aquinas, and Aristotle were all members.

Well, heck. Outside sources say the group was started by a guy named H. Spencer Lewis in 1915. A.D. Lewis was a spiritualist who claimed to be a Ph.D. but never attended college. The Rosicrucians were as substantial as Middle Earth until Lewis cribbed the name from a seventeenth-century pamphlet. He claimed special authority from certain Eastern masters to found the order in the Americas.

It follows that Jesus, Benjamin Franklin, and all the rest were not members of any order that Lewis founded. One suspects that the Rosicrucians are able to name-drop so freely because the parties in question aren't around to complain. I've never seen a list of ten *living* celebrities who are Rosicrucians.

Lewis first advertised for members in a New York newspaper; unlike other fraternal orders, the Rosicrucians encouraged both men and women to apply. Lewis drifted from New York to San Francisco to Tampa to San Jose, uprooting and reestablishing the organization as he went. He died — "experienced the Great Initiation" — in 1939. Upon his death his son, Ralph, took over as "Supreme Autocratic Authority," "Imperator for North, Central, and South America, the British Commonwealth and Empire, France, Switzerland, Sweden and Africa," and other titles that make it sound as though he's pretty much in charge of everything. Ralph is still Imperator.

Today the Rosicrucians operate out of a garish compound in San Jose, Rosicrucian Park, which occupies an entire city block. Palm trees frame a crazed architecture of obelisks and sphinxes, rounded domes and columns. What the Rosicrucians call the "See of the Worldwide Jurisdiction for the Americas, Australasia, Europe, Africa, and Asia" or "The Valley of Heart's Delight" includes administration buildings, recording and movie studios, a planetarium, a science museum, an auditorium, a temple, an art gallery, and a library. Collectively, this is a tourist trap big enough to rate mention in the AAA *Tourbook* (there's a discount for triple-A members) and membership in the local Chamber of Commerce.

The Supreme Temple is unexpectedly tasteful, as if the Memphis design group did a Las Vegas hotel. A red carpet crosses a black and white tessellated platform surrounding an altar. At one end of the room is a "view of the East": a fake Diamond Head surmounted by a crescent moon. Stone pharaohs stand on either side.

Pink and green "Rose-Croix University" operates for a three-week period each midsummer. Classes are offered to members of the order only, and students lodge in nearby motels. The college catalogue doesn't say so in so many words, but you'd probably have trouble transferring credits to Stanford.

The museums house an assortment of gaudy bric-a-brac — fancy

French furniture, jewels, human and animal mummies, and a mock-up of an Egyptian tomb. The planetarium's "intricately constructed dioramas depict the life and terrain of other planets," boasts a pamphlet.

A Rosicrucian Supply Bureau sells books, jewelry, and junk. There are coloring books for children, busts of Nefertiti, a "Master Jesus Plaque," and windshield decals.

The Rosicrucians have about a hundred lodges in the United States. There are 26 lodges in France, 21 in Brazil, 18 in Nigeria, 13 in both Canada and Mexico, 12 in England, 11 in Venezuela, and 8 in Australia. The number of members is debatable; one outside estimate put the number of *active* Rosicrucians at about 45,000. A newsletter for the New York City lodge reported fourteen recruits in three months. The membership is more itinerant than most, what with the mail order focus. The dues don't encourage backsliders to retain their membership.

Anyone who sends in a coupon gets some information and a request for the $20 fee — which is just the beginning. Those who write in are then expected to fork over $9.50 a month in dues, entitling them to a subscription to the monthly *Rosicrucian Digest,* a membership card, and the secret password for entrance into Rosicrucian lodges.

The seeker is then sent a booklet called *Mastery of Life.* The inside front cover has *World Book Encyclopedia*–style color lithographs of alleged Rosicrucians (such as Claude Debussy, who is identified as "Most famous French composer"). *Mastery of Life* is a rambling philosophical treatise. It asks so many rhetorical questions that you find yourself counting them. "If you could reach into a dependable source and produce helpful, constructive, intelligent ideas at a time when an important thought, a useful plan, meant the difference between discouragement and achievement, would you not feel equal to any circumstance?" asks the eighth of one unbroken string of questions. "Certainly, such a life would be far superior in its advantages," it finally declares.

The typeface is about 30% larger than that found in the average publication intended for grownups. A lot of *Mastery of Life* is jerky advice seemingly directed to high school–age kids. A picture of pairs of eyes is captioned: "You are several selves and personalities in one.

Stop being a stranger to yourself. There is no greater adventure than exploring the frontiers of the mind."

The book is a sales pitch for the lessons. You are assured that the lessons are printed in "large, *easy-to-read type*" with "suitable illustrations" and that no college education is necessary. The topics dealt with range from "How to Improve Your Daily Affairs" to "Creating Life out of Nonliving Matter."

There is a color picture of a leisure-suited man and woman studying the lessons in their game room, haloed by the flashbulb glare on the wood-paneled wall. "You select *one night a week* — any night will suffice — and that becomes *Your Lodge Night*" to contemplate the "wonderful disclosures."

About a week after the first packet is sent, there is a follow-up mailing. You soon find that you are on one of the monster mailing lists of all time. Within days I was getting junk mail pitches for study materials, some with a cover letter floridly signed by Lamar Kilgore (that can't be his real name), Grand Treasurer of the Rosicrucian Supply Bureau.

Kilgore offers an "economical associate membership" to those too cheap to become regular members. Associate membership costs $4.50 a month, which buys the *Rosicrucian Digest* and study materials. Associate members *don't* get the passwords, nor do they get the initiation.

You are on a mailing list even if you answer the ad and then decide to wash your hands of the whole business. My tardiness in sending in the $20 copped me a letter addressed to "Respected Seeker." This was worded like a collection agency's first notice: "Like a magnet, something pulled you toward the Rosicrucians. There was a sympathetic bond even if for but a moment. . . . What NOW concerns us is why the bond has not become stronger."

The first official mailing after one applies for membership comes in a folder fastened with a green paper seal marked SEALED BY THE ARCHIVIST. This would appeal, I think, to the same audience attracted by walkie-talkies and breakfast cereal prizes. There is a pervasive something that is not quite adult about the Rosicrucians.

Dare you break the seal, you find an ornate letter from Ralph Lewis, Imperator. It begins: "Hail Neophyte!" Ralph's signature is ornate, kind of like Lamar Kilgore's. (I compared them and they're different, so it's not the same person.) The membership card, needed to get into lodges, is a thin piece of plastic with the member's name and number typewritten on it. As the card itself says, it is good only when accompanied by a receipt showing that your dues are paid up.

The membership packet includes instructions for an "experiment" you're supposed to do: Stare at someone who is not looking at you and see if you can get his attention just by concentrating on him. The picture shows two men in a dentist's office, one reading while the other stares at him. Per Rosicrucian art direction, the background is wood paneling with reflection from the photographer's lights. The instructions promise that the person you stare at will often smile when he realizes you are looking at him. Is anyone enough of a dope to do this? The Rosicrucians think so. Experiments like this are a big part of the instruction.

Lessons take the form of "monographs," slim pamphlets bound in green paper. Most begin: "Fratres and Sorores, Greetings!" The first monograph is a pep talk: "You are going to be given the opportunity to be the master of situations rather than the victim of circumstances." It suggests setting Thursday night for study "because it is called Rosicrucian night throughout the world." It's okay to study during the daytime if necessary: "Many theatrical and professional people . . . have had to do this."

These monographs are serious business. You aren't allowed to show them to anyone. You are told to keep them in a box, preferably locked. The box *must* contain a written directive specifying that when you die, the monographs must be returned to AMORC, Rosicrucian Park, San Jose, California 95191.

Most monographs come with curious inserts. One is a novelty paper placemat intended for cheap restaurants. It shows an assortment of optical illusions ("This is not a spiral, but a series of complete circles"). It says nothing about the Rosicrucians. I think some Rosicrucian saw it at a luncheonette and thought it was neat.

Members are told to send in a recent photo for the lodge records. One mailing has a photo album of the Rosicrucian higher-ups. H. Spencer Lewis was a heavy, round-faced man with a mustache and a tiny goatee. Ralph Lewis looks a lot like Marlin Perkins. Lamar Kilgore has a beard and is wearing a suit with contrast stitching.

The Rosicrucians believe in ESP. Monograph No. 6 tells you to send a postcard or short letter to Rosicrucian headquarters whenever you miss your regular home study night so that they will know everything's okay. Apparently the Rosicrucian thought police know when you are meditating and know when you're shirking. I don't know why they need the postcard, then.

Many of the recommended experiments try to demonstrate ESP, auras, and the like. One, described in darkly lecherous detail, has you relax your body, organ by organ: "You can feel the pressure of the clothes . . . next, slowly come to the chest and breasts, one at a time."

The First Degree

Three secret, do-it-yourself rituals initiate members into this mail-order order. Sealed letters tell you what to do; you're pretty much on the honor system.

Novices are expected to study for about six weeks to prepare for the first degree. It takes three more months to reach the second degree, three more to reach the third. The persons who initiate themselves at home are called "sanctum members." The order sells optional audio tapes for initiation. Pop one of these into your stereo and "the voice of the Imperator takes you back to a romantic period of ancient history as he relates in an intimate style" the rituals with musical accompaniment.

The initiations go like this:

When it's time for the first initiation, you get a packet containing a sealed gray envelope. The envelope warns you not to open it until you have read the accompanying literature. Said literature tries to convince you that what you're about to do isn't stupid. It explains that you're going to act out a little drama. It mentions catharsis and symbolism. Privacy is essential for the initiations, you are told.

The instructions are printed in purple ink. Sheet music for the "Rosicrucian Chant" is provided. You need two candles, a mirror, and a dark room. The candles are placed on a table, dresser, or shelf in front of the mirror. You don't have to buy a *new* table or dresser just for the initiation, the instructions state. This table is given the grand name of "telesterion," which means a place of initiation.

There are two "characters" in the initiation. You have to play both the "Master of the Lodge" *and* yourself, sort of like Peter Sellers in *Lolita*. "Think of yourself as one of many other candidates who would be assembled to participate in a similar experience," the instructions advise. "In your mind's eye, visualize the ritualistic officers in attendance — who would direct and guide you — as standing in various places in the temple or lodge room. Only in this instance, we repeat, you are performing your own initiation."

As you light the candle on your left, you recite in your Master of the Lodge voice, "Sacred Light, symbol of the Greater Light of Cosmic Wisdom, cast thy rays in the midst of darkness and illuminate my path!" Then you light the right candle and say some more words.

You sit down and whisper, as yourself, "Before I cross the mental and spiritual Threshold of greater understanding I must courageously face those realities, those notions, that have for so long stood in the shadows of my mind to taunt and thwart me." You meditate a minute. Then you make the sign of the cross with your finger on the reflection of your face in the mirror. The oil from your finger is supposed to leave a faint mark. You stand back and say, "Hail, O sacred Symbol of Life, Love, and Resurrection! In the center of thy cosmic body shall come the Rose, the soul of Man's being, and thou shalt be my sign! Hail, Rosy Cross!" You fixate for a minute upon the sign of the cross.

Then — no kidding — you ask yourself nine ritualistic questions and answer them. The first is: "Wouldst thou know the mystery of thy being?" I guess you could say there aren't any right or wrong answers here. The initiation instructions don't say how you're supposed to answer the questions. Finally, you say some more words and snuff out the candles.

You are expected to write up a report of the initiation and send it to Rosicrucian headquarters. I said that I got a "cool feeling" when I ran through those nine questions. I figured they'd eat that up in San Jose. Several weeks later I got a reply. It was one of those mail-merge jobs that prints your name and address in the text of an obvious form letter: "We have enjoyed reading your report of the First Atrium Initiation. We are pleased to welcome you, Frater Poundstone, as an initiated member of the Rosicrucian Order."

The Second Degree

Shortly before you are eligible for the second initiation, you get an ominous letter from the Imperator's Sanctum. This warns that "not all who enter into the First Atrium are permitted to continue." Now remember, everything has been transacted by mail. It is hard to imagine what could get you on the blacklist — unless it is not sending in dues. The letter goes on: "Tests are met at times in ways that are not easily understood by new members . . . you will have a very pleasant surprise at the conclusion of a certain phase of the work; then you will know what careful investigationwe are making of your progress, how closely we keep in contact with our members." This seems to hint, not too convincingly, that they've got your house under surveillance.

The second-degree initiation uses a white cardboard triangle, a chair, incense, a dish, and two candles. The Rosicrucians hawk incense. You get a flyer suggesting India Moss Rose for your second initiation, twenty-four cubes for $3.75 from the Rosicrucian Supply Bureau.

I sent away for the stuff. The instant I opened the lid, I was reminded of movie theaters. India Moss Rose smells exactly like Jordan Almonds. Once ignited, a single brick is capable of making an apartment smell like Jordan Almonds for days.

The candles go at two corners of the triangle. The chair is near one candle. The dish holds the incense and goes in the center of the triangle. You stand at the third corner and cross your arms and touch your shoulders in a "sign of supplication." You recite more incantations, take the right candle, and go sit in the chair. Then you gaze into the burning incense while seated and try to pick up a message from your "Inner Self." After the initiation, you write this message on the form provided and mail it to San Jose.

The Third Degree

For the third degree, you face east and hold your hand over your heart while offering prayer. You take three deep breaths and read: "The

Divine essence which I breathe into my body brings with it an influx of the Soul of God; and I likewise breathe out of my body the exhausted essence which has given me life and maintained the Soul in my body. All evil influence surrounding my soul and contaminating my body went forth from my body with the passing of the exhausted and de-vitalized breath. With the newer breath, the sweet and holy air, I took into my body the purer essence, which is Divine and is God."

Then it gets *strange*. You raise your hand and make these animal-istic sounds: "Oo . . . ah . . . ee . . . oo . . . ah . . . ee . . . oo . . . ah . . . ee." You meditate five minutes and then repeat the sounds.

Then you set up the candles and mirror and say, "Ra, Ra, selah, Ra." This is claimed to draw the "herald of the Master." You tilt your head back and place your left hand over your heart to invoke the spirit of the "guardian." You have a pretend conversation with the guardian. Then you blow out the candles and sit in the dark for ten minutes, meditating on the Cosmic Temple.

The final step is to copy this oath, pausing after every seventh word to gaze into the mirror and repeat the word seven times: "I shall strive forever to deserve the approbation of all good Souls on earth and to serve silently and peacefully, not in fear of the future made, but in consideration of an unmade future, a realm of greater development. So mote it be."

Are the words you repeat (every seventh word, like in an old spy movie) supposed to be a secret message? It would read: "the earth not but a it."

Vestal Virgins

You can be a full-fledged Rosicrucian without ever setting foot in a lodge, but there are Rosicrucian lodges in the bigger metropolitan areas. What goes on there? A brochure for public dissemination says that "the Order makes no demands upon its members to conduct themselves in any manner that would cause public ridicule or con-demnation. The members are not required to dress, eat or act differ-ently from any intelligent and morally responsible man or woman."

What they don't tell the public is that the lodge ceremonies include a "Vestal Virgin." Inside each lodge is a triangular dais resembling a set in a Buck Rogers movie. A male "Master" and a female "Mater," sitting on opposite ends of the dais, co-chair the meeting. The Vestal Virgin is stationed near the Master. She is a young girl who "symbolizes certain virtues" and must resign at the age of eighteen. Her main job is to guard a sacred fire used to light the incense used in lodge ceremonies. For the "New Year Feast," held around March 21, everyone sits around and chows down on corn, salt, and grape juice.

Want to see all this for yourself? The three passwords you need to get in are *Reflection, Maat,* and *Moard-Moarc.*

· 4 ·

THE KNIGHTS OF COLUMBUS

*T*o be a Knight of Columbus is to undergo an initiation of blood, brutality, and crowd psychology. The Knights' secret rite is such a production that they wait until they have a sizable group, often a hundred or more, to initiate. *Bigger Secrets* got hold of the Knights of Columbus ritual book and found a Knight willing to corroborate its description of the initiation.

Secret Handshakes and Signs

The roughhouse initiation is all the more surprising given the lodge's ties to the Catholic Church. The Knights of Columbus were set up as a lodge for Catholics (the Church forbids Catholics to join the Masons and similar orders). "At best this organization can only be described as a consolation prize for the good boys who might otherwise be tempted into Freemasonry," wrote a waspish Mason in the anonymous work *Light Invisible*. The Knights are known mostly for selling insurance to members, getting Columbus Day declared a legal holiday, and offering a correspondence course in Catholicism. Many priests are members, and all cardinals, archbishops, and bishops are technically members whether they ever attend a meeting or not. One requirement for joining is proving that you made your last Easter duty.

41

According to the ritual book, the Knights' secret handshake is conventional, but one person tightens his grasp twice in quick succession and the other person responds with a single application of pressure. You're supposed to ask "What council do you belong to?" when giving this handshake.

My informant mentioned another secret recognition sign: move the hand in a vertical direction. The response is to move the hand in a horizontal direction, completing a "cross."

If any Knight is in trouble and in a crowd, he is supposed to yell "Are there any good men here?" This is the distress sign, and all Knights within earshot are supposed to lend assistance.

The most controversial of the Knights' secrets has been the fourth-degree oath. A Knight may earn several optional degrees after the first three mandatory ones; this is the oath taken in the first of the optional degrees. Evidently a group of anti-Catholics made up a false oath around 1912 and circulated it. The *false* oath goes like this:

> I, ———, now in the presence of Almighty God, the Blessed Virgin Mary, the Blessed St. John the Baptist, the Holy Apostles, St. Peter and St. Paul, and all the Saints, sacred host of Heaven, and to you, my ghostly father, the Society of Jesus, founded by Ignatius Loyola, in the pontification of Paul III, and continued to the present, do by the womb of the Virgin, the matrix of God, and the rod of Jesus Christ, declare and swear that His Holiness, the Pope, is Christ's vice-regent, and is the true and only head of the Catholic Church throughout the earth . . . I do further promise and declare that I will, when opportunity presents, make and wage relentless war, secretly and openly against all heretics, Protestants and Masons, as I am directed to do to extirpate them from the face of the whole earth; that I will spare neither age, sex, nor condition; that I will hang, burn, waste, boil, flay, strangle and bury alive those infamous heretics; rip up the stomachs, and wombs of their women, and crush their infants' heads against the walls, in order to annihilate their execrable race. That when the same cannot be done openly I will secretly use the poison cup, the strangulation cord, the steel of the poniard, or the leaden bullet.

The Knights offered a $25,000 reward to anyone who could prove that the false oath was legitimate. To prove the oath false without revealing the real, secret oath, the Knights of Columbus showed a copy of the real oath to a group of Freemasons. The Masons avowed that the real oath is harmless and does not even mention Protestants or

Masons. The Knights' ritual book does not even mention the fourth degree.

Initiation

Knights of Columbus lodges have an anteroom, a main room, and a "hot box" (to be explained shortly). All three degrees may be given in one night.

The first degree is a throwaway. The candidates are paraded from the anteroom into the main room to the strains of "Come Holy Ghost, Creator Blest" or another hymn. There the Grand Knight asks them some straightforward religious questions: "Do you believe in God?" In the Trinity? In the Catholic Church? "Do you pledge to obey the Church?" The Knights of Columbus? The candidates make the obvious replies and march back to the anteroom.

The second degree is a pious game show. Candidates again march into the main room to the accompaniment of organ music. The room is dark except for a light over the altar. The Grand Knight is quizmaster. He now asks candidates catechism questions — good, hard ones like "How many kinds of grace are there?" The point is for the candidates to flunk. This demonstrates that "most of them have no intelligent idea of what their faith consists of," according to the ritual. (If there are any priests among the candidates, they are excused from participation lest the priesthood be embarrassed by a wrong answer.) The Grand Knight exhorts the candidates to study the Scriptures.

The third degree starts as the candidates return to the anteroom. Unknown to them, there are decoys in their midst — lodge brothers playing the part of greenhorns. One brother is dressed as a priest, with Roman collar and rabat. Another is a "Secret Service man," as is later revealed.

Other lodge brothers order the candidates about. Their purpose is to work the candidates into a frenzy, "using the decoy priest as a last resort." They tell the candidates to get in line in the anteroom. No matter how conscientiously they queue up, the lodge brothers find fault with something — the line isn't straight enough, the candidates aren't facing forward, they aren't in order of seniority, and so on. If anyone doesn't follow orders, they imply that the offender may be kicked out. "Break the spirit of all, if possible," advises the ritual book, which has a dry, cynical tone throughout, and "make all timidly obey the smallest command of the team members."

A Captain of the Guard plays the goon. When a candidate balks at the rough treatment, they sic the Captain on him. The Captain comes in wearing a bathrobe soaked in whiskey. Decoy candidates murmur that he must be drunk just in case anyone doesn't get the idea. The besotted Captain tries to enforce order, shoving and insulting the candidates.

The fake priest leaves the line. When the Captain of the Guard asks where he thinks he is going, the priest says he is sick and needs a glass of water. The Captain tells him to get back in line. The priest says he feels as if he's going to faint. The Captain tells him to faint already. Two of the Captain's thugs force the priest back in line.

The Secret Service man (not yet known to be such) breaks out of the line in livid disgust and gets the priest a glass of water from a fountain. The Captain knocks the glass out of his hand. There is a picture of this scene in the ritual book so the lodges will know just how it is supposed to be.

"If the candidates have not yet gone beyond control, this always stirs them to fury," homilizes the ritual book. If all goes as planned, the candidates now threaten force against the Captain, and the plants egg them on. Someone yells that this is an insult to the priesthood. If things get *totally* out of hand, the plants protect the Captain, and the fake priest may calm the crowd by saying that the Captain is drunk and not really responsible.

Are candidates really taken in by this? Our informant said he and a friend weren't — "The violence was so obviously phony that we laughed at it." But other candidates "were taking it all seriously." The lodge used "an out-of-state initiation team noted for its histrionic skills."

That's just act one. Once tempers cool, the candidates are blindfolded and led back into the main room. They are led around the room several times to disorient them a bit. Then the blindfolds are removed.

The candidates find themselves facing an operating table supplied with surgical instruments and knives. Several lodge brothers dressed as "doctors" surround the table. All the other lodge brothers form a circle around the doctors; they are dressed in black monks' robes with hoods and masks.

44

The Chief Surgeon calls out the names of several candidates. Guards usher them to the operating table. One of the names called is that of a lodge brother. The Chief Surgeon selects this decoy, apparently at random, and has him lie down on the table.

Before they can proceed, the Surgeon says, the candidate must submit to a test. He is given a copy of a pledge he must sign in his own blood. The Surgeon hands the candidate a knife in order to draw the blood.

The decoy refuses to do it. The Surgeon says he has to; the doctors will make sure that he suffers no permanent injury. The decoy still refuses. The Surgeon tells the decoy to get off the table; he will be taken care of later. Another candidate, this time a real one, is called to the table and told to prick himself with the knife.

According to the ritual book, the unrehearsed candidate usually agrees to cut himself. But before he does anything, someone whispers something to the Chief Surgeon. He stops the candidate and says that they must first decide what to do with the previous candidate. For that, the other candidates must be cleared from the room.

Guards lead the candidates to the hot box. This is a very small room that is kept as hot as possible. "The Hot Box must be small enough to make it difficult to move about easily without jostling," says the ritual book. Masked monks lock the candidates in the room and guard the door.

The Captain of the Guard, just as contentious as before, is also in the hot box. This time the decoy priest complains about the sweltering heat. He has to get out, he says. The Captain refuses. The priest tries to force his way out, and the Captain slugs him in the mouth.

The priest has been chewing some red gum to make his saliva look like blood. When the candidates see the blood, they go ape. Spurred by the decoys, they pound on the door, demanding to be let out. If necessary, decoys station themselves between the Captain and vengeful candidates. Just as it seems the candidates will tear down the door, the guards let them out, and all come tumbling into the main room.

Now one of the decoy candidates gets on a chair and denounces the goings-on at the top of his lungs. This encourages the real candidates to do likewise. The most "hotheaded and devout" are usually the best orators, says the ritual book.

Once everyone has had his say, the Grand Knight restores order.

He says they must try the Captain immediately. Seven jurors are selected, their decision to be binding.

The Secret Service man is selected as a juror. The Grand Knight says that the jurors must empty their pockets of all valuables so that they will not be passing anything to one another during the hearing. He instructs the Captain of the Guard to collect all the personal effects.

Of course, the Captain of the Guard is the person on trial. There is general spleen-venting at having to give *him* the valuables. The Secret Service man refuses to surrender his valuables. A guard searches him and finds a gun.

The Grand Knight asks him why he has a concealed weapon. The man says that he is employed by the Secret Service. He is under orders to carry the gun and cannot let it leave his possession if he wants to.

The Grand Knight tells the Captain to take the gun. The Secret Service man yells that he wouldn't give it to the Captain in any case. They struggle. The Secret Service man grabs the gun and it goes off. The Captain drops to the floor. Blood oozes from a "bullethole" in his chest.

The action is faked with blank cartridges and a rubber bag of "blood" stashed in the Captain's robe which is punctured at the right moment. Priests rush up to the Captain to give him the last rites. The Secret Service man is taken out of the room by guards. The Captain is carried into the antechamber and presumably to a hospital. The doors are closed, locking the crowd in the main room to wait.

Decoys start nervous rumors. If the guard dies, they say, the incident will make the newspapers. *That* will be the end of the Knights of Columbus. After fifteen anxious minutes, the doors open and the Grand Knight walks in. With him are all the other lodge brothers who took part in the charade. The Captain of the Guard is cleaned up and in regular clothes. The Grand Knight turns to the priest and pulls off his collar. The decoy priest and Captain shake hands.

Appearances can be deceiving, the Grand Knight says by way of explanation. The candidates raise their right hands and take the oath of fealty to the Knights of Columbus.

• 5 •

FRATERNAL ORGANIZATIONS

The Bohemian Club

For two and a half weeks every July, two thousand of the top movers and shakers in business and government attend the Bohemian Club's summer encampment. Although highly selective, the club has a national membership and is among the most prestigious of affiliations in neoconservative circles. Its membership is known to include Ronald Reagan, George Bush, Gerald Ford, William F. Buckley, Jr., Frank Borman, Justin Dart, William Randolph Hearst, Jr., Caspar Weinberger, Charles Percy, George Shultz, Edward Teller, Merv Griffin, and a large proportion of the directors and chief executive officers of the Fortune 1000. Daniel Ludwig, the richest private citizen on earth, is a Bohemian. Conspiracy nuts think the Bohemian Club meets each summer to plot to take over the world. These guys *already* run the world.

The club's name harks back to its founding in 1872 by artists and journalists in the Bay Area; the club proper is at 624 Taylor Street in San Francisco. The annual summer camp is held at "Bohemian Grove," an isolated site in Sonoma County, California, near the town of Monte Rio. To get there, you cross the bridge over the Russian River and take the second left.

Signs warn off trespassers, and the Grove is guarded during the encampment. Visitors must have invitations and sign in and out; cooks and other workers have to wear ID badges. The club (and hired staff) is all male. There are no black Bohemians and just one Asian, the former Philippine president Carlos Romulo.

The club does a good job of avoiding publicity, although in 1980 Rick Clogher, a writer for *Mother Jones* magazine, managed to slip in to the encampment for four days with the help of an unidentified insider. Brooding over the Grove is a giant rock that looks like an owl. Clogher discovered that the rock is concrete, covered with moss to look natural. The Cremation of Care ritual takes place in front of the owl when, on the first night of camp, robed members burn a doll representing Dull Care.

Bohemian Grove includes 122 distinct camps in its 2,700 acres. The camps have whimsical names such as Whiskey Flat, Toyland, Owl's Nest, Hill Billies, and Cave Man's, and each one has its own kitchen-bar building — there is a lot of drinking — and sleeping quarters. The members of some camps sleep in tents; other camps have redwood cabins. Daily "Lakeside Talks" on geopolitical topics are given by prominent speakers, both members and nonmembers. It is claimed that Richard Nixon and Ronald Reagan conferred during the 1967 encampment, Reagan agreeing not to challenge Nixon for the presidential nomination.

The highlight of camp is the Grove play, which is written exclusively for the club. All the female roles are played by men in drag. The 1980 play was an adaptation of the Greek myth of Cronus and Zeus supplemented with fireworks, smoke bombs, and a light show. (One can only wonder if Reagan ever starred in a Grove play. He certainly has more acting experience than most club members.) The polished productions cost the Bohemians as much as $25,000 — for one performance.

The Independent Order of Odd Fellows

The Odd Fellows have a less tony image than, say, the Freemasons. Traditionally workingmen joined the Odd Fellows, and their bosses joined the Masons. In the mid- and late 1800s, the group attracted members with its free burials and benefits to widows and children of deceased members. Only white men may apply for membership, and anyone in the business of selling liquor is snubbed. The Odd Fellows have lodges throughout North America and in Europe and Australia.

The candidate for the IOOF's Initiatory Degree must promise to keep secret whatever transpires during his initiation. Once he makes this pledge, lodge brothers blindfold the candidate, put him in chains, and march him around the room in a mock funeral procession. The blindfold is then slipped off to reveal a skeleton lighted by two torches.

A *real* skeleton? Neither *Howard's Odd Fellowship* nor *Revised Odd Fellowship Illustrated* (both available from Ezra A. Cook Publications of Chicago, a supplier to lodges) says. I wrote to the Sovereign Grand Lodge in Baltimore, trying to broach this subject obliquely. I didn't claim to be an Odd Fellow, nor did I say I wasn't. "Is there any objection to using a plastic-material skeleton (such as are sold for use in schools) as opposed to a real skeleton?" I asked.

Robert W. Wepking, Sovereign Grand Secretary, answered, as if he gets this question all the time, "There is no objection or regulation prohibiting the use of Artificial Skeletons. Of course, your judgment should consider the quality of the Artificial Materials." That seems to imply that at least some Odd Fellow lodges use real, human skeletons. (Medical supply houses sell human skeletons for about $400 each.)

After the Initiatory Degree comes a series of three Lodge Degrees. Each degree's initiation is a skit performed by lodge members which the candidate watches. The playlet for the First Lodge Degree has the biblical David cutting off Goliath's head and taking it home to King Saul.

"The use of petards, guns, pistols, blank cartridges, explosives of all kinds, and every kind of firearms, or offensive, irritating, or over-powering drugs or chemicals in conferring degrees is strictly prohibited." The IOOF ritual is so specific, and even imaginative, about what *isn't* allowed that one suspects these injunctions are taken as suggestions.

Optional Encampment Degrees are offered to full members. The Golden Rule Degree is a weird minstrel show, with lodge brothers made up to represent the white, brown, yellow, red, and black races. According to the ritual, "The use of any animal, or representation thereof, or noises indicating the presence of any animal" is verboten,

as is any "character representing the female sex, either by imperson-
ation or otherwise."

In the initiation for the Patriarchal Degree, the blindfolded candidate
listens as a High Priest recites the Twenty-third Psalm. When the
High Priest says, "Let the torch be applied! Let the fagots be fired!"
this effect is simulated with fire or a red light. The High Priest raises
a knife as if to slay the candidate, but a rumble of artificial thunder
causes him to drop the knife.

The big enchilada for the Odd Fellows is the Royal Purple Degree.
The blindfolded candidate is subjected to assorted perils on a pretend
trip through dangerous terrain, and some lodges go hog wild with
jazzy special effects. According to the ritual, the candidate "shall not
be subjected to 'rain' during the storm, nor permitted to fall into the
river or otherwise wet. He shall not come into contact with electrical
or kindred appliances." No animal sounds are permitted except for
bird calls. The order boasts that "no degree in the ritual appeals more
strongly to intelligent and thinking men than does the royal purple."

The Knights of Pythias

The three degrees of the Knights of Pythias are called Page, Esquire,
and Knight. A candidate must be a white man in good health and of
able body. They aren't kidding about the latter: the Knights reject
amputees.

The initiation for Pages is a spook show similar to the IOOF's Initiatory Degree. The blindfolded candidate marches into the lodge room
and kneels. He takes off the blindfold, and in front of him is an open
coffin containing a skeleton. Two crossed swords are on the coffin,
supporting an open copy of the Bible. (I sent another skeleton letter
off to the Knights of Pythias headquarters. They never answered.)

The candidate recites pat answers to a series of questions and swears
not to reveal the "password, grip, signs or any other secret or mystery"
of the rank. "Stranger, by this vow, you are bound until death," a lodge
brother says.

The secret grip for the first degree: Extend the index and middle
fingers of the right hand, with a slight separation between them. Each
person then grasps the other's extended fingers and tries to shake

hands normally. A funny handshake is no good without dialogue to distract prying eyes, so they say this:

Q. Say, what is this?
A. A good thing.
Q. Most people would say so.
A. Some would.
Q. Oh, would they?
A. No doubt.

The Esquire candidate swears another secrecy oath: "I specially promise that I will not commit to writing any of the secret work of this order, so that it may become known; nor will I permit it to be done by another, if in my power to prevent." They go through some more rigamarole and then a lodge official known as the Keeper of Records and Seal gives the candidate some paperwork, a form asking for his name, address, age, occupation, and, just incidentally, the secret Knights of Pythias motto. If the candidate refuses to commit the motto to writing, fine. If the candidate has severe brain damage and does write down the motto, then the lodge brothers conduct a mock trial for his crime. Lodge members *live* for these trials. At the end, even the indiscreet candidate is inducted as an Esquire.

The Knight initiation is scariest. The candidate wears a knight's helmet and carries a shield. Lodge brothers pretend to be senators debating the merits of the candidate for Knighthood and discussing various tests of his mettle. A liberal senator says, Why bother with any tests? A second senator proposes a fencing match. A third says that would be unfair if the candidate didn't happen to be a good fencer. He suggests having the candidate jump on a bed of steel spikes set in a slab of solid oak. Yeah, let's do the steel spikes, everyone says.

Someone brings out a wicked-looking bed of spikes. The candidate is invited to inspect the spikes and convince himself that they are real. The bed of spikes is placed behind the candidate with an audible thud, and a set of three steps is placed facing the spikes.

The king says that there is one thing he wants him to know: A coward sometimes commits foolhardy acts out of social pressure, but a brave man won't "do violence to his manhood." He tells the candidate to "be the judge of what is prudent."

The visor of the candidate's helmet is lowered to serve as a blindfold.

He is ordered to take off his shoes and socks. The candidate ascends to the first of the three steps. This represents the Page degree. Then he steps onto the second step, representing the Esquire degree, and the third step, representing the Knight degree. The king says there is no way to appeal the decision; the candidate must jump barefoot onto the spikes. If he doesn't flinch or make a sound, he'll be accepted as a full Knight.

Of course, the spikes are removed before he jumps — that's the kind of wacky guys the Knights of Pythias are. If the candidate does jump, he lands on the floor and it's all a big joke. If he refuses to jump, lodge brothers grab him and hold him over the spikes so he can just feel the tips. In either case, the candidate is admitted. Maybe the Knights can't afford to be all that choosy. The final oath includes a vow always to pay lodge dues.

In 1936 President Franklin D. Roosevelt was initiated into the Knights of Pythias in the White House's diplomatic reception room.

The Loyal Order of Moose

Everything that happens in a Moose lodge is technically secret. A candidate for Moosehood must promise "that I will not — in any matter — communicate or disclose any information — concerning anything — I may hereafter hear, see or experience in this lodge or in any other lodge — of the Loyal Order of Moose — unless it be — to one whom I know to be a Loyal Moose — in good standing. By this vow I bind myself for all time."

Our sources say that the highlight of a Moose meeting is the Nine O'Clock ceremony. At precisely nine o'clock, all the loyal Moose face toward Mooseheart. This is a big swatch of Illinois real estate, forty miles west of Chicago, where the Moose have their world headquarters and run a sort of Boys' Town for five hundred Moose orphans. The Moose fold their arms and bow their heads in this prayer: "Suffer little children to come unto me and forbid them not for such is the Kingdom of Heaven. God bless Mooseheart."

Not to be confused with Mooseheart is Moosehaven, the Florida hamlet where Moose and their wives may spend their sunset years.

The Benevolent and Protective Order of Elks

A group of actors and singers founded the Elks in a New York City bar. The order's name was chosen capriciously after its founders saw a stuffed elk in Barnum's Museum. Franklin D. Roosevelt, Harry Truman, and John F. Kennedy were Elks. The Moose's hallowed Nine O'Clock ceremony seems to be a ripoff of the Elks' Eleven O'Clock Toast, which goes: "Wherever an Elk may roam, whatever his lot in life may be, when this hour falls upon the dial of night the great heart of Elkdom swells and throbs." At any rate, someone cribbed the idea from someone, and the Elks (founded in 1868) are older than the Moose (founded in 1888).

The parts of Elk anatomy that lodge brothers carry around are genuine. Geo. Lauterer Corporation of Chicago publishes a catalogue of Elk gewgaws. A "real elk foot" costs $7 (small), $8.50 (large), or $20 (made into a walking cane). Eighty-five dollars buys a pair of antlers "mounted in velour and set on a natural wood plaque."

Santeria

Santeria is an animal-sacrifice cult derived from elements of Roman Catholicism and the religion of the Yoruba tribe of southern Nigeria. Originally Cuban (Batista was said to be an initiate), it is prevalent in Miami and, to a lesser extent, in other U.S. cities with large Latin populations. In Miami, many initiates are Anglos. To Santeria's affluent initiates, the group's appeal may be similar to that of conventional lodges or country clubs — as a way of making business connections. Initiates include doctors, businesspersons, and drug dealers.

Santeria's secret initiation is gruesome and expensive (about $500). A detailed description of the ritual by an anonymous female initiate appeared in *Miami* magazine in 1982. The ceremony is performed by a *babalawo* (male "bishop"), a *madrina* (female "godmother"), and a *yubona* (female assistant to the *madrina*). A babalawo can earn well over $60,000 a year performing initiations.

A ubiquitous symbol of Santeria is a statuette of an American Indian, a miniature of the old cigar store Indian. How such a trinket came to have significance in a cult of African and Catholic origin is one of the

many unexplained mysteries of Santeria. The night before the ceremony, the candidate sleeps at the babalawo's house in a room with
the Indian statuette. In the morning, the madrina prepares a mixture
of grated coconut and coconut butter in the blender. Sometimes the
babalawo chews the coconut instead. Chunks of coconut meat are
dipped in the coconut purée and placed at certain points on the candidate's body: the forehead, the temples, the back of the skull, the
breastbone, the arms, the palms, the knees, and the feet. A white scarf
is placed on the head, and a candle is set out.

The madrina sprinkles water on the floor. She throws four cubes of
coconut fashioned to serve as dice: some faces are white, some are
black. The outcome of the throw augurs the validity of the ceremony.
If the throw is bad, it may be corrected by appropriate ritual. The
pieces of coconut are taken off the candidate's body and placed in a
paper bag. The bag must be thrown away "in the country." (In contemporary South Florida, a vacant suburban lot will do.)

A terrine, a live pigeon, sugarcane syrup, honey, and seashells are
taken by those assembled to a deserted beach. Weekdays and the off-
season (summer) are preferred, for privacy. The candidate is told to
find an attractive stone or shell as an offering to Olokum, a sea god,
and to fill the terrine with sea water. The yubona stands at the water's
edge with the pigeon. Grabbing the bird by the legs, she twists its
head off. Its blood is sprinkled in the water, and honey is poured into
the neck opening. Cane syrup is poured in the water. (The blood and
syrup are symbolic food for Olokum.) The yubona throws the coconut
cubes to determine if the gods were pleased.

The main part of the ceremony takes place back at the babalawo's
house. Some parts are so secret that the candidate is not permitted to
watch. A variety of herbs are prepared. The hosts may ask specific
favors from the gods on behalf of the candidate. A ceremonial liquid
is prepared, and a special meal of many dishes — meat, coffee, sugar,
rice, plantains, beans, eggs, and more — is set out for the gods. The
candidate must grab the various foods in his fists and rub them over
his body. The food is then thrown into a basket.

Small icons represent four gods of African origin: Eleggua, the
Trickster (a mask); Oggun, the Owner of the Knife (a pot containing
metal implements); Ochosi, Justice (a lyre with spears instead of

strings); and Oshu, the Head (a cup with a rooster head, containing beads and powders). The babalawo and *santeros* (priests) bring in four animals for sacrifice. A chicken is decapitated first and its blood sprinkled on the image of Eleggua. The babalawo pours honey into the neck opening, and the chicken head is placed next to Eleggua's icon. A rooster is sacrificed to Oggun. A pigeon is next, then a duck. The heads of the larger birds are severed with a knife. The babalawo cuts out the duck's tongue and a piece of vein from its neck and places them in a terrine. He lights a candle and throws the coconut dice to assess the gods' approval or disapproval.

All the animal carcasses are placed in a basket. A member of the party takes the basket to a river or the beach and throws it into the water. The new initiate may not leave the babalawo's house until the animals are disposed of.

Some initiations are more elaborate. It costs about $7,500 to become a santero, part of which goes to defray the cost of the animals used. The Miami River is said to be teeming with headless carcasses; the Dade County Water Control department finds decapitated chickens almost daily. Larger animals, including goats, pigs, and dogs, turn up about ten times a month. In Cuba, recurrent scare stories say that children are sacrificed on St. Barbara's Feast Day, December 4.

• 6 •

MANTRAS

Mantras are the secret words given to those who take Transcendental Meditation classes. Each person repeats his or her own individual mantra while meditating. The TM organization will not say how it doles out mantras. We're told that there are many different mantras and that they are assigned on the basis of personality.

Yeah, yeah, but it really works. If you take TM from one instructor and then switch, you are usually given the same mantra, it is claimed. How is that arranged?

TM's founder, Maharishi Mahesh Yogi, is a doggedly enigmatic figure who won't reveal his age, much less the mantra formula. (Most guess that Mahesh was born around 1911.) A vegetarian, he breakfasts on honey and distilled water. Mahesh does not insist on such asceticism among his followers, though they must renounce hard drugs and psychoanalysis. At one time or another, students of TM have included all the Beatles, Mia Farrow, Joe Namath, assorted Beach Boys and Rolling Stones, Efrem Zimbalist, Jr., Kurt Vonnegut's wife and daughter, and Major General Franklin M. Davis, many of whom would as soon not be associated with TM today. Mahesh's organization operates from Maharishi International University, a 232-acre spread that weirds out the natives in Fairfield, Iowa. Today's converts learn of Mahesh through his TV show, seen mostly on UHF and cable stations.

TM's use of mantras is a watered-down version of Eastern practices. Some believers in India have chanted ten hours a day for many years. TM recommends that its converts meditate for a mere twenty minutes in the morning and another twenty minutes in the evening. In principle, any word can be a mantra. The simplest traditional mantra is OM, sometimes spelled AUM. This is claimed to be the "cosmic sound" or "the perfect symbol of the impersonal aspect of the Godhead." "Hare Krishna" is another Eastern mantra. George Harrison has said that his mantra (assigned by Mahesh personally) is an English word included in the lyrics of "I Am the Walrus."

But a standardized system suffices for run-of-the-mill TM-ers. Mahesh reportedly realized that not all of his instructors could be as perceptive as himself, so he designed secret "foolproof" procedures for assigning mantras to the masses.

TM land has its malcontents. A few years back, a bunch of dissidents got together and published the *Transcendental Meditation Secret Manuscript*. According to them, just sixteen mantras are given out, and they are assigned by the age of the student. Lest there be any doubt of the *Manuscript's* accuracy, Scot Morris of *Omni* magazine reported that the magician Marcello Truzzi got hold of the list and built a mantra mind-reading act around it. The act amounts to guessing the person's age.

Okay, then. The next time a TM-er tries to sell you a flower in an airport, try yelling his mantra. The secret mantra lists goes like this:

Age of Student	Mantra	Age of Student	Mantra
0–11	ENG	26–29	SHIRING
12–13	EM	30–34	SHIRIM
14–15	ENGA	35–39	HIRING
16–17	EMA	40–44	HIRIM
18–19	AENG	45–49	KIRING
20–21	AEM	50–54	KIRIM
22–23	AENGA	55–59	SHAM
24–25	AEMA	60 and older	SHAMA

Note: Spellings are phonetic. Mantras are not supposed to be written down.

· 7 ·

THE SECRET TEACHINGS OF L. RON HUBBARD

Scientology, a cult, church, and self-development program, was founded by the reclusive science fiction writer L. Ron Hubbard. His worldwide organization offers counseling based on his best-selling *Dianetics: The Modern Science of Mental Health.* The Scientology organization actively recruits members. John Travolta, Chick Corea, Sonny Bono, and Karen Black are Scientologists; so is Sylvester Stallone's brother Frank.

In 1985 Larry Wollersheim sued the Scientology organization for not making good on its promise to increase his intelligence. One of the exhibits in the case was a copy of Hubbard's secret teachings, arcane wisdom that is revealed only to those who pay $12,100 for a special course. Thus the teachings briefly became a matter of public record. On November 4, 1985, about fifteen hundred Scientologists stormed the Los Angeles County Courthouse to request photocopies of the documents in order to keep outsiders from getting them. Less than three hours after the documents were made available, they were sealed on the request of Scientology's attorneys, who objected that disclosure would subject the cult to "ridicule, hatred, and contempt." *Bigger Secrets* got a look at those documents.

Getting Clear

The cornerstone of Scientology is "auditing," a form of analysis or confession using an "E meter," a homemade lie detector of Hubbard's invention. You hold on to two tin cans, and the E meter measures the resistance between them. That's it. While you are "on the cans" — that's what Scientologists call it — an auditor asks you embarrassing questions. If your palms sweat, the resistance goes down, the meter's needle jumps, and the auditor figures you're lying. Auditing costs about $300 an hour.

The goal of auditing is to confess all your painful thoughts and thus become "clear." In practice, Scientology students keep going to auditing sessions as long as their money or interest holds out. If the numerous lawsuits filed by former members are any indication, it is easy to drop anywhere from $5,000 to $40,000 on getting clear.

Scientology is big, big enough to have an espionage agency that has employed as many as five thousand spies. Scientology moles have infiltrated the IRS, the Drug Enforcement Agency, the Justice Department, and sundry other U.S. and foreign agencies believed to be critical of the organization, according to testimony at the trial of Hubbard's third wife. Hubbard had a thick dossier on Richard Nixon.

All those auditing classes pull in as much as $100 million a year. No one is quite sure what happens to the loot. Scientology has a string of dummy corporations based in no-tell countries like Liechtenstein, Luxembourg, and Liberia. It is unclear who is sincere and who is cynical in Scientology. Hubbard once quipped that the best way to become rich is to start your own religion. He never entirely shed suspicion that he was taking his own advice.

In 1975 Scientology tried to take over the city government of Clearwater, Florida (pop. 70,000). That never panned out. But the group is believed to have hidden enclaves in Dunedin, Florida, and La Quinta and Gilman Hot Springs, California. Scientology also has a secret movie studio out in the California desert.

Disillusioned Scientology graduates have charged that Hubbard has blatantly falsified his biography. He is supposed to have traveled in the Orient for inspiration as a teen. School records show he was attending high school in the Midwest. Biographies say he wrote the screenplays of *Treasure Island* and *Dive Bomber,* both produced by Columbia. The films were actually produced by RKO and Warner Brothers and credited to Lawrence Edward Watkin and Frank Wead and Robert Buckner, all well-known screenwriters with many other credits.

Hubbard made himself out to be a naval hero. "Blinded with injured optical nerves, and lame with physical injuries from hip to back, at the end of World War II, I faced an almost non-existent future," he claimed. Naval records show he never saw combat.

Off Oregon, Hubbard's ship engaged what they thought was a Japanese submarine. The navy thinks it was just a log. Hubbard's ship next sailed down the coast and opened fire on Mexico. Since we weren't at war with Mexico, the navy thought this was a dumb idea. Hubbard was discharged for arthritis and bursitis.

In 1966 Hubbard took to sea again. This time it was aboard the *Apollo,* a 330-foot customized ferryboat. Hubbard and his entourage steered a course for international waters, never to return until he got the "all clear" — news that the organization's mounting tax and legal troubles were over. It never came.

"Aboard the *Apollo,* Hubbard acted out his wartime fantasies as he sailed the world's oceans," *Time* magazine reported. "He was addressed as 'the Commodore,' his bevy of young women servants were called 'Commodore's Messenger Org' (for organization), while his uniformed 'Sea Org' elite formed his crew."

After almost a decade at sea, Hubard was believed to have gone into hiding in the Southern California desert. Widely reported rumors had it that he was dead or a pathetic mental vegetable. In an unexpected development, his literary career resumed in the wake of the death rumors. In 1983 his nine-hundred-page *Battlefield Earth: A Saga of the Year 3000* became a best-seller. It was followed in 1985 by *The Invaders Plan,* which was advertised as Volume One of a *ten-part* series. There has been speculation that Scientology's high command hired ghostwriters for these books to combat the dead-or-demented stories.

Finally in 1986, the Scientology organization conceded that Hubbard was permanently indisposed. The word *death* was studiously avoided, but we were given to understand that Hubbard "no longer had need of the encumbrance of the physical identity we have known as L. Ron Hubbard," in the words of Scientology President Heber Jentzsch. The Commodore's ashes were scattered in the Pacific.

The $12,100 Xemu Revelations

The longer a person stays in Scientology, the more layers of Hubbard's revelations he learns. The forbidden central core of Hubbard's philosophy is disclosed only to those who have been prepared by extensive auditing. Regular folks aren't ready for these shockers, according to the leadership, and such knowledge could actually be harmful to the uninitiated.

The organization charges $12,100 for a course on the secret teachings (this does not include the cost of prerequisite auditing). Scientology splinter groups have offered no-frills versions of the same course for as little as $1,500, but this was ruled a violation of Scientology's rights in 1985 by U.S. District Judge Mariana R. Pfaelzer. "It's the first time you've ever seen a decision that religious scriptures constitute trade secrets," a Scientology attorney claimed.

According to the documents Wollersheim placed in evidence — the documents that fifteen hundred loyal Scientologists tried hard to conceal — here is what Hubbard and his inner circle believe:

Seventy-five million years ago, the earth was called Teegeeach. It was one of a federation of about ninety planets. A bad guy named Xemu ruled the planets. The federation was overpopulated, so Xemu rounded up the surplus population and beamed them down to ten volcanoes on earth/Teegeeach. Then Xemu dropped H-bombs on the volcanoes, and they all died.

No, *really*. Then the spirits of the dead guys, the thetans, all stuck together in clusters. Xemu imprisoned the clusters of thetans in a frozen mixture of alcohol and glycol for thirty-six days. (*Note:* Glycol, synthesized by Charles-Adolphe Wurtz in 1856, is the main ingredient of Prestone antifreeze.) During the thirty-six days, Xemu put bad personality traits in the thetan clusters. When the thetans got out of the antifreeze, they attached themselves to humans and infested them with bad personality traits. All emotional illness and antisocial behavior come from the thetans. When a person dies, the thetans move on to another person. The upshot is, when you do something bad it isn't you, it's the thetans and Xemu. The practical side of the course tells you how to identify thetans and exorcise them.

Wollersheim didn't think this was worth $12,100.

• 8 •

GHASTLY ADOLESCENT RITUALS

*B*igger Secrets uncovered the loathsome secret rites of some of our most distinguished college Greek-letter societies. Then I checked the fraternities' history to see what prominent persons may have received or dished out similar treatment in their college days.

Alpha Sigma Phi

Famous Members: Vincent Price, Willard Scott, Tom Watson

The full significance of Alpha Sigma Phi's symbol — the phoenix — becomes known to pledges in the "flambeau" ritual of initiation. (The rite was revealed in 1985, when an Illinois Institute of Technology student was accidentally burned and sued the fraternity and the college.)

Pledges enter a darkened room decorated with skulls. In the middle of the room is a flaming pan of alcohol resting on a coffin. As the pledges draw close, they see the coffin has a glass window. Visible in the flame's livid light is the "dead" body of one of the lodge brothers.

Beta Theta Pi

Famous Members: James Arness, Chuck Colson, William O. Douglas, H. R. Haldeman, Mark Hatfield, Jerry Lucas, George Peppard, John Warner

Beta Theta Pi is one of many fraternities that practice "dumping." They get a pledge drunk, pile him into a car, and maroon him at some distant location with or without clothing.

Black Watch Cadet Corps

Famous Members: Names not released; traditionally, many of Canada's top military leaders

The Black Watch Cadet Corps is a prestigious military fraternity headquartered in Montreal. Most of the thousands who apply each year do not get in, even after grueling hazing details such as scrubbing toilets. A *Bigger Secrets* informant described this hazing stunt:

A group of several hundred pledges are taken into the wilderness for a survival test. They perform physical labors and attempt to live off the land. There is not enough wild food to support the large group, and several days later, the group is exhausted and malnourished.

Then a Black Watch member leads them to a circus-size tent set in the wilderness. The tables inside are set with a smorgasbord of hot foods, and the pledges feast. While the celebration goes on, the pledges are called away in groups of about a dozen and taken to a small building some distance away. The door is locked behind the pledges after they enter. Inside, a tablet is dropped into a pool of liquid. It fizzes, producing an evil-smelling gas. Most of the pledges throw up.

Our informant said some of the pledges feared death. The setup is clearly intended to resemble a gas chamber, where a pellet of cyanide drops into a vat of sulfuric acid and releases hydrogen cyanide gas. The informant did not know what chemicals were used in the Black Watch hazing.

Delta Kappa Epsilon

Famous Members: Alfred Bloomingdale, George Bush, Dick Clark, Tom Eagleton, Gerald Ford, William Randolph Hearst, Cole Porter, Winthrop Rockefeller, Teddy Roosevelt, Sargent Shriver, George Steinbrenner, Jonathan Winters

Initiates at Colgate University learn the secrets of the Deke Temple, a quaint brick building without windows near the Deke frat house. The temple was built in 1873 and is always locked. No one except Dekes knows what is inside. Whatever it is, it probably can't compare to campus rumor: the temple is said to house a swimming pool full of sparkling burgundy.

Omega Psi Phi

Famous Members: Count Basie, Benjamin Hooks, Jesse Jackson, Vernon Jordan, Jr., Walter Washington

Incredibly, Omega Psi Phi brands its members during initiation. Simulated branding is a common fraternity stunt: A pledge is told that he must take the fraternity's brand. He is blindfolded and a piece of ice applied to his skin, often the genitals. It's all a big joke, and the pledge usually understands that. Some fraternities brand with an iron placed in dry ice. This is claimed to produce a temporary scar lasting about six months.

But on many campuses the Omega Psi Phi initiation includes *real* branding with a red-hot coathanger. The Omegas, one of the oldest predominantly black fraternities in the country, were founded by students who failed other frats' "paper-bag tests." (Some black fraternities used to reject rushees whose skin color was darker than a brown paper bag.) Omega Psi Phi has 250 undergraduate chapters and 80,000 initiates. Not all chapters require branding, and the fraternity's national headquarters claims to be appalled by it. The branding iron is apparently made by straightening out a coathanger, the hook at the top becoming the Omega. Pledges are branded on the biceps, leg, or chest. Sometimes the brand is a pair of intersecting omegas or an omega and a small Z.

Omegas are also known for beating pledges with switches and "food gorges," in which pledges must eat without using their hands. Some of the food is doused with Tabasco sauce. Hence the rival frat Kappa Alpha Psi song that goes: "If I had a low IQ, I'd pledge Omega too."

Skull and Bones Society

Famous Members: William F. Buckley, Jr., George Bush, Averill Harriman, Henry Luce, Archibald MacLeish

On a designated "tap day" in April, masked members contact selected Yale seniors and invite them to become members. The initiation requires candidates to lie in a coffin and describe their sexual history to the members. (An absurd story claims that the candidates get $15,000 upon initiation.)

By tradition, a member must leave the room when the society's name is mentioned. Athletes from other schools sometimes yell "Skull and Bones" during matches in the hope that some of the Yalies will be in the society and have to leave.

Zeta Beta Tau

Famous Members: Leonard Bernstein, Stanley Marcus

Zeta Beta Tau pledges lie in a mock grave — a real grave dug in the ground.

Zeta Chi

Famous Members: No one famous has admitted being in this fraternity.

At the infamous Zeta Chi Spaghetti Dinner, pledges eat spaghetti and drink wine until they vomit. Trashcans are provided. After this, the pledges are supposed to keep eating.

• 9 •

MOUNT WEATHER

In the best-selling 1962 spy thriller *Seven Days in May*, the Joint Chiefs of Staff plot to overthrow the U.S. president. Their conspiracy centers on a place called Mount Thunder, a secret subterranean command post where government leaders would go in the event of a nuclear attack.

On December 1, 1974, a TWA Boeing 727 jet crashed into a fog-shrouded mountain in northern Virginia and burned, killing all ninety-two persons aboard. Near the wreckage was a fenced government reserve identified as Mount Weather.

Mount Weather is a real place: eighty-five acres located forty-five miles west of Washington and 1,725 feet above sea level, near the town of Bluemont, Virginia. In the event of all-out war, an elite of civilian and military leaders are to be taken to Mount Weather's cavernous underground shelter to become the nucleus of a postwar American society. The government has a secret list of those persons it plans to save.

The Federal Emergency Management Agency (FEMA) runs Mount Weather. When it has to talk about the place, which is rare, it calls it the "special facility." Its more common name comes from a weather station that the U.S. Department of Agriculture had maintained on the mountain.

The authors of *Seven Days in May,* Fletcher Knebel and Charles W. Bailey II, were Washington journalists who learned a lot about the then-quite-secret post. Few readers of Knebel and Bailey's fiction could have imagined how close to the truth it was. The novel gives detailed highway directions from Washington:

> ... the Chrysler wheeled onto Route 50, heading away from Washington. . . .
>
> In the jungle of neon lights and access roads at Seven Corners, Corwin saw Scott bear right onto Route 7, the main road to Leesburg. The two cars moved slowly through Falls Church before the traffic began to thin out and speed up. . . .
>
> At the fork west of Leesburg, Scott bore right on Route 9, heading toward Charles Town. . . . They began to climb toward the Blue Ridge, the eastern rim of the Shenandoah Valley. . . .
>
> West of Hillboro, where the road crossed the Blue Ridge before dropping into the valley . . . Scott turned left. Corwin followed him onto a black macadam road that ran straight along the spine of the ridge.
>
> ... Because of his White House job, Corwin knew something about this road that few other Americans did. Virginia 120 appeared to be nothing more than a somewhat better-than-average Blue Ridge byway, but it ran past Mount Thunder, where an underground installation provided one of the several bases from which the President could run the nation in the event of a nuclear attack on Washington.

Knebel and Bailey disguised the directions slightly. You continue on Route 7 west of Leesburg, turning left on Route 601 just west of Bluemont. It's Virginia Route 601 that runs right up to the gates of Mount Weather. Residents have long known there is something funny about that road; it is always the first road cleared after a snowstorm.

At one point, the government asked the local newspapers not to print any articles about the facility. But it is all but impossible to keep such a place secret. The Appalachian Trail runs right by Mount Weather, and hikers can get close enough to see signs and flashing lights. One sign reads: "All persons and vehicles entering hereon are liable to search. Photographing, making notes, drawings, maps or graphic representations of this area or its activities are prohibited." In the late 1960s an unidentified "hippie" is supposed to have stumbled upon the facility and sketched it from a tree. His drawing turned up in the *Quicksilver Times,* an underground newspaper in Washington.

Residents also tell of the time a hunt club chased a fox onto the site and triggered an alarm. The club had to go to the main gate to get its dogs back.

After the TWA crash, a spokesman "politely declined to comment on what Mt. Weather was used for, how many people work there, or how long it has been in its current use," the *Washington Post* reported. The *Post* published a photograph of the facility, citing far-fetched speculation that Mount Weather's radio antennas may have interfered with the jet's radar and caused the disaster.

You don't get into Mount Weather without an invitation. The entrance is said to be like the door to a bank vault, only thicker, set into a mountain made out of the toughest granite in the East. It is guarded around the clock.

Mount Weather got more unsolicited publicity in 1975. Senator John Tunney (D-Calif.) charged that Mount Weather held dossiers on 100,000 or more Americans. A sophisticated computer system gives the installation access to detailed information on the lives of virtually every American citizen, Tunney claimed. Mount Weather personnel stonewalled question after question in two Senate hearings.

"I don't understand what they're trying to hide out there," Douglas Lea, staff director of the Senate Subcommittee on Constitutional Rights, said. "Mount Weather is just closed up to us." Tunney complained that Mount Weather was "out of control."

Mount Weather has been owned by the government since 1903, when the site was purchased by the U.S. Department of Agriculture. Calvin Coolidge talked about building a summer White House there. In World War I it was an artillery range, and during the Depression it was a workfarm for hobos. Mount Weather as an alternate capital seems to have been the idea of Millard F. Caldwell, former governor of Florida.

There is a fallout shelter under the East Wing of the White House. No one believes it offers any real protection from a nuclear attack on Washington, however. FEMA has elaborate plans for getting the president and other key officials out of Washington should there be a nuclear attack.

In that event, the president is supposed to board a Boeing 747 National Emergency Airborne Command Post ("Kneecap"). That is presumed to be safer than any point on the ground. The president's plane can be refueled in the air from other planes and may be able to stay airborne for as long as three days. Then its engine will conk out for lack of oil. That is where Mount Weather comes in.

Government geologists selected the site because it has some of the most impregnable rock in the eastern United States. The shelter was started in the Truman administration, and it took years to tunnel into the mountain.

There is a whole chain of shelters for leaders and critical personnel. The Federal Relocation Arc, a system of ninety-six shelters for specific U.S. Government agencies, sweeps through North Carolina, Virginia, West Virginia, Maryland, and Pennsylvania. A duplicate of the Pentagon is located at a site called Raven Rock in Maryland. The administrative center of the whole system, and the place where the top civilians would go, is Mount Weather.

Mount Weather is much more than a fallout shelter; it is a troglodytic Levittown. In the mid-1970s Richard Pollock, a writer for *Progressive* magazine, interviewed a number of persons who had been associated with Mount Weather. According to them, Mount Weather is an underground city with roads, sidewalks, and a battery-powered subway. A spring-fed artificial lake gleams in the fluorescent light. There are office buildings, cafeterias, and hospitals. Large dormitories are furnished with bunks or "hot cots" — hammocks intended to be occupied in three eight-hour shifts. There are private apartments as well. Mount Weather has its own waterworks, food storage, and power plant. A "bubble-shaped pod" in the East Tunnel houses one of the most powerful computers in the world.

The Situation Room, a circular chamber, would be a nerve center in time of war. The Mount Weather folks set great store by visual aids and retain artists and cartographers at all times. A futuristic color videophone system is the basic means of communication within Mount Weather's subterranean world. "All important staff meetings were conducted via color television as far back as 1958, long before it was generally available to the public," one former staffer bragged.

The most surprising of Pollock's revelations is that Mount Weather has a working back-up U.S. Government *even now*. Undisclosed persons there duplicate the responsibilities of our elected leaders, making Mount Weather an eerie doppelgänger of the United States.

An Office of the Presidency is ensconced in an underground wing known as the White House. The elected president or survivor closest in the chain of command would make his way there and take over the reins. Until then, a staff appointed by FEMA would be carrying out duties said to simulate those of the real president.

Installed at Mount Weather are nine federal departments, their very names ironic in the context: Agriculture, Commerce, Health and Human Services, Housing and Urban Development, Interior, Labor, State, Transportation, and the Treasury. Miniature versions of the Selective Service, the Veterans' Administration, the Federal Communications Commission, the Post Office, the Civil Service Commission, the Federal Power Commission, and the Federal Reserve are there, too.

"High-level government sources, speaking under the promise of strict anonymity, told me that each of the federal departments represented at Mount Weather is headed by a single person on whom is conferred the rank of a Cabinet-level official," Pollock reported. "Protocol even demands that subordinates address them as 'Mr. Secretary.' Each of the Mount Weather 'Cabinet members' is apparently appointed by the White House and serves an indefinite term. Many of the 'secretaries' have held their positions through several administrations."

What do all these people do? Twice a month, Mount Weather stages a war game to train its personnel and explore various dire scenarios. Once a year they pull out all the stops and have a super drill in which *real* Cabinet members and White House staffers fly in from Washington.

General Leslie Bray, director of the Federal Preparedness Agency, FEMA's predecessor, told the Senate that Mount Weather has extensive files on "military installations, government facilities, communications, transportation, energy and power, agriculture, manufacturing, wholesale and retail services, manpower, financial, medical and educational institutions, sanitary facilities, population, housing shelter, and stockpiles." Additional information is kept in safekeeping at other shelters in the Federal Relocation Arc.

There is a body of opinion that considers Mount Weather obsolete. Mount Weather is a nonmovable target, and a very strategic one if the relocation plans work. The "toughest granite in the East" may have offered some protection in Eisenhower's time, but multiple strikes could blast the mountain away. It was reported that the TWA jet crash knocked out power at Mount Weather for two and a half hours. What would a bomb do?

The Soviet Union knows exactly where Mount Weather is — and almost certainly knew long before the Western press did. The Soviets tried to buy an estate near Mount Weather as a "vacation retreat" for embassy employees. The State Department stopped the sale.

The Survivor List

In 1975 General Bray told the Senate that the Mount Weather survivor list had sixty-five hundred names on it. Who might be included?

The president, of course, provided he survives his Kneecap command. The vice-president and Cabinet members are on the list because they take part in the annual dry runs. Beyond that, little is known, and the few existing accounts conflict.

For instance, what about Congress? General Bray said that his responsibilities included the executive branch only, not Congress or the Supreme Court. But in an interview in 1976, Senator Hubert Humphrey insisted that he had visited the shelter as vice-president and seen "a nice little chamber, rostrum and all," for postnuclear sessions of Congress.

Furthermore, Earl Warren is said to have been invited when he was Chief Justice of the Supreme Court. Warren refused because he was not allowed to take his wife. The protocol for ordering persons to Mount Weather specifies that messages not be left with family members answering the phone.

The vast majority of the persons on the list are believed to be ranking bureaucrats from the nine federal agencies with branches at Mount Weather. Pollock said he heard stories that some construction workers were on the list "because, the Mount Weather analysts reasoned, excavation work for mass graves would be needed immediately in the aftermath of a thermonuclear war." General Bray admitted that some others such as telephone company technicians are included.

Each person on the survival list has an ID card with a photo. The cards read: THE PERSON DESCRIBED ON THIS CARD HAS ESSENTIAL EMERGENCY DUTIES WITH THE FEDERAL GOVERNMENT. REQUEST FULL ASSISTANCE AND UNRESTRICTED MOVEMENT BE AFFORDED THE PERSON TO WHOM THIS CARD IS ISSUED.

· 10 ·

SECRETS OF STATE

Russian Spy Powder

The Soviets use a yellow powder to track U.S. Embassy personnel and others. According to government analysis, its formula is $NO_2C_6H_4CH:CHCH:CHCHO$ — nitrophenylpentadienal, or NPPD.

Although the State Department has been reluctant to explain how the powder is used — and the Russians deny it even exists — it probably works like this. The chemical is smeared on a doorknob or a steering wheel, say, that a certain person is sure to touch. (It was wondered if a cockroach powder used by Russian exterminators at the U.S. Embassy in Moscow might contain the substance.) That person then leaves traces of NPPD on everything and everyone he touches. If the Russians marked U.S. personnel with the powder and subsequently found traces of it in the apartment of a suspected spy, it would be strong evidence of dealings with the Americans.

Why NPPD rather than some other chemical? The Russians must be able to detect NPPD in extremely small traces. NPPD glows under ultraviolet light. Some embassy staff speculated that the Russians may use portable ultraviolet lamps to follow a trail. But ultraviolet lamps would be of little help unless the marked person was leaving visible smudges of the dust. More likely, Russian agents use chromatography or mass spectrometry on objects they suspect a marked person has touched. NPPD, or the preparation containing it, is believed to be extremely tenacious once it gets on the skin. It apparently does not come off in normal washing for a long time. American residents in Moscow were advised to wash with soap and water and then with an alcohol-based compound.

No one is sure how well the powder works. Suppose an NPPD-marked person attends a diplomatic reception and shakes hands with several hundred people. Will the KGB end up tracking them all? What about the people those people touch?

The FBI's License Plate Code

About twenty-five hundred Soviet and Eastern European officials reside in the United States at any time, and the State Department estimates that 30% to 40% of them are spies. That means maybe nine hundred working spies just in the diplomatic corps. Keeping track of their comings and goings creates jobs for a comparable number of American spies. One labor-saving device is a secret code used on diplomatic license plates that was revealed by the *Washington Post.*

The code applies only to diplomatic plates, a familiar sight in Washington and New York. These plates are red, white, and blue and say DIPLOMAT at the top. All diplomatic license numbers have a *D*. The two other letters code the nation. *SX* means the Soviet Union, for instance. FBI counterintelligence agents are given a wallet-sized card listing the codes for eighteen "problem" nations:

Albania	CP	Libya	FM
Bulgaria	OM	Nicaragua	QU
China	CY	North Korea	GQ
Cuba	DC	Poland	QW
Czechoslovakia	PH	Romania	ND
East Germany	TJ	South Africa	FY
Hungary	KH	Soviet Union	SX
Iran	DM	Syria	AQ
Iraq	TS	Vietnam	LD

The State Department was upset with the *Post* for publishing the code, hinting that Rambo nuts might start throwing rocks at Russian cars.

Cocaine in U.S. Money

There is a detectable trace of cocaine in U.S. paper money. It is not, of course, an ingredient in the paper or ink. It probably results from cocaine users snorting through rolled-up bills. Cocaine users handle $50 and $100 bills far more often than most other people do.

The fact first came to light in the 1984 trial of two Mexicans for laundering (figuratively) drug money. The defendants were nabbed by an agent of the presidential Drug Task Force when they purchased a number of cashier's checks from Atlanta banks for amounts just under $10,000. An amount of $10,000 or more requires special paperwork, so the purchases were suspicious. So was the fact that the defendants had $200,000 in $20 bills on them at the time of their arrest. But the agent found no drugs.

A chemist with the Georgia Bureau of Investigation was called in to analyze the money. The government reasoned that if the money had been touched by people who had handled drugs, or if it had been in the same room where drugs were being cut, there might be detectable traces of drugs in the money. The GBI chemist took a sample of the bills, washed them in alcohol, and did a radio-immunoassay on the solution. She found 100 nanograms of opiate and cocaine residues.

The defending attorney, Jack Martin, hired his own chemist, Atlanta toxicologist James Woodford. He had Woodford buy 6½ pounds of U.S. currency fragments — the shredded money that is sometimes sealed in a paperweight and sold as a gag gift. Woodford subjected his sample to a more exacting analysis than the government investigators had, including both a radio-immunoassay and a second-derivative nuclear magnetic resonance analysis. He found 15 milligrams of either cocaine or amphetamines in the first analysis. The nuclear magnetic resonance study confirmed that there was cocaine in the sample.

In short, Woodford's tests seemed to show that there was a detectable trace of cocaine in any old money. In the absence of any other evidence against them, the defendants were acquitted.

Similar results were reported in the 1985 trial of Maiano Ospina, a wealthy Colombian, in Miami. Ospina had been arrested when customs dogs snuffled and barked at some of Ospina's luggage. Inside the bags was $1.3 million in cash.

Ospina's attorney, Jack Denaro, hired Dr. William Lee Hearn. Hearn used a gas chromatograph–mass spectrometer to examine bills from local banks for comparison. Only large bills were tested — twenties, fifties, and hundreds. Hearn used $1,000 to $1,500 from each of seven Dade County banks. All seven samples showed traces of cocaine; in fact, the first sample made the machine go off the scale.

Okay, but that's Miami. Heard then tried samples of money from all over the country. Still, each sample contained cocaine.

If these findings are representative, there is a lot of cocaine in the money supply. Woodford found 15 milligrams in his 6½ pounds of money. Cocaine sells for something like $100 a gram. That means there was about $1.50 worth of cocaine in Woodford's sample, or about 23 cents' worth per pound of money.

The Deformed Foot on the $2 Bill

There is a strangely twisted foot in the picture of the signing of the Declaration of Independence on the $2 bill. Many have noted this peculiarity, and there have been the usual naive allegations that this is an anticounterfeiting device purposely implanted by the Treasury Department.

The vignette shows John Hancock seated at a table. Five signers stand in front of the table. From left to right, they are John Adams, Roger Sherman, Robert L. Livingston, Thomas Jefferson, and Benjamin Franklin. The corner of the tablecloth almost touches the floor. Just to the right of this corner is part of a foot. It seems to be paired with the foot to the left of the tablecloth. But unless Jefferson can bend his leg in the wrong direction at the knee, it is hard to see how this foot can be attached to his leg. If it's someone else's foot, he is standing in a more incredible position yet.

The $2 bill's picture is closely based on John Trumbull's *The Declaration of Independence,* a painting commissioned by Congress for the U.S. Capitol Rotunda. The perspective is easier to judge in that painting, and the foot in question (definitely Jefferson's) does not look so strange as on the bill.

SEX on the $5 Bill

Wilson Bryan Key, Ph.D., the guy who finds the word "SEX" embedded in advertising photos and even on Ritz crackers, is still at it. He claims that the offending word is to be found in Lincoln's beard on the U.S. $5 bill.

According to Key's description in *The Clam Plate Orgy and Other Subliminal Techniques for Manipulating Your Behavior,* you start by finding the diagonal line coming down from the left side of Lincoln's chin. This almost runs into a dark region representing the top of the beard. Go right about an eighth of an inch. Below this dark area is a white, horizontal stroke forming the top of Key's S. The purported letters S, E, X are white on the dark background of the beard, a little to the left of Lincoln's chin.

On a brand-new bill, I *think* I see what Key is talking about. But what I see doesn't look particularly like the word "SEX." It's just some white spaces between the black engraving strokes.

Key says, "Once you clearly perceive the three letters in Lincoln's beard, you can hold the $5 bill several feet away and the tiny letters stand out like a neon sign." If that's right, I must have a defective bill. Key claims that after a lecture in San Diego, a naval officer went to a bar and won over a hundred dollars by wagering that he could prove there is something sexy in the Lincoln portrait. I can just imagine how easily drunk sailors will pick this out in a bar. In any case, Key thinks the word "SEX" was put there on purpose, starting with the 1914 series of $5 bills. He believes it is intended to be perceived subconsciously and boost confidence in U.S. currency.

The Burp Defense

Burping during a breathalyser test invalidates the results. The test measures alcohol in the breath, and a person with a lot of alcohol in his blood will have alcohol in his breath. If a person burps during the test, vapor from alcohol that has yet to enter the bloodstream is introduced into the test balloon. That throws things off, giving a false positive reading.

It follows that anyone who burps during a test and gets a high reading can claim that the burp invalidated it. In 1981 a driver in Montrose, Colorado, used the burp defense to get himself off. Since then, word of the burp ploy has spread widely.

Some products are said to *reduce* a breathalyser reading. Lemon drops and Skoal chewing tobacco are often mentioned but probably don't work. Breath Fresh 502, a mouthwash sold via mail order was promoted as helping you beat the test until the Feds cracked down. The government's gripe wasn't that you couldn't sell something to help pass a DUI test but rather that it just didn't do what the ads claimed.

Secret Grass

An "invisible" type of marijuana has been invented on behalf of the U.S. Government. "Secret grass" is a freakish hybrid of hops and marijuana, and it is claimed that clever pot growers avoid detection by growing it.

Marijuana and hashish come from the same plant that produces hemp fiber. The navy used to use a lot of hemp rope, and so, in a modest way, hemp was vital to national defense. During World War II, the government sponsored research at the Carnegie Institute of Washington into finding a superstrong hemp plant that did not contain the drug principle. One of the angles they tried was grafting hemp to other plants.

Hemp will not graft to just anything. The closest living relative of *Cannabis sativa* is hops (*Humulus lupulus*), the bitter plant used to flavor beer. Government botanists discovered that the two plants may be grafted using the simple "wedge graft" of horticulturists. At the age of a few weeks, a seedling of one plant is chopped off a few inches above the ground. With a razor blade, the "stump" is split vertically. A scion of the other plant (a stem about the same size, trimmed to a wedge shape) is inserted in the split. The graft is tied with raffia and sealed with Vaseline to prevent loss of fluid.

Researchers tried grafting hemp onto a hops root and hops onto a hemp root. The first combination didn't grow. The second combination thrived. It was, however, the opposite of what the government was looking for. Aboveground, it was to all appearances an ordinary hop plant — a large rambling vine with lobed leaves something like a maple's. It didn't produce hemp fiber at all. But it was reported to contain levels of THC and other cannabinoids (hashish's active ingredients) comparable to an ordinary marijuana plant.

Synthetic fibers came into use shortly afterward, and the matter was dropped. But word of the experiments got around. Underground magazines told how to make the grafts. Supposedly untold numbers of marijuana growers sidestep the drug laws by growing secret grass, the hops/hemp chimera . . .

Secret grass may be little more than a pipe dream. In 1974 two British chemists, Leslie Crombie and W. Mary L. Crombie, repeated the grafting experiments using modern analytic techniques. In a 1975 study published in *Phytochemistry,* they found it easy enough to graft hops onto marijuana. But the Crombies failed to find THC and other cannabinoids in the top part of the resulting plant. At most, they found that the bottom, marijuana part of the plant might produce slightly more of certain cannabinoids for being grafted to hops.

The Umbra Secret

The federal government rates classified information as Confidential, Secret, or Top Secret, in order of increasing sensitivity. There are categories beyond Top Secret that are so secret that even their *names* are supposed to be a secret. Washington insiders say classification categories in current or recent use include Umbra, Ultra, Froth, and Canoe.

· 11 ·

THE TELEPHONE COMPANY

*T*he paisley vendetta against the phone company continues. Ever since the 1960s, the Yippies — who are still around — have probed the mysteries of the phone company. For years they staged an annual ritual of cracking the new telephone credit card code introduced each year. They usually succeeded the first week of January. Income from the sale of phone company secrets to people wanting to make free calls helped finance the Yippies. (A new, more secure code has stumped them.) Of late, the Yippies have uncovered scary new high-tech gimmicks the phone company doesn't talk about. They include unprecedently sophisticated means of spying via phone — even a phone that's on the hook.

• Campus mythology speaks of a forbidden issue of the *Bell System Technical Journal*. If you go to a college library and try to get this issue, you are told that it is unavailable. In it, a telephone company scientist innocently published a secret frequency that can be used to get free phone calls.

The secret frequency is an acoustical tone of 2,600 cycles per second: a slightly flat E three octaves above middle C. The phone network uses this tone to signal that a line is unoccupied.

This discovery sparked the phone hacking explosion of the 1960s and 1970s. Phone cheats devised a way of using the 2,600 tone to get free calls. They dialed an 800 toll-free number — say, of an airline or hotel chain, it didn't matter. They let the 800 number ring and then played the 2,600-cycle tone into the speaker of the phone. This fooled the phone company computers into thinking that the line was free, that the caller had hung up. The dialer would hear a click, a buzz, and then a faint background hiss. With a "blue box" device to play the standard tones, a knowledgeable person could then dial virtually any number in the world toll-free. As far as the billing computers were concerned, the caller had dialed a toll-free number and hung up without getting an answer.

The 2,600-tone is easy to generate. Persons with perfect pitch can whistle it. A free whistle once given away in Captain Crunch cereal hit the exact note. A one-line BASIC program will generate it on virtually any personal computer.

The days of "blue boxing" are pretty much over. The phone company now has an automatic "blue box alarm" that records the number dialed (and conversation, some claim) whenever this tone is transmitted from a phone.

• The phone company doesn't tell you, but you get a ten-second grace period when hanging up. Suppose someone calls and you answer on one phone but want to talk on another. If you hang up and can make it to the other extension in ten seconds, the caller will still be on the line. If both parties hang up, the connection is broken immediately.

• The phone company has a number that recites the phone number you dial from: 958 in New York City, for instance. The number is used by phone company employees to make sure that a new phone has been assigned the intended number. When you dial the number from your home, you hear a machine voice announcing your home phone number.

• The high numbers of a phone exchange (such as 836-9999 or 836-9998) are frequently used for "loops." A loop is a pair of consecutive phone numbers used in testing toll-free lines. Anyone calling one of the numbers of an active loop can hear anyone else who calls the other number at the same time. Pirate radio stations use this to allow listeners to phone in requests while preventing the FCC from tracing the calls.

- You can listen in on calls made with cordless phones using an ordinary radio. Many cellular phones transmit at a frequency just beyond the AM broadcast band. Set the radio on AM and tune it past 16 kHz, as far as it will go, and see what you hear. High-tech voyeurs have reported hearing of drug deals, adulterous liaisons, stock tips, and other minutiae of the glamorous lives of cellular phone owners. The FCC is worried that burglars may eavesdrop to find affluent people who are away from home. Newer cellular phones use less accessible frequencies (which can nonetheless be tuned in with a radio hobbyist's scanner).
- Many calls are transmitted by microwave, and it is accepted that espionage operations may tap into these conversations by sophisticated means (such as electronically "listening" to the ringing, comparing the phone number with a list of numbers of persons under surveillance, and recording relevant conversations). If you say the initials CIA, FBI, or NSA (National Security Agency) on long-distance calls, you may hear a click. It's rumored that the aforementioned agencies, or parties interested in their doings, have voice recognition devices that are able to record automatically any microwave conversation mentioning the agencies. One way or another, the NSA alone records and screens *thousands* of phone calls a day. (The agency is so secret that employees are not allowed to admit that they work for it.) Until 1978, the NSA spied extensively on domestic phone calls. Now legislation (theoretically) restricts surveillance to calls out of the country.
- The ultimate in phone spying is REMOB, remote observation. The phone company is said to have certain secret numbers — one is in Iowa — that can be used for listening in on other numbers. You call the REMOB number with a Touch-Tone phone, then punch in two access codes and the phone number you want to tap — which can be anywhere in the country. The tapping is done by a sophisticated technique that does not create a telltale click, hum, or beep. It's all done automatically, without an operator, and anyone knowing the number and access codes can spy on anyone anywhere.

The Infinity Microphone

Then there is something called an infinity microphone. This is a device, or a technique, that allows you to hear room conversations through a phone *still on the hook*, thereby turning any telephone into a bug.

Descriptions of the infinity microphone vary and are usually secondhand. By some accounts, it requires planting a small device in the phone to be tapped. By other accounts, no extra hardware is necessary. It is claimed that plans for infinity microphones are published in various electronic hobbyist magazines under "babysitters." That name refers to their alleged use in checking on an infant at home. The Yippies claimed in the March 1978 *YIPster Times* that the phone service was "now ready to place at the disposal of any U.S. government a capacity to search out and monitor interesting phones that would make the Gestapo green with envy — especially inasmuch as one additional modification in your local switching office enables [phone company] Security to turn any phone into a bug by amplifying the minute vibration of the bell circuit caused by room noise, whether it's on the hook or off!"

In modest ways, at least, the phone company can spy on you when the phone is on the hook. Each phone is connected to the phone network via red, yellow, and green wires. The buttons in the phone cradle are switches that disconnect the green wire. A live 48-volt circuit passes through a telephone on the yellow and red wires whenever the phone is on the hook. There is no way to turn a phone completely off, short of pulling it out of the wall.

The 48-volt circuit rings the phone. The red and yellow wires go to two induction coils and a capacitor. This simple circuit has a resonant frequency of 20 hertz. It's like a wineglass that vibrates when just the right note is struck. When someone is calling you, the phone company sends out a 20-hertz signal on the red and yellow wires. This signal, which may be very weak, builds up on the phone's ringer circuit and triggers the ringing mechanism. When you pick up the phone, the circuit drops to 6 volts.

Since every phone is always electrically live, the properties of the circuit can be measured at any time. An electrical quality called impedance can be measured easily from the phone company's switching offices. On a standard phone, this impedance is determined by the two induction coils and the capacitor inside the phone. Extra equipment added to the phone circuit may change the impedance.

Adding an extension phone changes impedance. Some phone companies automatically check the impedance of each line every day to catch customers who might try to hook up an extension themselves without paying for it. Phone hackers found that you can attach extension phones undiscovered as long as you disconnect the ringer circuit on the extensions. (The extension phones won't ring, of course.)

Bigger Secrets asked New York Telephone whether it was technically feasible to eavesdrop on room conversations via the ringer circuit. The spokesman didn't know much about the matter and cited federal and local laws regulating the use of phone company switching equipment.

Plans for a typical "babysitter" are included in *Electronic Telephone Projects* by Anthony J. Caristi. Caristi's gismo does not qualify as an infinity microphone, but it is in the ballpark. It is a 4½-by-3-inch circuit board studded with a resistor, capacitors, diodes, and the like, all readily available at your neighborhood Radio Shack. It is too bulky to hide inside a telephone,and it has its own microphone and AC plug. When the babysitter is switched on, it acts something like a phone answering machine. When someone dials the number, the babysitter prevents the phone from ringing (that would wake the baby) and automatically switches the audio from its microphone into the phone line.

Through clever design, the babysitter does not change the electrical character of the phone line. When the babysitter detects an incoming call, it directs the phone line current through a 150-ohm resistor simulating the resistance of a phone that has been taken off the cradle. The phone company is unable to detect that it has been added.

Bigger Secrets asked Caristi about infinity mikes and the Yippies' claims of eavesdropping on an unmodified phone. He confirmed that infinity microphones are no fantasy. All that's required is a small microphone hooked into the phone line and drawing, say, 1 milliampere of current, says Caristi. The microphone could be hidden inside the base of the phone, powered entirely by the 48-volt direct currect of the phone circuit. It would not affect the normal operation of the phone.

The 48-volt current comes from continuously recharged batteries at the phone company. Since this voltage is never interrupted, not even during a general power failure, the microphone would constantly impress the room noises on the phone line. Given the 900-ohm impedance of the phone line, a 1-milliampere microphone would produce an audio signal of 0.9 volts in the line. This could be amplified easily. The signal could be picked up anywhere on the phone line — where the wires leave the house, in the basement of an apartment building, at the switching box down the street, or at the phone company switching office.

All this at least requires that the phone be modified. According to Caristi, it would be difficult, but probably not impossible, to detect room noises via the ringer circuit of an *unmodified* phone on the cradle, too. The ringer circuit is not particularly sensitive to ordinary sound vibrations. The resulting "signal" would therefore be extremely weak and difficult to amplify. Caristi conjectures that a well-financed government agency might be able to solve the problems of amplification should it so desire. The Russians are known to have eavesdropped on the American embassy by detecting vibrations in windowpanes, and that would seem no less far-fetched.

PSYCHOLOGICAL TESTS

You are not supposed to see the tests psychologists use to measure personality. You are not even supposed to know how answers are interpreted. Copyright regulations prevent us from reproducing these tests in their entirety, but here are excerpts of some of the tests most widely used for employment screening and clinical diagnosis.

The Children's Apperception Test

The Children's Apperception Test (CAT) is a surreal blend of nursery rhyme innocence and primal terror. As cartoons and comic strips attest, children identify with animals. The CAT has children aged three to ten make up stories to go with test pictures of animals. These stories help the examiner — a child psychologist, teacher, guidance counselor, or social worker — understand the child's personality. Sex, violence, and scatology are high on the CAT agenda. Populating the CAT pictures are a pregnant cat, a monkey about to be eaten, and a deer with an enema bag. The pictures' cheery, Curious George style only lends a perverse frisson. Test authors Leopold and Sonya Bellak commissioned Violet Lamont, a children's book illustrator, to do the test cards. CAT proponents argue that the test is relatively free of cultural bias. No humans inhabit the CAT world. The animals defy categorization by race or class; age and gender are blurred into uniformity.

Animals can represent themes that would be hard to illustrate with humans, like return-to-the-womb fantasies. Some Freudians hold that children's fascination with kangaroos stems from such suppressed wishes. Stories playing out these desires may be particularly significant when an older child is identifying with the pouch baby. Children under six, however, often don't know about marsupials and think the mother and baby are one freakish two-headed animal.

The way children explain the kangaroos' hurry reveals their worldview. If they are fleeing from danger, children may see the world as a hostile place. Sometimes children note the milk bottle in the basket and mention its being spilled — a possible sign of a bedwetting problem. Pyromaniac themes (the house burning down) in this or other pictures may indicate bedwetting, too.

The small bears have their eyes open, a disarmingly clever way of getting children to talk about what they saw or heard when their parents thought they were asleep. The CAT manual explains that the pictures were designed in part "to learn about the child's relationship to the parents as a couple — technically spoken of as the oedipal complex and its culmination in the primal scene: namely, the child's fantasies about seeing the parents in bed together."

No parents are visible, just some bunched covers on the double bed. The child is free to fill in his own observations or speculations. Most children have absorbed enough sexual taboos to be reluctant to talk about sex. Some children see just one parent, omitting the one who seems to play the lesser role in the family.

In the CAT, animals' tails represent phalluses. Stories of the tiger biting off the monkey's tail are held to signify castration fears. Likewise, a picture of a monkey holding its tail represents masturbation, and a picture of a cat looking at its tail in a mirror probes body image. Perhaps due to the Freudian, male-oriented slant of the test, there is no comparable visual shorthand for female sexuality.

Most children mention the monkey's obvious peril. But children having trouble dealing with aggression — in others or in themselves — may be so defensive that they describe this as a peaceful scene.

The axiom of CAT interpretation is that the children's made-up stories
are largely about themselves. The monkeys on the couch are unflattering
caricatures of the adult world, talking about the little monkey behind
his back. This picture inspires thinly veiled autobiographical stories of
misbehavior and punishment or treachery at the hand of grownups. The
androgynous monkey with the earring is a parental figure that may be
interpreted as suits the story. This monkey's finger is extended as if
making a point. The position of the other hand is equivocal. The large
monkey may have its arm around the little monkey or may be spanking
him.

*This picture lays bare the sins of the bathroom. Stories about toilet
training or masturbation are normal responses. For some, this picture
hits too close to home. These children protest too much and come up
with evasive, sanitized stories. Bellak cites the response of a child with
chronic psychosomatic constipation: an exasperated "Nothing's gonna
happen!"*

The object on the wall is an enema bag. It is included to identify children being given enemas by hysterical parents. Children with more conventional toilet training simply don't recognize the bag. The way the small deer is looking at the large deer suggests themes of curiosity about the adult body and incest fantasies. The picture may help to identify cases of child abuse.

This and other pictures from the CAT's Supplement are used only with children in special situations — in this case, children of expectant mothers. The pregnant cat elicits anatomically confused stories about where babies come from. "Explosive" stories, where the mother bursts, are common.

The Menninger Word Association Test

The word association test of the Menninger clinic's D. Rapaport, M. Gill, and R. Schafer uses a standard list of sixty words. That way, responses can be compared to tabulated responses to this list. The examiner says to "call out your words as fast as you can because I will be timing you." That is a trick to get you to say the first word that comes to mind. The more revealing test words like "breast" are preceded by innocuous words so that they catch you off guard.

The analysis of responses to this or any word association technique is often common-sensical. People in a normal state of mind favor synonyms, opposites, or complements of the test word. An overuse of neologisms — dubious words like "foodless" for "hunger" — are held to indicate low intelligence. Psychotics favor non sequiturs. Here are the sixty words of the Menninger test.

1. Hat	21. Suicide	41. Cut
2. Lamp	22. Mountain	42. Movies
3. Love	23. Snake	43. Cockroach
4. Book	24. House	44. Bite
5. Father	25. Vagina	45. Dog
6. Paper	26. Tobacco	46. Dance
7. Breast	27. Mouth	47. Gun
8. Curtains	28. Horse	48. Water
9. Trunk	29. Masturbation	49. Husband
10. Drink	30. Wife	50. Mud
11. Party	31. Table	51. Woman
12. Spring	32. Fight	52. Fire
13. Bowel movement	33. Beef	53. Suck
14. Rug	34. Stomach	54. Money
15. Boyfriend	35. Farm	55. Mother
16. Chair	36. Man	56. Hospital
17. Screen	37. Taxes	57. Girlfriend
18. Penis	38. Nipple	58. Taxi
19. Radiator	39. Doctor	59. Intercourse
20. Frame	40. Dirt	60. Hunger

The Porteus Maze Test

Stanley D. Porteus's maze test, used to assess mental retardation, is not supposed to be difficult for persons of average intelligence. The examiner rates you largely on speed, whether you start to enter blind alleys, whether the pencil point touches a maze wall, and whether your lines are too wavy. Neatness counts. Here is the Adult I version.

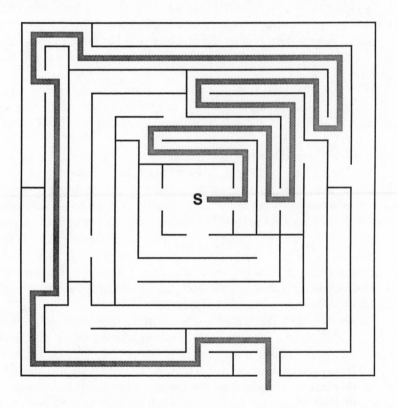

The Minnesota Multiphasic Personality Inventory

The Minnesota Multiphasic Personality Inventory (MMPI) is the true-or-false test used by the armed forces and many employers to screen personnel; it's the most widely used general-purpose psychological test in America today. It is also among the most tightly guarded of tests. Only credentialed psychologists may purchase the test. *Bigger Secrets'* request for permission to reproduce sample items from the test was denied. The copyright holder, the University of Minnesota Press, says it never allows test items to be printed in books or periodicals for the general public.

In format, the MMPI is little different from a *Cosmopolitan* quiz. The subject marks each of 550 first-person declarative sentences as being true or false of himself. But there is more to the MMPI than appears at first glance. "Trick questions" tip off the examiner to subjects deliberately answering incorrectly.

The MMPI was created in 1940 by Stark R. Hathaway and J. C. McKinley to take the place of routine psychiatric interviews. It attempts to be cheatproof — a tall order for a simple true-false test. Hathaway and McKinley realized that self-assessment has its limits. Early questionnaire personality tests simply asked subjects to identify psychiatric symptoms applying to themselves. Answers were taken at face value. A schizophrenic or a compulsive liar cannot be counted on to answer questions truthfully, however. Results could be highly inaccurate, especially for those most in need of attention.

Rather than rationalize how a schizophrenic, say, *ought* to answer questions, Hathaway and McKinley concerned themselves with how known schizophrenics *did* answer. They assembled a long list of items they felt touched on most aspects of personality and common disorders. Persons with known disorders and "normal" persons (healthy visitors recruited from hospital waiting rooms in Minnesota) took the test, and their answers were tabulated. The MMPI is scored by comparing responses to those of Hathaway and McKinley's sample groups. If a subject answers in much the same way as previously tested schizophrenics have, he is judged likely to be schizophrenic also.

Because interpretation is statistical, it is not always possible to say why a particular answer correlates with a particular state of mind. One item asserts that all foods taste the same. Significantly more schizophrenics mark this item true than do normals. A true answer counts as one point on the schizophrenia scale.

To a degree, it doesn't matter if the subject evades or misrepresents. For all anyone knows, schizophrenics may be lying when they say everything tastes the same. If the subject's personality compels him to lie on certain questions, his answers may well agree with those of others who lied for the same basic reasons. Deceit is factored in.

Persons taking the MMPI for employment screening never learn what their answers mean. There are ten clinical scales (sets of responses to items that are scored to get a point total): hypochondriasis (hypochondria), depression, hysteria, psychopathic deviate (aggressive, antisocial behavior), masculinity-femininity, paranoia, psychasthenia (obsessive-compulsive tendencies), schizophrenia, hypomania (manic behavior), and social introversion. Many items count toward more than one scale.

No single answer means anything. Only total scores count. On some questions, both true and false responses count toward pathological scales. A normal individual scores some points on all the scales.

Fifteen items are designed to detect lying. Unknown to the subject, they are all in the last rows of the top and bottom halves of the answer form (items 15, 30, 35, 60, 75, 90, 105, 120, 135, 150, 165, 195, 225, 255, 285). That way, the examiner can check them at a glance.

These items make up the lie scale. Each is an admission of a petty fault or vice: lying, sneaking into a movie without paying, laughing at dirty jokes, and so on. Psychologists assume that most of these statements are true of everyone. If an answer sheet has more than 7 of the 15 items marked false, chances are the subject has lied — not only on these questions but on the whole test.

One miscellaneous set of items, the correction scale, fine-tunes the scores on other scales. Roughly speaking, the correction score measures how frank the subject is in admitting his shortcomings. Those with high correction scores are defensive and may not admit abnormalities. Those with low scores are "confessors" who tend to exaggerate slight deviations from normalcy. A fraction of the correction scale total is added to the raw scores for some of the other scales to get a corrected score.

One scale (validity) is composed of extremely unusual answers to items — such as saying that you see animals, persons, or things invisible to others. A person trying to feign psychosis might mark this as true. In fact, this is a rare response even among the emotionally ill. Responses claiming out-of-body experiences or suspicions of being poisoned are other examples. Each aberrant response counts as a point toward the validity score.

Validity scale items deal with a wide assortment of topics and were chosen so that they do not form any pattern. Even if a person *does* believe he is being poisoned, he is not likely to give unusual responses on the other validity scale items. A high validity score indicates that something is wrong. The subject may be simulating illness, may be unable to read the test form, or may be writing T and F randomly.

Many test items concern physical complaints. The back of my head feels sore, says one. These items identify hypochondriacs. Persons with genuine physical illness acknowledge only their own symptoms and score only somewhat higher than average on the hypochondria scale. Hypochondriacs usually claim a far wider assortment of symptoms.

The use of the MMPI for employment screening has occasioned controversy because of the many personal topics that seem irrelevant to job performance. Religion is amply covered. I am more religious than most people, claims one item; another says that faith healers can cure with the laying on of hands. True answers to these items count on the validity scale (a high validity score is suspicious). Admission of atheism counts on the same scale. False to an item asserting that Christ will return counts on the depression scale. The MMPI is stacked against fundamentalists and freethinkers alike.

The masculinity-femininity scale was developed using two sample groups felt to epitomize masculinity and femininity — 54 soldiers and 67 airline hostesses. Items are scored one way for males, the opposite way for females. The masculinity-femininity score is actually a measure of deviation from the traditional gender roles. A high score ostensibly means femininity in a male or masculinity in a female. High scores are associated with homosexuality, though the correlation is not so clear-cut as Hathaway and McKinley anticipated.

Some masculinity-femininity items are simple enough. I like magazines like *Popular Mechanics*, says one. A false counts a point for a male subject; a true counts for a female. Other items are among the hardest to figure on the test. An item asserting belief in the Devil and Hell is scored when false for males and true for females. To oversimplify for the sake of clarity, women who believe in a Devil are more likely to be lesbians.

Much of the psychological thinking underpinning the MMPI has changed since the test was created. Some of the scale names (such as hysteria) are more or less obsolete as diagnoses. Psychologists increasingly regard the scales as measures of facets of personality rather than diagnoses. These days, MMPI responses are analyzed by computer and the scales plotted as a simple line graph. Connecting the dots yields patterns recognizable to experts. Common MMPI constellations include the Paranoid Valley, the Conversion V, the Psychotic Tetrad, the Hysterectomy Profile, and the Scarlett O'Hara V — an inverted caret resulting when you plot a high psychopathic deviate score, a low masculinity-femininity score, and a high paranoia score. This indicates a demanding, insecure woman whose exaggerated femininity prevents her from expressing her hostility directly.

We can't reproduce the items, but we can give you a sample of the subjects covered by the test, along with their significance:

Detective and mystery stories:
Disliking them counts on the hysteria scale.

Profanity:
Not swearing every now and then implies depression, hysteria, and (via the validity scale) falsified responses.

Passing old school friends on the street, pretending not to recognize them:
This counts on the depression and schizophrenia scales.

Biblical prophecy:
Not believing that things are turning out as they said it would in the Bible counts on the depression scale.

Megalomania:
Admitting that you are an important person counts on the mania scale.

Teasing animals:
Saying you *don't* do it counts on the depression scale.

Morbid fear of blood:
Hemophobia counts on the hysteria scale.

Vomiting blood:
Admission of vomiting episodes counts on the depression scale. Surprisingly, saying you have never vomited blood counts on the hypochondria scale.

Fear of losing your mind:
It counts on the depression, obsessive-compulsive, and schizophrenia scales.

Flirting:
Not liking to flirt counts on the depression and introversion scales.

Sweating on cool days:
Reporting it counts on the mania scale. Saying you *never* sweat on cool days counts on the depression scale.

Hypnotism:
If you believe someone is trying to hypnotize you, it counts on the paranoia, schizophrenia, and validity scales.

Alice in Wonderland:
Liking the story suggests femininity in a man; disliking it suggests masculinity in a woman.

Counting light bulbs in electric signs:
It suggests obsessive-compulsive behavior.

Fear of knives and pointed objects:
A point on the schizophrenia scale.

· 13 ·

THE NOBEL PRIZE SPERM BANK

*T*he Repository for Germinal Choice is a garage eugenics outfit run out of a small office in Escondido, California. Better known as the Nobel Prize sperm bank, it has no connection with the Nobel Prize committee. At one time, only Nobel Prize winners were allowed to donate sperm. Lately, an Olympic gold medalist and others have been accepted. The premise of the bank is that sperm from geniuses, athletes, or other achievers is more likely to produce children with desirable traits. The Repository does not name names, but the notoriety of the donors has piqued curiosity. The bank's "catalogue" for interested women gives only physical descriptions and certain general information about the donors. Only one donor has owned up to participating: William Shockley (physics, '56), a co-inventor of the transistor and a proponent of sterilization for persons of low IQ.

Graham and Muller

The guy who invented shatterproof plastic eyeglass lenses is the guy behind the Nobel Prize sperm bank. The Repository is funded and run by Robert Klark Graham, an optician, inventor, entrepreneur, and former Bausch and Lomb executive. Graham is the father of eight — by

103

conventional means, that is — and a member of Mensa, the club for those with a high IQ. His ancestors include a signer of the Declaration of Independence.

Repository literature credits the American geneticist Hermann J. Muller (1890–1967) as a cofounder. In fact, Muller was the inspiration for the Repository for Germinal Choice. He took the Nobel Prize in physiology or medicine in 1946 for demonstrating that radiation can produce mutations.

In experiments with fruit flies at Columbia University, Muller demonstrated the phenomenon of genetic crossover. He later became professor of zoology at the University of Texas, Austin. In 1932 Muller suffered what is described as a nervous breakdown. His marriage to mathematician Jessie Marie Jacobs was failing. A utopian socialist, Muller felt frustrated by the conservative political climate of Texas and believed he had not received due credit for his work. He penned a suicide note, put it in his pocket, walked to a nearby woods, and swallowed an overdose of sleeping pills.

Muller survived and traveled to Europe to escape scandal, accepting a post in the Soviet Union. Muller saw the USSR as a new, experimental society that might be open to eugenics on a national scale.

While in Russia, in 1935 Muller published *Out of the Night: A Biologist's View of the Future,* a book advocating eugenics; "germinal choice" was Muller's phrase. He thought technology was interfering with natural selection, and he feared a future in which everyone would be a hopeless cripple due to accumulated genetic defects. He argued that it is necessary for society to make sure that the healthiest and most talented people have more children than those less favorably endowed.

"In the course of a paltry century or two," Muller predicted, ". . . it would be possible for the majority of the population to become of the innate quality of such men as Lenin, Newton, Leonardo, Pasteur, Beethoven, Omar Khayyám, Pushkin, Sun Yat Sen, Marx . . . or even to possess their varied faculties combined." Muller foresaw little hope for eugenics in a capitalist society. In the hands of American free market forces, he wrote, eugenics would ensure "a maximum number of Billy Sundays, Valentinos, Jack Dempseys, Babe Ruths, even Al Capones."

He sent a copy of his book to Stalin, who wasn't much interested.

For this and other reasons, Muller became disillusioned with the Soviet Union and left for a position in Scotland in 1937. He returned to the United States permanently in 1940, becoming a professor at Indiana University in Bloomington from 1945 until his death.

In 1963, Graham met Muller and offered to put up the money to start a genius sperm bank. Muller tried to drum up interest for the bank among prominent scientists. Then Muller and Graham had a falling out. Muller was acutely aware of how the Nazi Lebensborn movement had blackened the name of eugenics. He wanted to breed for qualities such as altruism as well as intelligence. Graham was interested mostly in IQ and was also much more conservative politically than the socialist Muller. In a letter, Muller chided Graham for wanting to include the sperm of people like Barry Goldwater. The collaboration dissolved.

Muller died in 1967. His widow, Thea, has been an outspoken critic of the Repository as it exists today. She has tried, to no avail, to stop Graham from printing stationery and brochures listing Muller as a cofounder. "There are quite a few crackpots who supported this idea," she told a reporter in 1983. "When they came to my husband and wanted to join, it was difficult to keep them out. He felt he was losing control of the project, that it had fallen into the wrong hands."

Geniuses and Outstanding Bodies

Graham's version of Muller's dream has produced fifteen children thus far. The bank is in Graham's backyard in Escondido, near the San Diego Wild Animal Park, in a bathroom-size concrete cubicle six feet underground on Graham's ten-acre estate. The semen is kept frozen in liquid nitrogen in a cylindrical container with quarter-inch lead shielding to protect it from natural radiation. According to the Repository, the half-life of semen at the temperature of liquid nitrogen is more than a thousand years.

Semen is shipped via Federal Express in a 58-pound cryogenic container that contains enough nitrogen to preserve the temperature for four insemination cycles (about three months). Applicants must pay a $500 deposit (refundable, less depreciation) for the shipping container.

"When I went to his house several years ago, he had a donor right there," Repository consultant Steve Broder said in a newspaper interview. "I showed them how to do it."

The nonprofit bank does not pay anyone for semen, nor does it sell it, taking in only nominal fees from recipients. One employee travels around the country collecting sperm, and several others handle administration. The payroll and operating expenses, over $100,000 a year, are footed by Graham.

The Repository started soliciting donations in late 1977 and went public in a 1979 Mensa newsletter. Initially the bank accepted sperm only from Nobel winners in the hard sciences; peace and literature Nobelists weren't good enough. "The electric light bulb has been more useful to me than any poem I can think of," Graham said.

The bank has since broadened its scope. Graham suggested in a 1980 press conference that others might start banks for "Olympic gold medal winners, or artists or movie stars." In 1984 Graham invited an Olympic gold medalist to donate to his bank. According to Graham, "Our present donors are all geniuses. Now we're also emphasizing outstanding bodies."

Only married women may receive sperm from the bank. They are asked to provide evidence of their IQ or scholastic or career achievement and a $50 application fee. About half the women who apply are accepted. Once a woman is accepted, there are no further fees other than the deposit on the cryogenic container. Semen is supplied in plastic "straws" sent to the recipient's physician or to her home. "Strongly motivated couples find little difficulty with home insemination, providing the husband learns how to find the external os of the cervix," the Repository says. Recipients are allowed to order straws from two donors to try in alternate months.

Sperm donors fill out a detailed personal history questionnaire, which has them report everything from "exposure to mutagenic agents" to transvestism to "delusions of greatness or omnipotence." The Repository's sperm catalogue identifies donors only by a color and a number: Fuchsia #1, Coral #36, Turquoise #28, and so on. The catalogue gives weight, height, age, IQ, color of eyes, skin, hair, outstanding characteristics, hobbies, notes about athletic and musical abilities, and number of offspring.

Critics

In February 1980 the *Los Angeles Times* learned of the bank. At that time, Graham said that the bank had three Nobel Prize–winning donors and that all the donors were from the San Diego and Stanford-Berkeley areas. Edward Chen of the *Times* tried to track down all the Nobel laureates in California to identify the donors. The *Times* staff got in touch with twenty-three of them.

Most of the Nobelists contacted by Chen and other journalists dismissed the bank, regarding the bank's criterion as too arbitrary. There was concern about the advanced age of most Nobel laureates. (Evidence suggests that the incidence of Down's syndrome increases with the age of the father as well as the mother.) Critics included:

David Baltimore (physiology or medicine, '75): "I don't think we can allow an individual who's got the resources to define what he thinks are the appropriate genes for the next generation."

Owen Chamberlin (physics, '59): "There are a lot of great people and scientists in the world who have not won Nobel prizes. My feeling is that the importance of the prize is being overrated."

Max Delbrück (physiology or medicine, '69): The bank is "pretty silly."

Renato Dulbecco (physiology or medicine, '75): "It's too late for me. I was vasectomized long ago."

Richard P. Feynman (physics, '65) and Murray Gell-Mann (physics, '69) responded through an aide: "Neither one of them wanted any part of it because they don't believe in the concept."

Robert W. Holley (physiology or medicine, '69): "What surprises me is that any woman would want this."

Arthur Kornberg (physiology or medicine, '59): "Off the top of my head, it sounds like a rather poor criterion. It's a very narrow selection and not necessarily a proper one."

Linus Pauling (chemistry, '54, and peace, '62): "The old-fashioned way still seems best to me."

Burton Richter (physics, '76): The bank is "somewhat weird."

Charles H. Townes (physics, '64): The bank is "snobbish."

George Wald (physiology or medicine, '67): "Oh, this is a crushing blow, to be left out of this sperm bank. I felt bad enough when I only made it into President Nixon's second enemies list."

Somewhat more positive was Felix Bloch (physics, '52): "I really have no strong opinion on that. But I think I'm half convinced." He said he did not remember ever being contacted by Graham.

Francis Crick (physiology or medicine, '62) has spoken out in favor of Muller's views on eugenics. But he told journalist David Rorvik that he had not contributed to Graham's bank: "I'm not so sure I have such a high opinion of Nobel laureates that I want to see them as fathers of the population."

William Shockley

Of the Nobelists contacted in 1980, only physicist William Shockley of Beckman Instruments admitted donating sperm. Shockley has not been a PR coup for the bank. For all his accomplishments, he is known to nonscientists mostly for his belief that blacks are genetically inferior to whites. In the 1960s Shockley proposed a plan whereby stupid people would be paid $1,000 for each IQ point below 100 if they agreed to be sterilized. Most of the payment would be kept in trust on the assumption that the recipients would not know how to manage the windfall. "Bounty hunters" would receive a finder's fee for each low-IQ person they convinced to be sterilized, since these persons might not find out about the program otherwise.

Shockley is not one of the color-coded donors in the Repository's current sperm catalogue. The oldest donor currently listed was born in the 1920s; Shockley was born in 1910. If there was a continuing demand for a given donor's sperm, he would have to donate regularly. That may not be convenient, especially when the donor lives some distance away. Evidently the Repository is out of stock on Shockley's sperm.

The Missing Nobelists

There are only so many Nobel laureates in California. Graham said the original donors were all from the Stanford-Berkeley and San Diego areas. And we can eliminate those who criticized the bank in the press. Who does that leave?

According to the *Nobel Foundation Directory,* thirty-four Nobel laureates were associated with California institutions at the time of their prize. (Pauling won two prizes.) Seven of the thirty-four won their prizes in 1980 and later, so Graham couldn't have been talking about them in early 1980. That leaves twenty-seven.

Willis Lamb (physics, '55) won his prize at Stanford but moved to Yale in 1962. He has been at the University of Arizona since 1974. Eliminating him makes twenty-six.

Then there are Nobelists who won prizes elsewhere and moved to California. A search of Nobelists' biographical sketches in *Who's Who* turned up six additional Nobelists who were associated with California institutions from late 1977 to early 1980. All told, that makes thirty-two Nobel laureates working in California when Graham was soliciting the first donors.

Eliminate the nine from Cal Tech and UCLA. Then there are twenty-three, all from the Stanford-Berkeley and San Diego areas.

Of these twenty-three, Owen Chamberlain, Robert Holley, Arthur Kornberg, Burton Richter, and Charles Townes were critical of the bank in interviews. Felix Bloch and Francis Crick had some good words for the idea but denied being donors. Renato Dulbecco had a vasectomy. Eliminating them leaves fifteen.

Maria Goeppert-Mayer (physics, '63) is a woman. Take her off the list.

Ernest Lawrence (physics, '39) died way back in 1958. Cross him off.

Kenneth Arrow (economics, '72) won in a "soft" category.

Shockley, the known donor, is already accounted for.

That leaves eleven, two of whom are now dead. *Bigger Secrets* attempted to contact each of the nine living Nobelists by phone or registered letter.

Luis Alvarez (physics, '68), Melvin Calvin (chemistry, '61), Roger Guillemin (physiology or medicine, '77), and Edwin McMillan (chemistry, '51) denied being donors.

The widow of Paul Flory (chemistry, '74) recalled that Flory had been contacted by the Repository, but he did not donate.

These five denials compress the list to six names. If Graham was speaking truthfully, if no one falsely denied being a donor, and if no other California Nobelists have escaped notice, then two of the remaining six ought to be donors. The list runs:

William Giauque (chemistry, '49) of Berkeley, who won his Nobel Prize for his studies of matter at near absolute zero temperatures. Born in 1895, Giauque seems relatively unlikely to have been a sperm donor on account of age — he would have been about eighty-four years old. Giauque died in 1982.

Donald Glaser (physics, '60) of Berkeley, inventor of the bubble chamber.

Robert Hofstadter (physics, '61) of Stanford, who probed the inner structure of protons and neutrons.

Joshua Lederberg (physiology or medicine, '58), who studied gene recombination in *Escherichia coli* bacteria. Lederberg left Stanford in 1978, so he is just barely in the time frame (Graham started contacting California Nobelists in late 1977). Lederberg is currently president of Rockefeller University, New York.

Glenn Seaborg (chemistry, '51) of Berkeley, codiscoverer of the chemical elements plutonium, americium, curium, berkelium, californium, einsteinium, fermium, medelevium, and nobelium and long-time member of the Atomic Energy Commission.

Emilio Segre (physics, '59) of Berkeley, who won his Nobel for his role in the discovery of the antiproton. He is also the discoverer of the element technetium and codiscoverer (with Seaborg and others) of plutonium. Segre wrote "no answer" to *Bigger Secrets*' inquiry.

Current Donors

None of the above men match any of the donor descriptions in the current catalogue. If they were donors, the bank must have run out of their sperm, as with Shockley. The fact is, the Repository for Germinal Choice has quietly lowered its standards. Most of the twelve donors listed in the current catalogue are too young to be Nobelists. Some aren't scientists (or world-class athletes) at all.

Light Green #40 is a graduate student born in the late 1950s. Coral #36 is a "professional man of very high standing in his field." Yellow #19 is a financial consultant. Orange #26 is an engineer. You have to wonder if a future race of financial consultants and grad students would be so different from what we have today.

Light Blue #14 and Lavender #20 are high-IQ scientists born in the late 1940s. George Kohler (medicine, '84), the only Nobel scientist born then, does not match either description.

Silver #24 is a "gifted research biologist at a world-renowned research center." Turquoise #38 is a "top science professor at a major university" and "head of a large research lab." Both were born in the early 1940s. That would limit the field of Nobelists to Brian Josephson (physics, '73), and he does not match either description.

White #6, a "scientist involved in sophisticated research," and Dark Blue #10, an "accomplished chief scientist, Ph.D., from a major university," were born in the 1930s. Twelve Nobelists were born in the 1930s, but there is no particular reason to believe that White and Blue are Nobelists.

Brown #15

The sperm catalogue saves its most glowing description for Brown #15. An "internationally renowned research scientist," he is "responsible for one of the major medical advances of our time." If any of the current crop of donors are Nobel Prize winners, Brown #15 ought to be.

Born in the 1920s, Brown earned his M.D. at the age of twenty-one. He's 6'1", 200 pounds, with medium brown, wavy hair. He has three children, all of them Ph.D.'s and all tall — 6'2" to 6'4". Brown had a coronary bypass operation at age fifty. His hobbies include classical music and singing.

Twenty physiology or medicine winners were born in the 1920s. Most are Ph.D.'s rather than M.D.'s. This and number of children rule out all but three Nobelists: Gerald Edelman ('72), David Hubel ('81), and Daniel Nathans ('78).

Nathans *did* have a coronary bypass in 1979. Since he was born in 1928, he would have been fifty or fifty-one. Despite that rather amazing coincidence, Nathans cannot be Brown #15 if the description is accurate. He earned his M.D. at the age of twenty-six, not twenty-one.

(Neither Hubel nor Edelman earned their M.D. at twenty-one, either.) In a press photo of Nathans posing with other Nobel winners, he seems shorter than 6'1".

Disowned by one Nobelist and snubbed by dozens, the Repository seems not to have a single Nobel laureate among its current donors.

Fuchsia #1

Fuchsia #1 is the code name of the Olympic gold medalist. According to the Repository, he is not only "one of the most accomplished athletes in the world" but also a "successful young business man." He's described as being 6'4", 195 pounds, of English ancestry, with brown eyes, fair skin, and thick dark brown hair. He was born in the 1950s and is "very handsome."

According to the *New York Times,* Graham started soliciting athlete donors with the 1984 Olympics in Los Angeles. (Graham has not explicitly stated that the donor is an American or that he was in the 1984 Los Angeles Olympics, however.) Out of curiosity, I went through the list of summer 1984 American gold medal winners, comparing their biographical information with Fuschia #1's description. Fairly detailed physical information on the 1984 American Summer Olympic team is contained in the *United States Olympic Team Media Guide/ Record Book,* published by the United States Olympic Committee. Photographs and further vital statistics of the athletes were found in newspaper and magazine coverage and in the spate of souvenir and coffee table books.

Ruling out women, nonwhites, and those not born in the 1950s compressed the list of gold medalists to fourteen athletes. Of them, only two were reported to be 6'4" tall. One was wrestler Jeff Blatnick. But Blatnick can't be Fuschia #1 — he's far too heavy (248 pounds), Blatnick isn't an English name, and he suffers from Hodgkin's disease (an ailment on the Repository questionnaire's checklist and not mentioned in Fuschia #1's description).

The other 6'4" gold medalist is rower Brad Alan Lewis, who won the double sculls competition on Lake Casitas with teammate Paul Enquist. Lewis seems to fit Fuschia #1's description in every respect that can be checked from the writeups of his victory. Photos show that he has full, dark hair, a beard, dark eyes, and fair skin. Lewis is a financial analyst; his surname is English. And Lewis hails from Corona Del Mar, California — just 15 miles from Escondido.

Graham said that his "tall, dark and handsome" gold medal winner's sperm is in greater demand than any of the scientists'.

· 14 ·

BASEBALL'S PERFECT CRIME

*C*heating in baseball is largely a matter of friction. Saliva — plain or mixed with tobacco, licorice, or Slippery Elm lozenges — Vaseline, hair tonic, fly fishing line cleaner, shampoo, Ivory soap, K-Y Jelly, flour, rosin, and/or Metamucil all decrease the air resistance of the surface to which they are applied. Scratching the ball's surface with sandpaper or a tack increases the air resistance. The shape, the texture, and even the tactile properties of the baseball are so finely tuned that almost any such adulteration has an effect.

Cleveland Indians pitching coach Dave Duncan has asserted that almost 50% of major league pitchers tamper with the ball somehow. Said Orioles coach Ray Miller, "Someday I expect to see a pitcher walk out to the mound with a utility belt on — file, chisel, screwdriver, glue. He'll throw a ball to the plate with bolts attached to it."

Hyperbole notwithstanding, the trajectories of altered balls are dead giveaways. It's tough to get away with blatant cheating — yet players boast it is possible. Ordinary kitchen appliances figure in a novel way to cheat at baseball. The method leaves no lasting evidence of any kind. It is baseball's perfect crime.

Corked Bats

Of the new, more sophisticated breed of ruses, tampering with bats has probably been the most successful, for it leaves no clues on the balls. But this scam was exposed dramatically on September 7, 1974, when the top of Graig Nettles's bat came off during a Yankees game in Detroit. The incident has attained the status of legend. Fans of any number of teams claim it was *their* team the Yankees were playing, and they know because they were there and saw it. Accounts also differ on what happened to Nettles's bat. A book called *Playing Dirty,* by Mike Barry and Bob Buck, reports a common version of the story: "Nettles hit a shot, and the bat came apart in his hands, splintering debris everywhere. Among the items bouncing around on the field were several rubber 'superballs.'"

Back issues of newspapers say that the bat was filled with cork, not superballs. A *New York Times* article by Murray Chass reported that "as the Yankees' third baseman hit the ball, the top of the bat flew off. Freehan [Bill Freehan, the Detroit catcher] alertly noted the presence of cork inside. Freehan called it to the attention of Lou di Muro, the plate umpire, who called Nettles out for using an illegal bat."

The understandably less charitable *Detroit News* said, "Graig Nettles stood at first base looking like a bald man whose wig had blown away. . . . After the game, surrounded by questioning reporters, the New York third baseman acted like the straight man in a comedy act, denying that he had used an illegal bat to hit a game-winning home run. Those around him couldn't hold back the chuckles." Both papers agreed that the bat contained cork.

Cork is believed to give the bat a springy play. The usually proffered explanation says that the bat is a couple of ounces lighter with the cork core, so you can swing it faster.

Maybe so, but the momentum of the bat is proportional to its mass, so what you gain in bat speed is exactly canceled out. It's like driving faster when you're low on gas to get home before you run out.

And what is to be made of those who put lead in their bats to make them heavier? The corkers and the leaders can't both be right. Nettles recalled a minor league player who filled his bat with mercury to give it more oomph. The player was so lousy that it didn't seem to make much of a difference.

The preferred corking technique is to drill a twelve-inch bore into the thick end of the bat. Sometimes the bat will splinter and have to be discarded. Ground cork and glue are stuffed into the bottom of the hole, leaving an air pocket of several inches at the top, which is resealed with wood putty and sanded. A careful job is virtually undetectable. But Nettles's bat was crudely done: "About an inch and a half was cut from the top of the bat, then glued back on after the cork had been inserted," the *Times* said.

"I didn't know there was anything in the bat; that was the first time I used it," Nettles protested too much. "Some Yankee fan in Chicago gave it to me. He said it would bring me luck. I guess he made it. I've been using the same Walt Williams's bat the past three days and I guess I picked this one up by mistake. It looked the same and it felt the same. As soon as the end came off, I knew there was something wrong with it."

Frozen and Microwaved Balls

The cleverest approach of all leaves no incriminating evidence. Get this: Balls stored in a freezer become sluggish; they don't fly as far as normal balls, given an equal swat. The difference is reportedly quite marked. This effect, or at least some of it, persists as long as the ball's core is still cold, even though the surface may have returned to normal temperature.

A new twist is microwaving balls. A microwave oven heats them evenly, inside and out. It's the same principle in reverse: Heated balls fly farther.

Enter baseball's equivalent of the stabbing-with-an-icicle murder plot. It is to a team's advantage to foist frozen balls on the opponent batters (or 'waved balls on your own batters). Even a modest change in the ball's elasticity could mean a few runs in the course of a game. After the game, the balls return to normal, and there is nothing to conceal.

Umpires are charged with dispensing the balls, so it requires some knowledge of their routine to switch balls successfully. Another pitfall is that overly cold balls might collect dew on humid days. The most lackadaisical umpire would be alert to moisture on a ball.

At least one player has confessed to using frozen balls (Art Fletcher of the Philadelphia Phillies, way back in 1925), but no one has ever been caught at it. It is even debatable whether the rules against tampering apply.

Most of baseball's illegal pitches are spelled out in rule 8.02, adopted in 1919 and effective for the 1920 season:

The pitcher shall not: (1) apply a foreign substance of any kind to the ball or his glove; (2) expectorate on the ball or his glove; (3) deface the ball in any manner; (4) deliver what is called the "shine" ball, "spit" ball, "mud" ball, or "emery" ball. The pitcher, of course, is allowed to rub the ball between his bare hands.

Despite its mention of such quaint exotica as the mudball (a ball weighted with cinders or phonograph needles pressed into the stitches), the rule says nothing about temperature. In any case, a suspicious ump would have to cut open a ball immediately, measure its core temperature, and then provide evidence that a ball would not naturally be at that temperature in order to prove anything.

Both the American and National leagues use cork-center Rawlings balls made in Haiti. As an experiment for *Bigger Secrets*, I tested the official balls to see how they were affected by temperature.

No two swats of the bat are exactly alike. The characteristics of a ball are better measured by dropping it from a fixed height and measuring the average height of the first bounce. For instance, when either the American or National League ball is dropped from 60 inches onto a hard surface, the bounce is about 21 inches — a 35% rebound. The actual bounce varies, depending on whether the ball bounces on the stitches or the smooth part of the leather.

A Rawlings ball was kept in the freezer overnight to chill it down to the cork core. Immediately out of the refrigerator, it rebounded only about 15½ inches (26% rebound) — and that with a thud. An hour later, after the surface had warmed, it bounced about 19 inches (32%). Two hours later, the bounce was about 20 inches (33%). The curve leveled off, and it took about eight hours for the ball's performance to return to normal.

The ball's surface felt cold only for a couple of hours. If a team took a ball from the freezer two hours before the game, it would be virtually indetectable and might give the other team a 2% disadvantage if the rebound trials are any indication.

Microwaving may give a comparable edge. A Rawlings ball and a cup of water (to prevent damage to the oven) were cooked at the high setting of a 500-watt microwave oven until the water started to boil. The ball became hot, but not so hot that it couldn't be handled. Right out of the oven, the ball did worse than a normal ball in the rebound test — 18 inches, or 30%. That was because the leather had softened. An hour later, the leather had firmed up and the ball was very active, bouncing 22½ inches (38%).

The ideal would be to have your team hitting the hot balls and the other team hitting the cold balls. If the rebound tests are a fair indication, that could mean a 5% edge.

· 15 ·

CONCEALED BLACKJACK COMPUTERS

*I*n 1977 electronic engineer Keith Taft rigged up a homemade computer programmed for blackjack strategy and took to the tables of Las Vegas. Taft worked with family members and Ken Uston, a notorious scientific blackjack player. The computer, bandaged to a player's leg, figured the best way to play each hand and transmitted this information to a signaling device in the shoes of Taft's confederates. In twenty-two days they won over $100,000. The setup was indetectable, they thought. Then, at Harvey's Club on May 11, Taft's son Marty was busted by casino security. "We're going to bash your brains in with a two-by-four," a casino goon said after they found the computer in Taft's pants. The casino had FBI agents dissect the computer. They decided that it was not against any law.

The powers that run Las Vegas and Atlantic City see trouble ahead. We are rapidly entering an age in which computer technology will change gambling forever. Taft was an isolated hacker soldering his own microprocessors. Of late, concealed computers for blackjack have gone commercial.

As of 1985, at least two models of covert computers were being marketed, albeit by word of mouth, sotto voce. Rumblings in the Las Vegas and Atlantic City subcultures claim that the people using computers don't want to talk about them. They're cleaning up, and if their identities were known, they would be barred from the casinos for life. Even the size and shape of the computers are not discussed for fear of telling pit bosses what to look for. The State of Nevada took the matter seriously enough to pass a bill barring computers in its gaming pits.

I obtained the most popular make of blackjack computer to see what it looked like and how it worked. Then I went to Atlantic City to see it in operation.

RULES OF BLACKJACK

Blackjack is a game of counting. You play against the dealer, and he or she must follow a simple, mechanical strategy.

Wagers are placed using chips bought at the table. You bet on your hand only, and must bet before any cards are dealt. After the bets have been placed, the dealer deals everyone two cards. In Atlantic City the players' hands are dealt face up, as knowledge of the other players' hands makes little difference. The dealer always deals himself a hand with just one card visible.

You look at your cards and add their values. A 2 (of any suit) counts as 2; a 10 counts as 10, and so forth. All face cards count as 10 as well. The ace may be counted as a 1 or an 11, whichever is better. A 5 and a queen, for example, total 15. The suits never make any difference.

The object is to attain the highest score possible without exceeding 21. In this you compete against the dealer. Twenty-one is the best possible hand; you cannot lose (though you may tie).

"Blackjack" is an initial hand of an ace and a 10-value card for a total of 21. A player with blackjack immediately turns the cards face up (Las Vegas) or the dealer declares blackjack as the second card is dealt face up (Atlantic City). Provided the dealer does not also have blackjack, the player wins one and a half times his wager. So if he bet $20, he gets back $50 (his $20 bet, plus winnings of one and a half times $20).

Players who do not have blackjack may elect to draw additional card(s) in hope of raising their total. Additional cards are dealt face up one at a time. When satisfied, the player "stands" — declares that he wants no more cards by holding his open palm to the dealer. The risk in drawing is that you sometimes "bust" — end up with a total of more than 21. Any player who busts automatically loses his bet.

After all the hands have been played, the dealer reveals his hole card (the card dealt face down). He then plays out his hand according to specified rules that vary slightly from one casino to another. Although the dealer has seen the players' hands, this never enters into his decisions.

In nearly all the Las Vegas and Atlantic City casinos, house rules require the dealer to stand if his hand's total is 17 or more and to hit otherwise. In most cases, the dealer must stand on 17, even if it is a "soft" 17, such as an ace and a 6. A soft hand is one in which an ace is counted as 11. Otherwise a hand (like 10 and 7) is "hard." Hitting a soft hand cannot bust it, since the ace can always be counted as 1 if necessary to keep the total from exceeding 21.

If the dealer busts, then all the players who did not bust win. If the dealer does not bust, his total is compared to the totals of the players still in the game. Players with totals higher than the dealer's win. Those with the same total "push" or tie. Those with lower totals lose. The basic bet in blackjack is double-or-nothing. If you bet $20 and win, you get back $40 — your original $20 bet plus even money from the house. If you lose, the house keeps your $20 bet. In the case of a push, you simply get your bet back.

Several special bets are allowed. You don't need to bother with them to play, but they are frequently to the player's advantage.

Doubling down is an option that lets the player double his bet after seeing the first two cards. The obvious advantage is tempered by the restriction that the player must draw one and only one card. Doubling down is most favorable with a total of 10 or 11 (Reno casinos often restrict it to these totals). Even then, you are out of luck if your third card is low — you cannot draw another.

If the player's first two cards have the same point value, he may split the pair. The player must ante an additional amount equal to the original bet. The two cards are spread apart, and each becomes the first card of a new hand. The player plays both hands normally, and wins are paid off as separate hands. An ad hoc rule stipulates that only one card may be dealt to each split ace. Even so, splitting aces — and 8s — is to the player's advantage.

The insurance bet is a fraud; it does not "protect" a good hand as the name and some dealers' explanations suggest. It is offered only when the dealer's visible card is an ace and before the players have played their hands. It is really a side bet on the dealer's hand. When you take insurance, you are betting an additional amount, equal to half your original wager, that the dealer has blackjack — that his hole card is a 10. If the dealer has blackjack, you lose your main bet but have the consolation of winning the smaller bet. The insurance bet is almost always bad for the player (and profitable for the casino).

Such are the rules. Knowing when to hit, stand, double down, and split pairs is something else. The average tourist plays hunches — and probably loses anywhere from 5% to 15% of the amount he wagers in the long run.

It is possible to do better without resorting to anything fancy. Four statisticians — Roger Baldwin, Wilbert Cantey, Herbert Maisel, and James McDermott — analyzed blackjack using mainframe computers in the mid-1950s. They published a "basic strategy" for the game in 1956 in the Journal of the American Statistical Association. *The basic strategy, usually presented as a table, tells you the best thing to do for every possible situation that might come up in a game. This strategy is based solely on the player's current hand and the visible card of the dealer. It doesn't take into account which cards have already been discarded from the deck. You will not get rich using the basic strategy. You can expect to lose about 0.5% of your wagers when playing basic strategy in a typical four-deck game in Las Vegas. If you can find a single-deck game, you ought to just about break even in the long run.*

Provided you know what you're doing, blackjack is so close to being an even game that any slight additional edge ought to put you over the top and slant the odds in your favor. That's what concealed computers attempt to do.

The Basic Strategy

	2	3	4	5	6	7	8	9	10	A
Pair of 2s	H	Sp	Sp	Sp	Sp	Sp	H	H	H	H
Pair of 3s	H	H	Sp	Sp	Sp	Sp	H	H	H	H
Pair of 4s	H	H	H	D	D	H	H	H	H	H
Pair of 5s	D	D	D	D	D	D	D	D	H	H
Pair of 6s	Sp	Sp	Sp	Sp	Sp	H	H	H	H	H
Pair of 7s	Sp	Sp	Sp	Sp	Sp	Sp	H	H	S	H
Pair of 8s	Sp	Sp	Sp	Sp	Sp	Sp	Sp	Sp	Sp	Sp
Pair of 9s	Sp	Sp	Sp	Sp	Sp	S	Sp	Sp	S	S
Pair of 10s	S	S	S	S	S	S	S	S	S	S
Pair of Aces	Sp	Sp	Sp	Sp	Sp	Sp	Sp	Sp	Sp	Sp
Ace and 5 or less	H	H	D	D	D	H	H	H	H	H
Ace and 6	D	D	D	D	D	H	H	H	H	H
Ace and 7	S	D	D	D	D	S	S	H	H	S
Ace and 8	S	S	S	S	D	S	S	S	S	S
Ace and 9 (or 10!)	S	S	S	S	S	S	S	S	S	S
Hard 7 or less	H	H	H	H	H	H	H	H	H	H
Hard 8 as 2 & 6	H	H	H	H	H	H	H	H	H	H
Hard 8 as 3 & 5	H	H	H	D	D	H	H	H	H	H
Hard 9	D	D	D	D	D	H	H	H	H	H
Hard 10	D	D	D	D	D	D	D	D	H	H
Hard 11	D	D	D	D	D	D	D	D	D	D
Hard 12	H	H	S	S	S	H	H	H	H	H
Hard 13, 14, 15, 16	S	S	S	S	S	H	H	H	H	H
Hard 17 or more	S	S	S	S	S	S	S	S	S	S

Do you have a pair? If so, use the first section of the table. If not, do you have an ace? If so, use the middle section. If you have neither a pair nor an ace, use the bottom section. Add the point values of your cards and find the total at bottom right. A jack and a 2 is a "hard 12," for instance. Most of the time you will use the bottom section, but it is important to make sure you do not have a pair or an ace first.

Find the dealer's up card at the top. Move down the column until you come to the row representing your hand. The abbreviation at the intersection tells you what to do: S is stand; H is hit; D is double down; and Sp is split the pair.

If you hit, use the middle section on subsequent decisions as long as you still have a soft hand; use the bottom section when you have a hard hand.

This strategy is strictly correct for a single-deck game. A few marginal decisions are different in a multiple-deck game.

Counting Systems

You might wonder how a computer can help at a game of chance. Blackjack hands are dealt from a "shoe" of one to eight decks of cards shuffled together. Completed hands are discarded and not used again until the next shuffle. If you could keep track of which cards have been played, you could determine the composition of the undealt portion of the deck. That is, you could if you could write down the cards and if you had enough time, which you can't and don't in a real situation. Knowing the composition of the deck would give you a real advantage.

When you try to do this, or something like it, in your head, it's called counting cards — a statistically valid but difficult technique that has been around for decades. A concealed blackjack computer can implement such techniques more extensively and more accurately than anyone can do mentally.

No one knows who thought up card counting. A near-mythic character known as Greasy John seems to have devised a naive counting strategy long before the math professors and their computers got into the act. The Henri Rousseau of counting, Greasy John was a grossly overweight player who usually brought a bag of fried chicken to the casinos. He would play the Vegas tables for twenty hours at a stretch, snacking as needed. The decks had to be discarded every few deals because of the grease marks. Greasy John liked to play alone. His sleazeball persona generally did the trick. He supposedly won a fortune before the casinos had any inkling that blackjack could be beaten. Greasy John is said to have retired and died of a heart attack. He never made any effort to publicize his secret.

The modern card-counting phenomenon is the result of a 1962 book, *Beat the Dealer* by mathematics professor Edward O. Thorpe. Thorpe's counting system was designed from a computer analysis of the game conducted at MIT and later at IBM. Dozens of counting systems have since been devised and often sold for large sums. The DHM Expert system of D. H. Mitchell (no longer on the market) had takers at a price of $1,500.

Counting systems do not track each and every card. All the counter usually tallies is the relative abundance of high cards remaining in the deck. The counter notes all the cards — in the player's own hand, in other players' hands as they are revealed, and in the dealer's hand — and adds or subtracts them from a running total. The higher the count, the richer the deck is in high cards.

High cards are good. That is, they're good for the player and bad for the casino. Counting systems have you make bigger bets when the count is high. When the count is negative, you make minimal bets. If it's *really* negative, it might be a good idea to move to another table.

Why is a deck rich in high cards so good? For one thing, an abundance of high cards increases the chance of getting blackjack. Although the dealer is just as likely to get blackjack as the players, the payoffs favor the player. The player wins one and a half times his bet for his blackjack. But he does not forfeit one and a half times his bet for the dealer's blackjack — he merely loses his wager, as in any loss. Also, blackjack strategy often requires the player to stand on a weak hand in hopes that the dealer will bust. The dealer (who always hits totals of 16 or less) is more likely to bust when there is an excess of high cards in the deck.

"We can plot and scheme and sneak through glittering palaces like James Bond on a secret mission," muses Arnold Snyder, publisher of *Blackjack Forum,* a newsletter for counters. "Every successful counter

I know has this attitude. You must thrill to being a conniving under-
cover spy on a mission of grave importance, knowing full well you're
just trying to make a buck and get away with your act." That said,
card counting is hard work. Few people really make money with it.

George, David, Casey, and Fred

Keith Taft's first concealed blackjack computer was built in 1972. He
called it George. George was a slow, boxy kludge that weighed a ton —
well, fifteen pounds. When in use it was taped to Taft's chest with an
Ace bandage. He wore a heavy pea coat, and no one noticed. No one
much cares what you look like in Las Vegas.

Taft registered the values of cards by wiggling his toes. A sensor in
his shoe was connected by a fine wire to the computer. Another wire
ran out from the collar of his shirt into his hair and up to his eyeglasses.
The computer signaled actions through a row of seven twinkling light-
emitting diodes in the horn-rim frame. All the diodes switched on
meant to stand. When all the diodes were off, it meant to hit. Other
options were encoded similarly.

Taft made smallish bets the first weekend and won $500. He con-
tinued to play on weekends and did well. Taft's success upset his deeply
religious wife, who considered gambling to be of the devil. Taft tried
to justify it as a way of getting hands-on experience in computer design.
"I want to build industrial robots to free people from drudgery so they
can do something more meaningful," he said, as quoted in *Sports
Illustrated*. "In that sense I'm mixing Christianity and blackjack. I'm
God's gambler."

Taft was doing so well, he decided to increase his bets to the $200
range. The first weekend he did this he lost $2,600. He tried again
the next weekend and dropped another $1,800. Taft told *Sports Illus-
trated* that he thought this was a sign from God to stop gambling.

But he continued tinkering. In 1977 he teamed up with Ken Uston,
one of the high gurus of the card-counting world and the man usually
credited with originating "team play." Uston would work with a crew
of experienced card counters who would play at different tables, making nickel and dime bets, counting cards, and looking like average
tourists. When a table's count became strongly positive, the counter

would signal the "big player," Uston. Dressed like a deranged Shriner in gold chains, diamond watch, and shiny sport jacket, Uston would place a few huge bets, chugalug a double Scotch, and hop to another table. Uston obviously was not counting; he just seemed godawful lucky.

Taft designed a second computer, George II, for team play. George II came in two parts. The counter's unit was bandaged to the thigh of one person, who stayed at one table, making small bets and entering card values on a keyboard concealed in a pocket. The keyboard was connected to the computer proper. A radio transmitter relayed signals to a vibrator, in the heel of the big player's shoe, which tapped out a code telling the big player what to do. The person carrying the computer and keying in the cards did not get the benefit of the computer's advice.

The Tafts and Uston hit Las Vegas on April 19, 1977, with a bankroll of $50,000. In less than a week they doubled it. Until the bust, they won $130,000 total.

The radio transmitter was George II's downfall; it must have interfered with the casino's security system. A Harvey's Club employee with a radio receiver zeroed in on Marty Taft, spirited him off to a back room, and found the computer in a strip search. They also strip-searched his partner, but couldn't find her shoe vibrator until she showed them.

The pair were turned over to Las Vegas police and released on $2,000 bail each. The computer itself was packed off to Washington, D.C., for examination by FBI agents. They determined that it merely analyzed information that was available to everyone at the table. It did not change the way the cards fell and thus was not a cheating device. Harvey's Club dropped the charges.

The law has since changed. A 1985 law outlawed computers — or any "device" for analyzing the odds in a casino game — in Nevada. As far as I can tell, no other place where gambling is legal has outlawed computers (at this writing, anyway).

Computers are legal in Atlantic City. What that means, basically, is that you can't be convicted of any crime if you're found using one. You *can* be barred from the casino; casinos are free to bar anyone they please.

The June 1984 issue of *Blackjack Forum* ran a letter from a computer user who was discovered. He was playing the graveyard shift at the Golden Nugget, betting $100 to $200 a hand. After seven hours of play, he was ahead $500. When he tried to cash in his chips, he was taken to a back room. When casino personnel discovered the computer, "they really got excited," he wrote. "They started calling in other people to examine the computer. They asked me questions for over two hours. I answered most of their questions but I wouldn't give them any names." They asked him if he expected to leave with his winnings. "I said yes and one of them said something about accidentally crushing my switches. They assured me they would send my picture to every casino in Las Vegas if I left with the $500."

He finally gave the money back and returned to his hotel, the Marina, where two guards arrested him and took him to another back room for the same sort of ordeal. The Marina gave him thirty minutes to hit the road. He went to the Riviera. There he was taken into another back room and the computer confiscated. (He had to retain a local lawyer to get the computer back.) All this, remember, happened when computers were perfectly legal.

Despite the harassment of users, concealed blackjack computers have gotten slicker. The March 1984 issue of *Blackjack Forum* noted several makes.

Keith Taft's George computer went through several more incarnations: George III, George IV, and George V. Taft never advertised his George computers, but it seems that he built some Georges for anonymous parties who got in touch with him. No further Georges are being manufactured, but there is a resale market in used Georges.

Then there is the Casey computer. This is a bootlegged George that was sold for $10,000 by a former partner of Taft's. *Blackjack Forum* rated this as a very capable model; it is no longer being manufactured.

Taft later came out with the David computer. Miffed at the success of the Casey, he decided to sell this improved George on the open market. At this writing, a brand-new David sells for $4,000. Prospective buyers are to contact Taft through *Blackjack Forum* (2000 Center Street, #1067, Berkeley, California 94704).

The ideal blackjack computer would calculate the best strategy for each hand from scratch, given the known composition of the remainder of the deck. It would hash out all the possible cards that could be drawn, figure the consequences, and tally the results. It would know with complete assurance the statistically best strategy. No currently available pocket computer works this way. The number of calculations required is just too vast. But the David uses a relatively sophisticated technique called linear approximations. The computer keeps track of the cards remaining in the deck and figures the effect of each card on the situation at hand using a value that has been derived from previous computer analysis. It then tells you what to do.

The David computer is believed to be the size of a deck of cards. Along with a battery pack, it fits in a jockstrap. Card values are entered by wiggling the big toes of both feet. The computer prescribes play by a dot-dash code that the player feels from a vibrator in the left shoe.

The Fred computer was created by a British player who goes by the alias of Frank Dracman. Fred is not for sale, but Dracman does rent the device for team playing.

Comp-U-Count

The most widely used device is the Comp-U-Count, sold for about $800 by Jerry Patterson Blackjack (One Britton Place, Voorhees, New Jersey 08043) and manufactured by Compu-Tek (P.O. Box 5412, Canyon Lake, California 92380). Patterson is a well-known professional blackjack player and teacher. Like most such guys, he does not allow photographs to be taken of him for fear of casino reprisals. A brochure for one of his blackjack courses shows him wearing a black satin mask. According to *Blackjack Forum*, the Comp-U-Count is easy to learn and has "ingenious methods of relaying information to the player."

Comp-U-Count's secret is a digital watch — a high-tech black model that says Timex Quartz on the face. On the back it is identified as a Timex K Cell, assembled in Korea. The watch has a liquid-crystal display giving the hour, minute, and date. Only — you guessed it — it's not a watch at all. It always reads something like 23:50 DATE 21, and the 0 is the only digit that changes, to inform you of deck conditions. (The watch is a man's model; there doesn't seem to be any provision for female players.)

A rainbow-stripe nine-strand flat cable runs out of the back of the watch. It's a bit showy for something so incriminating, but your shirt-sleeve hides it. The cable is about a yard long and terminates in a plug in the boxy main unit, which goes in your left hip pocket. It is larger (4″ by 3″ by 1″) than what you would probably have in your pocket. Still, it's not as if you have to pass it off as a portable kidney machine. It uses a nine-volt battery (not included). At the top is an on-off switch and three sockets. The unit's instructions tell you to cut a small hole in the inner lining of the pocket for the wires' egress.

Two more flesh-colored wires run down each pants leg from the main unit. They go inside the tops of your socks and out through holes you cut in the socks' insteps. Each wire ends in a foot switch, a sandwich of foam rubber and green plastic. Before using the unit, you have to trim a sheet of plastic to fit inside your shoes. You are instructed to put lipstick on your big toes, put on your shoes, and wiggle your toes. The smudges on the plastic tell you about where to position the foot switches for comfortable manipulation. The switches are self-adhesive.

Once you're wired up, operation is a breeze. Flick the main unit's switch on, and the watch's active digit becomes a liquid-crystal hyphen. You first tell it how many decks are being used in the game. This is done, Clever Hans fashion, by tapping with your right toe. Press down once and the dask becomes a 1. Press down again and it becomes a 2. If you overshoot, pressing with the left toe decreases the number of decks. The Comp-U-Count can handle up to eight decks. When the right number is displayed, you press down with both toes simultaneously. The display's active digit changes to 0.

There is no way you can walk without pressing the toe switches, so you always have to clear the machine when you sit down at the table. This is done by pressing down with both toes and holding them down for two seconds. Clearing the machine sets the count back to 0 (but does not change the number of decks). You clear the count every time the dealer shuffles.

During the game, you enter cards with your toes as seen. Every time you see a low card (a 2, 3, 4, 5, or 6), you press down with your right toe. When you see a high card (10 or ace), you press with the left toe. For neutral cards (7, 8, and 9), you press briefly with both toes.

The watch immediately displays a count, adjusted for the number of cards remaining. The active digit is the current count. A blinking digit means the count is negative and you should place only minimum bets. A steady digit means the count is positive. When the count is greater than 9 or less than -9, it is displayed as a steady or blinking dash.

The Comp-U-Count simply keeps count for you. It gives a "true" count, one adjusted for the number of cards remaining, rather than a running count. Since most counters are not able to keep track of how many cards have been discarded in addition to the running count and then divide to get a true count, this is a considerable advantage over a mental count. Still, it is stretching things a bit to call it a computer. In capability it is more like a special-purpose calculator. The reason you use the Comp-U-Count and not a calculator is the James Bond–like watch disguise. You still have to know the basic strategy and adjust your actions according to the count.

A Test Drive

As an experiment for *Bigger Secrets,* I pitted the Comp-U-Count against the Sands and Del Webb's Claridge casinos in Atlantic City. I wanted to see how it worked and, just as important, how detectable it was. I played in three sessions. At the start of each, I bought $100 in chips. I played at the tables with the lowest betting minimums available, using the table minimum as the betting unit. I played until I got tired (maybe forty-five minutes to an hour) or until an overly fast dealer replaced the dealer at my table and I couldn't find another table.

The Achilles' heel of the setup is the foot switches. To begin with, the chairs at the Sands were too high. I sat down at a table and discovered that my feet did not touch the floor. You can't work the toe switches unless your feet press against the floor. I had to stand up and half lean against the chair. I preferred the lower seats at the Claridge.

The switches take rather a lot of pressure to work at all. They're quirky. Sometimes a tap will do; other times they won't register even when you're afraid to apply any more pressure for fear of crushing them. There's no click or other feedback to tell you that the card has registered. In practice sessions, I found myself watching the display to make sure it was working. That isn't possible in a casino. The 7s, 8s, and 9s were the worst: sometimes just one of the toes would register, screwing up the count. In a practice session at home, I once pressed too long and cleared the machine by accident. After a little experimentation, the switches seemed to work fine, but it was awkward.

I wondered if I would get so confused by the mechanics of noting and entering the cards that I would play my hand wrong. Fortunately I didn't. The problem was entering all the cards in the brief time between deals.

Most dealers are fast, and casinos like to keep the game as fast-paced as possible. More hands dealt mean more money for the house. At first it was difficult to enter all the cards. I was missing almost half of them. That shouldn't invalidate the Comp-U-Count's readings, but it would make the periods with a high positive count all the rarer. I got better with practice. There is a huge difference in speed among dealers, so I learned to watch a dealer before I sat down to make sure that he or she was relatively slow. Dealers are switched frequently; if a replacement dealer was too fast I went to another table. Players who deliberate over their hands help slow the pace, too.

I tried several ways of tapping in the values of the cards. The simplest, at least in a place where the cards are dealt face up, is to tap in the cards as they are dealt. The trouble is, even the pokiest dealers dealt faster than I could enter the cards. I tended to tap in everyone's first card, falling slightly behind the dealer, then tap in the second and any additional cards as the players played their hands. I found I liked sitting in third base — to the dealer's extreme left.

As far as I can tell, the Comp-U-Count is indetectable in ordinary play. The most incriminating action was the constant glancing at my watch. At first I was doing an Ed Norton routine of hitching up my sleeve, stretching my arm, and checking the time before I could bet.

Cameras in the dark-glass hemispheres on casino ceilings can focus in on the values of cards. They can probably read the Comp-U-Count's display, too, if someone had a mind to. I learned to keep the watch half covered with my shirtsleeve and rested my arm on the table in the same line of sight with my cards. Then I could see the count without appearing to be checking the time. The main unit was hidden by my jacket.

The betting strategy you have to use with the Comp-U-Count (or with a mental counting system, for that matter) may be more of a giveaway than the hardware itself. You are supposed to bet more when the count is positive (not blinking) and high. Casinos regard wager variations as suspicious, though. Most counting systems recommend that your maximum bet, for high positive counts, be no more than twice the minimum bet. So at a $5 table, my maximum bets were $10 ($20 when doubling down). This may have been overcautious, considering that I was at a cheap table.

I ran into a pair of regular, low-tech card counters at the Claridge. Sitting at first base (the seat at the dealer's extreme right, favored by counters) was a gray-haired man in a maroon plaid jacket and a hat. A few minutes after I arrived, a younger man in a blue short-sleeve shirt bought in. "I like to sit over there," he said, pointing to Plaid Jacket.

"I'm sitting here!" Plaid said.

"What difference does it make?" Blue Shirt asked.

"I'm sitting here, all right?"

"I just usually sit there."

"I don't care where you sit."

"You know why I want it?"

"Yeah."

Blue Shirt sat down in the middle of the table.

Another half superstition is that bad players jinx the fall of cards. "I can't stand being at a table with people like that," Blue Shirt said after a bad player left. The bad player had gotten two blackjacks in a row.

The pit boss came over to our $3 minimum table and gave us a half-hour notice that they would be raising the minimum to $4. Plaid Jacket announced that he was going to check on them to make sure they gave us the full half hour. Then he looked in my direction and asked, "What time you got?"

I wasn't wearing my real watch, just the Comp-U-Count fake. I couldn't deny having a watch since he had probably seen it. I could say the watch was broken, but then it would look suspicious when I kept glancing at it during the game. So I looked in another direction and pretended not to notice he was talking to me. Luckily, the dealer showed him her watch.

At the end of my first session, I was ahead $15 — three betting units, since I was playing at a $5 minimum table. In the second session I won $10, and in the third, playing at a $3 table, I won $3. All told, I ended up ahead just $28.

I'm not quite sure what to make of that. Few people come away from the blackjack tables with a net profit, however measly. Still, I was ahead by no more than three betting units for each session, and I suspect that is not statistically significant. If I played at each table for about forty-five minutes, then the hourly gain came to a little over $12 — nothing to get excited about.

At the right tables, I could have been betting ten or even a hundred times as much (with equally greater risk). But then the pit bosses and spy cameras would have been inspecting my actions a lot more closely.

The Comp-U-Count should be a lot more effective in Las Vegas (where it is illegal). Major fluctuations in the composition of the deck are most likely near the end of the shoe. In Atlantic City the shoe is composed of four or six decks, and they deal down only to a yellow marker that is inserted about two-thirds of the way into the shoe. This makes positive counts rare. In contrast, some Las Vegas casinos deal from a single deck and may deal as much as three-fourths of the way to the end. High positive counts would be much more common.

· 16 ·

THREE-CARD MONTE

*T*hree-card monte is the crooked gambling game played on urban streets. All it takes is three bent playing cards on a cardboard box. (The box can be abandoned if the police approach.) Dealers can earn as much as a successful dentist. A typical operation consists of a dealer, two shills, and one or two lookouts. Only the dealer is apparent to the naive player.

The game is simple. The cards are shown face up. Two are of the same rank and suit; the third is different. Often the like cards are black and the odd card is red. The dealer turns the cards face down and mixes them as in a shell game. Then a player bets money that he knows which face-down card is the odd one.

In current Manhattan operations, the payoff–table limits are often "40 gets you 100, 100 gets you 250." This means that if you put down $40, the dealer puts down $60. Pick the odd card, and you take the $100 pot. Pick one of the other two cards, and the dealer keeps the $100.

These seem to be decent odds. Suppose you can't follow the dealer's hands at all. The *worst* you can do is to guess a card completely at random. Then you would expect to win one in three times. Betting $40 each time, you'd spend $120 and get back $100. That's no worse than you'd do playing the slot machines. Of course, that's the worst possible case. If you could follow the card some of the time or if you could find some giveaway pattern in the dealer's behavior, you might tip the odds in your favor.

The dealer's legerdemain prevents that. In normal play, anyone you see win is a shill, the dealer is that good. The wins of these accomplices help attract a crowd of onlookers and convince people that they can win, too. The dealer is so good, in fact, that the shills can't always follow his manipulations, so he communicates the correct card through a code.

Often the code uses a body movement that is opposite the position of the odd card. A cigarette or toothpick in the left side of the dealer's mouth signifies that the winning card is the one on the dealer's right—and vice versa. When the card is in the center, the dealer positions the cigarette in the center of his mouth. Nonsmokers may hold the money in the hand opposite the location of the winning card. Another dealer may rest his left hand on the box when the card is on the right, both hands when it's in the center.

Some operations are bold enough to use verbal codes. "Seaside" means the winning card is in the middle. "Raider, raider" or similar-sounding words in the dealer's patter tells the shill to place a bet. "Slide" (said by the lookout) means the police are coming. Verbal codes are more changeable than the body language codes, but you may be able to discern them in a few minutes of observation.

That doesn't mean you can win. Even when a mark chooses the correct card (which happens one-third of the time no matter how good the dealer is), the dealer is covered. A shill may quickly put down a larger bet on a wrong card. The dealer may then cite a rule allowing him to accept bets on one card only. He will accept the shill's bet and annul yours. Or the dealer may accidentally knock over the box, spilling the cards.

More elaborage cons have shills "cheating." In one game I watched, the dealer was trying unsuccessfully to get a prosperous-looking sort to bet on which card was the odd one. This "businessman" was probably a shill. He pleaded that he wasn't interested in betting and walked away. The dealer ran after him, leaving the cards unattended. While the dealer was gone, a ragged-looking person in the crowd (unquestionably a shill) peeked under the cards, revealing the odd one. The dealer returned, having been unable to convince the businessman.

Once again he asked for bets. Now the shill who had peeked put his money on the card he had shown to be the winner. This made it look like a sure win, and other people in the crowd (the unknowing victims) put their money on the same card. When the dealer turned up the card, it was the *wrong* one, thanks to his sleight of hand.

In another common variation, the shill marks the winning card while the dealer conveniently isn't looking. The shill may bend a corner or dust it with chalk. After the bets are placed, the mark mysteriously "moves" to another card.

How do they manage *that*? An expert monte dealer who will remain nameless revealed the secret. Here goes.

The Hipe

The hipe is the basic move of three-card monte. You hold two cards in a packet, face down. Then you throw the top card on the playing surface. The suckers assume you let the bottom card drop. There's nothing mind-boggling about this deception, but after a few hipes, most observers lose all track of the odd card.

If you want to go through the motions, take three cards and crimp them by holding their right and left edges with the left hand (assuming you're right-handed). Put your right thumb on the bottom edge and right fingers on the center of the top edge, and give the packet a stiff pull toward you. Place the three cards in a row on a table in front of you.

You handle monte cards about the same way you bent them — with the right thumb at bottom center and the right index finger at top center. Pick up one card this way and place it on another. The left edges of the cards should touch, but keep the right edge of the top card suspended a fraction of an inch above the playing surface. With the right *middle* finger, grasp the bottom card at top center. Pick up both cards as a packet. The index finger holds the top card, the middle finger holds the bottom, and the thumb secures both.

Now jerk the hand to the right, releasing the index finger. This throws the top card. Quickly grasp the remaining (original bottom) card with the index finger, and let go with the middle finger. It takes practice to do this in one natural movement, but there you have it.

The Underthrow

The underthrow is the legitimate counterpart to the hipe. You pick up two cards just as with the hipe and throw the *bottom* card. The idea is to have the hipe look just like the underthrow. Mixing hipes and underthrows confuses even those spectators who may be wise to the hipe.

A Typical Routine

Start with the odd card in the center: red, black, red.

1. Pick up the right card ("Right" and "left" refer to your right and left in this description) with the right hand and show it to the marks: red.
2. Pick up the left card with the left hand and show it: red.
3. Lay the right card on the center card, then pick both up and show the bottom card: black.
4. Hipe the top (red) card to the left. The marks think this is the black card and keep their eyes on it.
5. With the left hand, throw down the other red card to the center position. Now both red cards are face down on the playing surface.
6. Throw down the black card to the right. This leaves the cards positioned red, red, black, most observers thinking the black card is on the left.

Now you show off:

7. Pick up the black card, on the right, with the right hand. Lay it on the leftmost red card, and show the bottom card of the packet: red.
8. Underthrow the red card to the playing surface. The black card remains in the right hand.
9. Lay the black card on the other red card. Pick it up and show it: red.
10. Hipe the black card to the left of the card on the playing surface. The observers think you threw the red card you just showed.
11. Now show the card remaining in your right hand: red. You have just shown all three cards, and all were red.

The Bent or Marked Card

In the bent card trick, the dealer *unbends* the card the shill has marked (the odd card) and bends another card (a losing card).

To accomplish this, you pick an unbent card with the right hand and show it. The next action the observers will see is you laying this card on the bent, odd card.

Hold the unbent card with the thumb at bottom, the middle finger at top. Your ring finger is curled, the fingernail pressing lightly against the top of the card. The little finger lifts up the corner of the card while the ring finger pushes down. This opposing force bends the corner neatly.

Place the freshly bent, losing card on the bent winning card and show the packet as one. Hipe the top card, leaving the odd card in your right hand. While the left hand picks up, shows, and throws the other (unbent) card, you unbend the odd card. Hold it between the thumb and middle finger. Grasp the corner between the ring finger (on bottom) and the little finger (on top). Pull up the ring finger while the little finger goes down. The scissors motion unbends the corner.

HOW TO FIX A COIN TOSS

Yep. There is a way to rig a coin toss. Not heads-I-win-tails-you-lose, but a physical trick long known to carnies and fellow travelers. It works best with large coins such as silver dollars or 50-cent pieces. A quarter is okay. It's very difficult with nickels or dimes.

No switches or false moves are used. The toss is fair in every respect — except that you know the outcome before the toss. Place the coin in the middle of your palm. The side you desire to force is down. Toss the coin in the air, jerking your hand back at the instant the coin leaves the hand. Catch the coin in the palm. It should show the same side up as before the toss. Slapping the coin onto the opposite forearm reverses it, yielding the desired outcome. It takes a little practice to learn just when to pull your hand back. Try it with a silver dollar or half dollar. It isn't hard to achieve an accuracy of 90% with a 50-cent piece.

Given the corruptibility of the wholesome coin toss, it should come as no surprise that a throw of dice can be tricked. Make a loose fist with the throwing hand. Place the (legitimate) dice in the hollow formed by the middle and ring fingers and the palm. The index finger on one side and the little finger on the other close the hollow. The dice can be rattled without changing their orientation. This "lock grip" makes it relatively easy to throw the dice with some control. It's not perfect, but it's good enough to slant the game in the cheater's favor.

· 18 ·

VIDEO GAMES

*H*ard-core video game addicts know you can play many games for free. Hidden deep in read-only memory are tricks that give savvy players unlimited play for a token or two. It's anyone's guess if these tricks are intentional or just bugs in the game program. Certainly tales of free play help maintain interest in the games, driving a lot of players to spend more than they would have otherwise just *looking* for these tricks. Other games have secret special effects that are triggered only by high scores, hot dog strategy, or unspecified right stuff on the part of the player. Our informants reveal how to blast the most infuriating arcade games into hyperspace.

Pac-Man

Namco/Midway

Pac-Man has a "hiding place," a special location in the maze where the Pac-Man is invulnerable. Provided a monster isn't hot on your trail as you enter the hiding place, you're safe. The monsters run around the maze and never find the Pac-Man. You can go have a pizza, a gym class, or a midlife crisis — as long as no one touches the joystick or unplugs the machine.

143

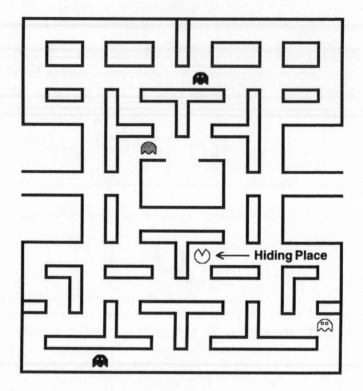

Pac-Man

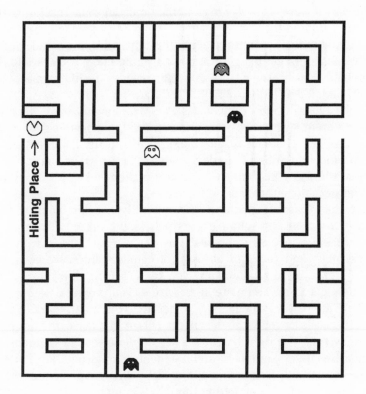

Ms. Pac-Man Maze 3

At least it works this way most of the time. On some machines, the monsters *do* find the Pac-Man after a while. Most arcade games have an internal difficulty control that may be adjusted by the arcade owner if the customers get too good and don't pump enough coins into the machines. Possibly the factory-set game includes the hiding place, but it is eliminated at higher difficulty settings.

In the generally more difficult Ms. Pac-Man, the mazes are different. Four different layouts appear in rotation, and the monsters show more initiative. There is at least one hiding place in Ms. Pac-Man, but it doesn't show up until the third maze. It's at upper left, at the entrance to the "tunnel" (the door in the gate wall that takes Ms. Pac-Man around to the opposite side of the maze).

A badge of arcade machismo is "byte rollover." The point of Pac-Man is to eat all the yellow energy pills in the maze without being killed. If and when you accomplish this, a new maze appears with new energy pills, and you start all over (of course, your score keeps increasing). If you're good enough, you keep clearing new mazes. The monsters get faster and more aggressive as you progress.

There are players who manage to get up to the 255th maze. If they then successfully gobble all the energy pills in that maze, the machine goes haywire. The right half of the screen dissolves into a jumble of particolored letters, numbers, and fragments of monsters. The left half of the screen still looks normal, but play halts. If you're the sort of player who is capable of getting through 255 mazes, this is either an annoying halt to your winning streak or a welcome Götterdämmerung.

The largest number a five-digit car odometer can display is 99999. Drive another mile, and it resets to 00000. Byte rollover is the same thing with binary numbers. A byte is an eight-digit binary number, and the largest eight-digit binary number is $11111111_{(base\ 2)}$ — 255 in ordinary numbers. When Pac-Man was designed, no one dreamed that anyone would ever clear 255 boards. So if a player clears the 255th maze, the count drops back to $00000000_{(base\ 2)}$ — the zeroth maze.

There is no provision for a maze #0. The first maze, the one that pops up when you put in a quarter and that has a cherry in it, is maze #1. The machine's attempt to produce a maze #0 gums up the works, so you get garbage. Byte rollover occurs in other games, too, always after the 255th of something.

Space Invaders

Taito/Midway

The holy grail for some video gamers is an enigmatic *something* hidden in Space Invaders. The something is believed to be a graphic, animation, and/or sound effect. The Taito Company, which manufactures the game in Japan and licensed it to Midway in the United States, won't say what the secret is but will say that it's there. By today's standards, Space Invaders is crude indeed — the screen is black and white. But the quest for Space Invader's secret has sustained interest in the game since 1978.

Space Invaders is a Godzilla-mentality game where you eventually lose no matter how good you are. As Taito says in a pamphlet: "Space Invaders gives a feeling of tremendous tension." By 1980, there were over three hundred thousand arcade machines installed. In Japan particularly, many of the machines are cocktail-table style so they can be used in coffee shops while patrons are dining. At the height of Japan's Space Invaders mania, there was a national shortage of the 100-yen coins used in the machines.

Taito says the game took over a year to devise. "The Space Age Theme was chosen because of its popularity then and now in Japan."

The player is kinesthetically linked to a "laser cannon" at the bottom of the game screen. Above is a barrage of fifty-five slowly descending Space Invaders. The invaders drop bombs on you while you try to blast them away.

Three bunkers are just above the level of the laser cannon. They protect you, sort of. Both the invaders' bombs and your laser blasts take bites out of the bunkers. The bunkers have a crumbly, sandcastle consistency as they erode pixel by pixel. Good players blast off their own bunkers right away to have a better shot at the invaders.

Part of the Space Invaders mindset is the annoying sound effects. Everything that happens happens loudly. When an invader's blast blows up your cannon, it disintegrates with a sickening crash. You get two more cannons after the first, with a bonus cannon if you score 1,000 points.

The three kinds of invading monsters are called skulls (lower part of the formation), toasters (middle), and coneheads (top). You get 10 points for each skull you zap, 20 for each toaster, and 30 for each conehead. Periodically a flying saucer sweeps across the screen. You get 50 to 300 points for annihilating it.

The invaders move back and forth across the screen in a huge flock. As the formation touches one side of the screen, the whole bunch move down a notch. Shooting down an invader provokes retaliation from the surviving invaders. And as invaders are exterminated, the survivors move faster. If they are not destroyed, the invaders eventually mow through the bunker ruins, then land. If even a single invader lands, you lose.

If you kill them all, then you get to start over with three new lasers and a new complement of invaders. In principle, you can play forever for a quarter.

It would be simple enough if the secret effect were triggered by an exceptionally high score. Space Invaders has a regressive scoring system. Try the game a few times, and you think you're doing really well to score 800 points. Then you find out that *lots* of guys have broken 100,000, and someone in Japan hit 300,000. (In its original release, the arcade machine could display scores only up to 9,999. Taito had to retool it to display larger scores.) Breaking 100,000 does not produce the effect, however.

Space Invaders' secret has been triggered by rare players. It goes like this: You have to kill every invader but one *and* that last one must be a skull. Normally, the skulls are the first to go. They're on the bottom, and you're shooting up through them. So leaving a skull as the last invader seems all but impossible.

Each blast travels in a straight vertical trajectory from its point of fire. Meanwhile, the monsters are moving laterally. It's just barely possible to shoot laser blasts up in advance of the monster fleet, timed precisely so that the coneheads run into them. You can take out the toasters the same way. Of course, it requires flawless reflexes and absolutely stupendous eye-hand coordination.

If you can manage this, leaving just one skull, the effect is activated. The last skull leaves a ghostly trail of scan lines. When it hits one side of the screen, it reverses and erases the trail. When it reverses again, it starts over. (You still have to shoot this invader before it lands to continue playing.)

The Deluxe (color) version of Space Invaders has a more elaborate effect. The last invader must be one from the bottom two rows — which, in the Deluxe version, includes three toasters as well as the skulls. Zap all the other aliens, and this one leaves a trail. If and when you then blast this last invader, the result is a "rainbow," a multicolored wedge covering most of the screen. It's orange, yellow, and green (top to bottom).

Donkey Kong, Jr.

Nintendo

This trick will give you true unlimited play for one player. Select a two-player game. You play Player 1's game normally. Every time the nonexistent Player 2 has a turn, do this:

Donkey Kong, Jr., starts out on a green island at lower left. Move Junior to the right, stopping just short of plopping him in the water. He should have one foot on the green turf and one foot dangling. A "snapjaw," which looks like a Johnson Smith catalogue set of chattering teeth, will descend down a nearby vine. When it comes to the end of the vine, it will plummet into the water. Make Junior jump for the snapjaw, hitting it as it touches the water. (This is a fairly easy maneuver.)

You're actually "throwing" Player 2's turn, since Junior dies. But a bonus turn will be awarded to both Players 1 and 2. That means you continue with normal play (as Player 1), and you will be able to do the same maneuver again as Player 2. For two tokens, you can play all day.

Dig Dug

Atari

Dig Dug is a fairly sicko game (the point is to smash small creatures with rocks) with a secret trick that lets you take a break. You maneuver a subterranean robot through the ground, digging tunnels as it goes. Dragon-like creatures called Fygars and cuter creatures called Pookas are killed by dropping rocks on them or pumping them full of air until they burst. In normal play, killing all the monsters on one screen brings up a new screen with new monsters.

To put the game on hold, you have to kill all the monsters but one. Then you must kill the surviving monster twice. Lead this monster to a position two spaces under a rock. Then pump it full of air — not enough to kill it, but enough to paralyze it. Dig up under the rock so that it comes loose. Quickly move out of the way and resume pumping the monster full of air so that he bursts just as the rock falls on him and smashes him. In a fit of moral indignation, the machine will take a powder and not move on to the next screen. You can move the Dig Dug around the empty maze to your heart's content. Some people dig their initials in the "dirt."

You can't score points when the machine is in this state, but you can take a rest. When you want to resume normal play, you have to commit suicide. Have Dig Dug excavate a rock and let it fall on him.

Defender

Williams Electronics

To put Defender on hold, you have to get all ten humanoids on the ground in the same place. Let a lander pick up the humanoids. Shoot down the lander, and catch the humanoids before they fall to the ground. Find a point above an unobstructed part of the landscape. Cut the forward thrust and use the altitude control to drop straight down. This should deposit all ten humanoids in a stack.

The number 500 is next to each humanoid. If the 500s are not moving or changing color, the game has been arrested. Nothing will move, and you can go eat lunch.

To resume, push the thrust button.

Galaga

Namco/Midway

There's a trick to Galaga that stops the bugs from firing — not just temporarily, but for the remainder of the game. Since the bugs' firing is the main impediment to survival, you can then play forever and rack up astronomical scores.

150

The bugs come in two species, red and blue and blue and yellow. The trick requires that you blast away all of the bugs except for one blue and yellow guy. This remaining bug must be one of the two leftmost in the formation. Then you have to dodge this lone bug and its fire for about fifteen minutes. This is difficult unless you're pretty good at the game.

At the end of this time, the bug will stop shooting. The next step is to let the bug wrap around through the top of the display (disappear off the top and reappear at the bottom) four times after it has stopped shooting. This disables firing permanently. Then you can shoot the lone bug. A new swarm will appear, but none will fire. As long as you don't smash into a bug (which is still fatal), you can pick them off indefinitely.

Xevious

Namco

Video game companies usually do not give the games' designers screen credit. But many game authors have hidden their names in the game, to be revealed under certain circumstances. One of the slickest concealed credits is in Xevious. Your chance to trigger it comes right at the beginning. You fly a delta-shaped space shuttle over a landscape that looks like a fancy country club's greens map. You start over wooded area. Move to the right edge of the screen and start bombings. Rings, the least aggressive enemy aircraft, will appear but not attack. Wait until the rings are near your shuttle, then shoot them.

This triggers the author credit. "NAMCO ORIGINAL program by EVE-ZOO" appears at the bottom of the screen.

• 19 •

MALL HORROR STORIES

The Medium Is the Muzak

Some retail stores sneak subaudible messages into their background music. This much has been admitted by the manufacturers of such systems, which include Proactive Systems of Portland, Oregon, and Behavioral Engineering Center of Metairie, Louisiana. Proactive claims that 120 stores use its system. Neither firm will name the stores using subliminal persuasion.

The messages are not sales pitches (as far as anyone knows) but mottos discouraging theft. "Don't steal," or something of the kind, is repeated subaudibly beneath the background music. The idea is that words too faint to be heard nevertheless register in the subconscious mind. Marketers of the devices claim dramatic reductions in shoplifting — up to 65%, according to Proactive.

Proactive's system is computerized. Sensors automatically adjust the volume as the level of background noise varies. Message programs come on magnetic disks.

Which stores use the messages? Just one has admitted it: Jay Jacobs, a chain of clothing stores for adolescent girls. Jay Jacobs sells things like fun furs, metallic earrings, and tops with cat faces on them. If you want anything with a unicorn on it, this is the place. I snooped around the Eagle Rock Plaza store in Los Angeles. It had rock background music, different from the Muzak-y tunes in the mall. I could not hear any messages. At the front left corner of the store was a case that seemed to hold the music system. Inside the case was a black box marked Auditron.

According to Proactive, the messages run: *Obey the law. Stay honest. Don't steal. We welcome honest shoppers.*

Appalled in Boston

A "Dear Abby" reader called "Appalled in Boston" insinuated in a 1984 column that many finer department stores have peepholes and two-way mirrors in their dressing rooms. Abby told Appalled she was "full of beans." Three follow-up letters assured Abby that the specter of security cop voyeurism was for real.

One reader, "Got an Eyeful," said he had worked as a detective for a fancy California store that had both peepholes and two-way mirrors in the men's and women's dressing rooms. Got an Eyeful's store had a policy preventing male detectives from monitoring the women's dressing rooms. It was okay for female detectives to monitor the men's rooms, though, and the rules weren't enforced much, anyway. Got an Eyeful said the covert surveillance went on even in states having laws forbidding it. Detectives making a bust would claim to have seen the shoplifting take place on the floor. Got an Eyeful admitted, however, that he had emotional problems and was fired after *he* was caught shoplifting.

"Still Appalled in Boston" (who seems to be no relation to the original Appalled) claimed to know "for a fact" that Bloomingdale's and Saks spied on their customers in the dressing rooms and she had it "on good authority" that Lord & Taylor did the same. Still Appalled mentioned signs in the Bloomingdale's and Saks dressing rooms informing customers of the monitoring.

Then "Reads You in Paterson" told of an unnamed woman in New Jersey who complained about two-way mirrors in two stores seven years earlier. According to Reads You, "An employee revealed that not only detectives were looking, some of the store personnel also took turns looking. He said they were in hysterics when a fat lady tried on a bikini and did a little dance in front of the mirror! Another time the men lined up in front of a peephole to get a look at an unbelievably well-built woman 'everyone had to see.' "

Apparently in response to the "Dear Abby" columns, State Senator Eugene Migliaro introduced "Peeping Tom" legislation in 1985 to ban the mirrors and peepholes in Connecticut. Migliaro's bill states: "No department or clothing store shall install or in any manner use a closed-circuit television system, a two-way mirror, a peephole or any other surveillance device in any dressing room available to the public. Any person convicted of a violation of this section shall be fined not more than five hundred dollars or imprisoned not more than three months or both." Migliaro argued that surveillance jobs attract "perverts" who like their jobs too much. "Nobody has the right to view you in any state of dressing or undressing," Migliaro contended, claiming that there are other ways of keeping inventory from walking out the door.

Bigger Secrets asked Migliaro how he knew that this sort of thing was going on. Did he know any specific stores that did it? Had he spoken to a retired head of security who was willing to break the silence? Migliaro said, "It is virtually impossible to furnish an accurate count of stores, since such an admission by a store could subject it to civil suit and potential loss of business."

I checked out dressing rooms in the flagship Bloomingdale's and Saks Fifth Avenue stores in New York. In each I went to a department geared to a younger crowd (which would likely have the stickiest fingers) and took two pairs of pants into a dressing room.

I found nothing that could have been a peephole. Some of the dressing rooms had no ceilings, and someone could have been watching from above, but all I saw were exposed pipes.

The "two-way mirror" is a matter of lighting. It is simply a pane of glass that is partially silvered. One side of the pane, the observer's side, is in relative darkness. The other side is brightly lit. The dressing rooms are well illuminated, of course. Still, if you could turn off the light or block it with your hands, it might be possible to see through the mirror if the store security people have some form of lighting on their side.

Shielding the light with my hands, I looked into the mirror in a Saks dressing room. At one point I thought I saw something move, but I couldn't be sure. The dressing room was one of a row lining a wall.

There was a door marked EMPLOYEES ONLY in the wall. A store employee went through it, but the door closed behind him before I could glimpse what lay beyond. I picked up a pair of pants and innocently blundered through that door, as if I was trying to find my way out.

Instead of a darkened spy operation, I found a brightly lit office space behind the door, with desks on the side of the wall opposite the mirrors.

Of several persons queried who had worked in various stores' security, none knew of two-way mirrors or peepholes. Mostly, they said, stores have someone outside the dressing rooms to note how many garments people take into a dressing room compared to how many they take out.

• 20 •

PARAPHERNALIA

Are Life Savers Deadly?

Wint-O-Green Life Savers shoot yellow sparks when you crunch down on them. So do Wintergreen Certs. This fact led two Illinois physicians, Dr. Howard Edward, Jr., and Dr. Donald Edward, to write to the *New England Journal of Medicine* warning of possible dire consequences if, God forbid, someone chomped down on a Wint-O-Green Life Saver in an oxygen tent, an operating room, or a space capsule.

To see the fireworks, go into a dark room with another person or a mirror. Chew forcefully, keeping your mouth open. (The lower the humidity, the better.) With luck, this will produce a modest paranormal phenomenon in your mouth. Life Savers spark a lot more than Certs. It may take several attempts to get a good display. If it works at all, it works on the first crunch or two. Once the candy gets wet, the show's over.

Most of the time, the "sparks" are a pale aura. Other times, they look almost like a yellow sparkler. The sparking seems to be a simple glow rather than a detonation of volatile oils in the candy. I have never been able to feel shock or heat or anything while this is going on.

What makes Life Savers spark? According to the label, Wint-O-Green Life Savers contain "sugar, corn syrup, artificial flavor & stearic acid." Wintergreen Certs with Retsyn are a more complex sweetmeat made from "sugar, corn syrup, artificial and natural flavoring, activated partially hydrogenated cottonseed oil, magnesium stearate, copper gluconate, and artificial colors (including FD&C yellow no. 5)." Unlike Life Savers, Certs have little green specks. This makes it look as though you are eating a small bathroom tile. At first I thought that the green specks were Retsyn, but close viewing of Certs commercials established that Retsyn is a liquid. Retsyn, as you have probably guessed by now, is an iffy substance that you are not going to find in the periodic table of elements. The Certs label informs you that the jazzed-up cottonseed oil and copper gluconate are what they're calling Retsyn.

I tried regular, Pep-O-Mint, and Tropical Fruit Life Savers, and none of them sparked, even though their ingredients are the same. So the wintergreen flavoring must be crucial. While neither Life Savers nor Certs reveals its flavorings, there can be little doubt of the formulas. Wintergreen is, along with vanilla, one of the easiest natural flavors to simulate synthetically. Hardly anyone bothers with natural oil of wintergreen. The synthetic is called methyl salicylate ($C_8H_8O_3$).

Life Savers' "Manager of Candy Technology" admitted that methyl salicylate was the flavoring but didn't seem to know much else about the sparking. The Certs people were more helpful. They reported that the sparks had been the subject of at least partially serious research at Yale and Temple universities.

The Edwards' 1968 letter inspired a spate of experiments and responses from the *New England Journal of Medicine*'s readers. One correspondent suggested keeping the mouth shut while chewing, a folkway Emily Post always favored anyway. Research at Yale revealed that Wintergreen Necco wafers spark. Others ticked off Life Savers flavors that *don't* spark (practically all others are duds). Clove Life Savers *do* spark.

Since Life Savers spark with just a trace of wintergreen oil, it stands to reason that a pure crystalline form of wintergreen oil would spark all the more. Some graduate students froze wintergreen oil in liquid nitrogen. When they smashed it with a hammer in a dark room, it was like the northern lights.

The term for this sort of thing is triboluminescence, the emission of light when a crystalline substance is crushed. Substances such as wintergreen and clove oil favor triboluminescence. The "sparking" is actually a cold luminescence rather than a real spark. The *Journal* judged Wint-O-Green Life Savers safe for oxygen tents and gas stations.

Mae West on the Camels Pack

Some people see a picture of Mae West hidden in the benday dots of the Camels cigarette pack. A brown and navy blue pattern on a light brown background represents the nap of the camel's hair. The Mae West effigy is on the left, the camel's upper leg corresponding to West's legs. The tip of the large pyramid at far right is level with West's neck.

As usually pictured, West is wearing a low-cut gown with a suggestion of cleavage. A minority opinion holds that she is nude. She has both hands on her hips (this detail nails down the ID). The face is featureless except for the hair. The head seems to be pointed right while the rest of her body faces left. Some also manage to see a lion (the MGM lion?) in the camel's hump. There are eyes, a nose, a mouth, ears, and a mane.

One of the oldest essentially unchanged package designs for a consumer product, the camel picture has been reproduced more than 162 billion times, according to the R. J. Reynolds Company. The Reynolds people in Winston-Salem, North Carolina, deny that there are any intentional hidden images in the package art. To those who inquire about Mae West, they send an illustrated historical brochure.

One picture in the brochure shows the prototype Camels pack. Created in 1913 by company artists in Richmond, Virginia, it depicts a gangly, not-very-realistic dromedary. The company wasn't very happy with that picture. When the Barnum & Bailey circus came to Winston-Salem, Roy C. Haberkern, R. J. Reynolds's secretary, took a picture of the circus's dromedary, Old Joe. This photograph, reproduced in the brochure, shows Old Joe with his eyes closed and his tail slightly raised. The camel kept fidgeting until its trainer, an obese man in a raincoat, slapped him on the nose. The trainer holds Old Joe still with a harness in the photo.

This picture was used as the model for a redrawn camel. Even such details as the closed eyes and the Mona Lisa smile (of the camel, not the fat guy, who looks pretty grim) are copied directly from the photograph. Here's the surprise — Mae and the lion are in Old Joe's fur. The light areas that form Mae's head, arm, and breasts and the dark regions of the lion's ears, eyes, and mouth are all there in the photograph.

They're not real markings. It's just the way the light fell on the pile of the coat the instant the shutter snapped. The translation from photograph to cigarette pack changed certain details and left others out. Mae and the lion are more prominent on the Camels pack than in the photograph.

The Camels pack is but one example of the erotica some find on packaging. A split apple on the Mott's Apple Juice can is said to depict a vulva.

The Publishers Clearing House Sweepstakes

If you're looking for an excuse not to send in your Publishers Clearing House sweepstakes ticket, here's one: The odds against winning are 181,795,000 to 1.

You'll never hear this from the Publishers Clearing House people. Letters to Publishers Clearing House and several other sweepstakes organizers asking about the odds brought only short, evasive replies. The Publishers Clearing House people responded that "with 7 lucky numbers the odds of winning are 1 in 3,080." That doesn't tell you much unless you know the odds of getting seven lucky numbers. They didn't give that.

The law in most states requires an organization running a large contest to file certain information with the state. That information usually includes the odds of winning. These figures — from the New York secretary of state's office — are the odds that apply nationwide, for such information is required on the New York registration form.

Contest	Odds for Grand Prize
Reader's Digest	1 in 84 million
Publishers Clearing House	1 in 182 million
American Family Publishers	1 in 200 million

The odds are more than twice as good in the Reader's Digest sweepstakes (which has relatively modest grand prizes) than in its two best-known competitors. The odds on the American Family Publishers and Publishers Clearing House contests seem to require that almost every man, woman, and child in America enter. Maybe they have a lot of people entering more than once.

If you divide the amount of the grand prize by the odds, you get the real worth of the contest — what your chance of winning would be worth to an oddsmaker. The results:

Contest	Grand Prize	Expected Winnings
Reader's Digest	$334,500 (maximum)	0.4 cents
Publishers Clearing House	$2 million	1.1 cents
American Family Publishers	$10 million	5 cents

The Reader's Digest contest is the worst deal. The per-entry value of the grand prize is approximately the cash value of four S & H green stamps. The Publishers Clearing House grand prize works out to about a penny. The American Family Publishers contest is far and away the richest — to the tune of a nickel. You don't have to subscribe to a magazine to enter these contests. You do have to send in the envelope, and that costs a stamp.

Slug Wars

Unscrupulous Necco Wafer eaters have discovered that the candies sometimes work in toll booths. Neccos are almost exactly the diameter of quarters, through twice as thick. About 59 cents buys you a roll of thirty-nine. A Chicago disk jockey publicized this gimmick, spurring a small epidemic of toll cheating. But it works only one time in a hundred, according to an Illinois State Police estimate, and the candies can gum up the machines.

Other fake tokens are all too effective. A staggering variety of bogus tokens and coins are accepted by New York City's subways. Most notorious are the Connecticut Turnpike tokens (17½ cents in value) issued from October 1982 to December 1985 and still occasionally turning up. The Connecticut tokens not only look like New York City subway tokens ($1 at this writing) but were made by the same company. The Connecticut token is a hair bigger (0.880 inch diameter vs. 0.875). When the subway turnstiles were calibrated so that they could distinguish between the two, they rejected slightly irregular genuine tokens. (New York City collected a million of the Connecticut tokens, and, so it wouldn't be a total loss, asked Connecticut to redeem them for 17½ cents apiece. Connecticut offered 2½ cents each, the minting cost.) Recently, cheats have discovered that the Mexican 5-centavo coin also works in the subway turnstiles.

The Mexican peso, worth about ½ cent, is the same size as the tokens used for New York City's Verrazano-Narrows, Bronx-White-stone, Throgs Neck, and Triborough toll bridges and the Brooklyn-Battery and Queens-Midtown tunnels, which sell for $1.50 at this writing. The Triborough Bridge and Tunnel Authority collects about 7,300 pesos a month from its toll machines. Some Greek, Chilean, and Israeli coins are substituted for U.S. quarters in exact-toll lanes.

The Italian 100-lire coin works in 1-franc slot machines at European casinos. A hundred lire are worth about as much as a nickel; a franc is worth a dime. Even with a 75% payoff rate, a lire cheat can come out ahead — unless someone has already filled the machine with 100-lire coins. In some French and Swiss casinos, about half the coins removed are the Italian coins.

Is Your Cadillac Spying on You?

Auto trade magazines commented darkly on the onboard computer on Cadillacs with V8-6-4 engines. Supposedly, it keeps a record of driving habits, or something of the kind. And some think GM plans to use that to weasel out of warranty repairs by using the data to prove that the driver violated the 55 mph speed limit, did not change the oil often enough, and so forth. The *Wall Street Journal* quoted a spokesman for GM's Cadillac Division as saying, "Any suggestion that there is any equipment in our cars designed to spy on a driver is pure hogwash."

Rolls-Royce *does* concern itself with the habits of its drivers, if on a more modest scale. Access to the chassis requires removing some of a set of sixty-four nuts painted bright yellow at the Rolls-Royce factory. By examining the nuts, a Rolls serviceperson can tell if any non-R folks have worked on the car.

Cigarettes in the Turkey

Campbell's Soup was embarrassed a few years ago when the government objected that the soup in its ads was photographed with glass marbles in the bottom of the bowls. The marbles held up the vegetables, making it look like, well, you could eat the stuff with a fork. Campbell's ad agency had to get rid of the marbles, but the fact is that commercial photographers cheat. For instance:

Baby oil is the almost universal cosmetic of food ads. It makes food look moister.

The steam in pictures of Thanksgiving turkeys is smoke from a concealed cigarette.

Soufflées and poultry are stuffed with cotton or toilet paper to look plumper.

Whipped cream may be shaving cream. (Whipped cream melts too fast under the lights.)

The semen in pornographic movies is Ivory Liquid dishwashing detergent.

Gremlins

Gremlins are practical jokes hidden in computer software. For instance, the programmers of the Apple IIc hid their names (Ernie Beernink, Dick Huston, and Rich Williams) in read-only memory. The names may be revealed by typing a three-line BASIC program:

```
IN#5
INPUT A$
PRINT A$
```

A secret animation called Mr. Macintosh is rumored to be hidden in Apple's Macintosh computer. Supposedly, after you turn the computer on so many times, an animated figure will appear on the screen, zip around a bit, and then disappear, not to be seen again.

There is some credibility to this. The Macintosh contains a battery that powers a small part of the computer memory even when the computer is turned off. The computer "remembers" some information, such as the time and date, from one work session to the next. The Macintosh's engineers did hide some secret gimmicks, at any rate. On the interior of the Macintosh case — where no one but a serviceperson would normally see them — are the embossed plastic signatures of forty-seven Apple employees. Apple cofounder Steve Jobs's signature is at upper center; Steve Wozniak (signed "Woz") is at lower right.

Bigger Secrets asked Andy Hertzfeld, a programmer who worked on the Macintosh's operating system, about Mr. Macintosh. According to him, Mr. Macintosh was Steve Jobs's idea circa 1981. The plan was that every ten-thousandth time, say, that the user displayed a menu of commands, an animated figure would appear. It became clear that Mr. Macintosh would require more memory or disk space than could be justified for pure whimsy, however. The idea was dropped.

Even so, the Macintosh operating system is built to accommodate Mr. Macintosh. Whenever a menu is to be displayed, a part of the operating system called the Menu Manager checks a certain memory address. This address is not revealed in the technical manual, but a dedicated hacker could probably find it, Hertzfeld suggests. Normally, this memory location contains 0. But when it is not 0, Mr. Macintosh is — or would be — activated. A programmer could create a Mr. Macintosh subroutine and insert it in the Macintosh system files.

Considerably more malicious software gremlins go by the name of Trojan horse programs. One is an IBM PC program called EGABTR. Someone has been putting EGABTR on computer bulletin boards, where unsuspecting persons have been downloading it and running it. EGABTR claims to be a handy program that somehow fine-tunes the IBM Enhanced Graphics Adapter display and indexes disk files. When you run EGABTR, it accesses the computer's hard disk (if present) and prompts the user to insert floppy disks. You don't question the computer, so most people comply. Then the screen displays "Got you! Arf! Arf!" The user discovers that the program has erased vital information (the file allocation tables) on the hard and floppy disks. This could mean the loss of all business data and thousands of dollars worth of software.

Exploding Toilets

The combination of Sani-Flush and Comet cleansers can explode. Comet (sodium hypochlorite and grit) is a common all-purpose abrasive, and Sani-Flush (a.k.a. sodium bisulfate) is designed to keep toilet bowls clean. Many think that the combination ought to work all the better.

The Sani-Flush label warns consumers not to mix it with a chlorine-containing cleanser lest hazardous fumes be released. But few people know which other cleansers contain chlorine, and in any case the label says nothing about explosions. In 1985 Hilton Martin of Satellite Beach, Florida, cleaned the bowl of his toilet with Comet and then hung a Sani-Flush dispenser inside the tank. He noticed the water starting to bubble when the phone rang. While he was in another room on the phone, the toilet detonated. American Home Products has denied that Sani-Flush poses an explosion hazard.

Is Dr. Bronner Really the Firesign Theatre?

Dr. Bronner is the most enigmatic figure in toiletries today. The labels for his soap contain an unrepentantly weird monologue that is both hilarious and a little scary. *Gentlemen's Quarterly* deemed the labels "an eccentric work of art." Many believe Bronner must be a hoax. Some think he is a fabrication of the Firesign Theatre comedy group.

Dr. Bronner's soap is sold mainly in yuppified health food stores. The "Peppermint 18-in-1 Pure-Castile-Soap" is the most popular variety, a dishwater-hued liquid smelling uncannily like Wrigley's Doublemint gum. It has "No synthetics! None!" in Dr. Bronner's own rhetoric, which soon becomes familiar, even contagious. The unadorned label is jam-packed with fine blue and white print.

It hits you gradually. Right below the big print of the product name is a list of ten deceptively sane uses for the stuff. You can clean dentures . . . repel ticks . . . wash pesticides off fruits and vegetables. There's no mention of the telegrams to Nikita Khrushchev yet. Nothing about Easter Isle bondage or Hedy Lamarr. There is a reassuring cadence to this nuts-and-bolts advice. Like, "Don't drink soap! Keep out of eye! Dilute! Dilute! OK!"

You figure the rest of the fine print is the macrobiotic household hints of some earnest ex-hippie. Maybe you use the soap for weeks, leave it out where the kids can get it, without reading any further. Then you read a little too far into the blue part of the label, and it hits you. Dr. Bronner is some weird dude. If things can be taken at face value, he is a nephew of Albert Einstein's, a man who sent ten telegrams to Nikita Khrushchev in 1963, a rabbi and a minister, and the entrepreneur behind a health food called Cheezon Corn. He survived the Holocaust and believes that Halley's Comet is the messiah.

Hidden on the inside of the outer wrapper for Dr. Bronner's Magic Soap are instructions for a bizarre, homespun birth control method. It is based on pH, which seems to preoccupy Bronner more than it does most people. It requires Vaseline, oil, cream, or butter, "juicy lemon pulp," and Dr. Bronner's soap. In that respect it is like those recipes on Tabasco sauce bottles that call for an awful lot of Tabasco sauce — only, remember, this is gynecological advice. Bronner instructs you to apply the Vaseline, oil, cream or butter to the vagina (presumably; the label discreetly sidesteps saying where you apply it) and then insert a teaspoon of lemon pulp. Lemon pulp has a pH of 2, Bronner explains, and conception is supposedly impossible below pH 3. The following day, you are to douche with a quart of soapy water (pH 8) to restore a natural pH of 5.

Mostly the label expounds Bronner's worldview. The amount of philosophy you get is proportional to the size of the container, and for the full gestalt, you need the quart bottle. Bronner's Molly Bloom persona speaks of "5 Amish-Amway-AT&T profitsharing jobs," "CO2 bombers," and "USA-USSR-H20-silicon-synthesis for 144 billion battery banks powering every car-factory-farm-home-milorganite-mono-rail-railroad." Bronner sees connections that other people don't, connections that may not exist. Every time he seems to be winding down, he says something like "Jellyfish! Dinosaurs!" and catches a second wind.

Every now and then the label lapses into coherence. One lucid passage gives as much of a bio as is to be found. It seems that Bronner built three soap plants in Germany between 1929 and 1944. Then, "after losing father-mother-wife, almost his own life, tortured, blinded, he deeded to All-One-God-Faith all of his patents, plants, products, profits & 2 new industries."

Bronner describes a deathbed message. "In '46, this 76 word death-bed message saved his life: 'Atom bombs can be controlled because uranium is rare! But hydrogen bombs cannot be controlled because hydrogen is everywhere! In 1910 night turned into day when Halley's Comet (almost) exploded! So if I don't get out of here, a hydrogen bomb chain reaction may explode God's spaceship Earth! I am fighting for peace no matter who you are, because in One world with atom bombs we're All-One, All-One, or we're none! All none!" The "his" refers to Bronner because he is being spoken of in the third person in this paragraph, even though, I think, he wrote it.

Then there's the time Bronner talked some sense into Khrushchev. He sent ten telegrams to the Soviet leader from Heilbronn, West Germany, congratulating him on destalinization. After the telegrams, Khrushchev gave every farmer an acre of free land. Bronner does not hesitate to see a connection here. It is, by the way, no simple matter to decide whether the label's politics are ultra conservative or ultra libera. But they're ultra something.

Among the many sputniks orbiting the doctor's private exosphere are Herbert Marcuse, the Black Panthers, Alpha Centauri, and Rabbi Hillel. Long, unexplained lists mention an Asimov, a Dumas, a Kipling, a Sanger, and a Spitz who seem to be Isaac, Alexandre, Rudyard, Margaret, and Mark. Is "Sills" Beverly? Is "Boscalia" a misspelled Leo? There's an Abba who may be Eban or the Swedish pop group. I wonder who Fred is.

Most everyone buys the soap, the first time anyway, because some-one has clued them in to the weird craziness on the label. There seems to be a strong repeat business, though, making one wonder if Bronner is not crazy like a fox.

There are several competing conjectures about Dr. Bronner. You can take the label at face value and figure that the soap is made by Albert Einstein's mad nephew, who is really serious about this. Or you can figure that there is a real Dr. Bronner, but that the labels are all one big joke.

Maybe Dr. Bronner is a new wave Betty Crocker, a persona created to appeal to somebody's target market. Or maybe Dr. Bronner is a hoax, perpetrated by person or persons unknown.

A 1976 article from the *San Francisco Bay Guardian* claims that Bronner is quite real. According to the *Guardian*, Bronner's sister committed him to an Illinois mental hospital in March 1946. He was released, then recommitted. Then he escaped three times and was captured twice — and is still at large. "In recent years he has bought and given away 60,000 copies of a *Reader's Digest* article about how innocent people get put away in mental hospitals for no reason."

The soap labels invite you to send $1 for Essene Scrolls. I did and got a reply in the official All-One-God-Faith envelope. The envelope had four stamps, three of them upside down and one on its side. Does Bronner, sightless, stamp his own correspondence?

The scroll turns out to be a poster that is like a super label. It refers to something called paraldehyde vodka. One-quarter ounce of this "innocent drink . . . turns the strongest man into a stuttering idiot within just 3 seconds; convincing his most loving wife that — 'he's so much better off dead!' " From 1917 to 1973, the Russians are supposed to have murdered over two million Americans with the stuff — including Wendell Willkie, according to a Mailgram Bronner sent to President Reagan and Phil Donahue.

The scroll says Bronner is a member of the Universal Life Church. *This* is none other than the famous mail order outfit usually characterized as a tax evasion scam. Thanks to ads in *Popular Mechanics* and the like, the Universal Life Church has ordained over eight million people. How would Bronner hook up with a quasi-legit religion? Or is this further evidence that there is something fishy about this so-called Dr. Bronner?

The labels give two telephone numbers for Dr. Bronner's organization. I called one, got a secretary, and within twenty seconds was talking to Dr. Bronner himself.

You can't read Dr. Bronner's prose without assigning a mental voice to it, and the one I favored was that of the wimpy guy who owned the candy store in the Bowery Boys movies. Well, Bronner doesn't sound like that. He has a German accent but speaks English fluently. He sounded vigorous and alert; his voice did not sound like that of a madman. I once interviewed the members of Firesign Theatre, and Dr. Bronner didn't sound like any of them, either.

I wasn't quite sure how to ask him if he was for real, so I asked him how the business was doing. He said there were six million users in the United States, Australia, and England. He said that when he came to this country they wouldn't print what he had to say, so he put the messages on the soap bottles. When I commented that the labels were very interesting, he said, yeah, he could get four thousand words on a quart bottle.

I asked him if he was really Albert Einstein's nephew. He said he was. This launched him into a monologue that to my satisfaction established him as *the* Dr. Bronner. He did mention Halley's Comet, and I asked him about that. "Halley's Comet is the messiah, as sure as I'm talking to you on the phone," he said. "Things are gonna start happening."

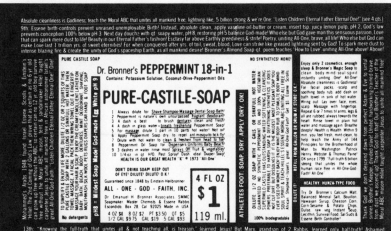

· 21 ·

IS THE INDIAN ROPE TRICK FOR REAL?

Botched attempts to capture the Indian rope trick on film abound. In the 1930s, a traveling fakir performed the trick for the British Resident. The Resident asked the fakir to repeat the trick a few days later in front of some other Westerners. The British minister hid a cameraman on the Residency grounds. He got eight pictures, which were subsequently published in a London weekly in 1934. None showed the rope in the air — only the coiled rope on the ground, a boy to the side.

A Major G. H. Rooke presented a photograph of the trick at a London meeting of the East India Association in 1936. Taken by one of Rooke's men, it shows only a seated holy man, the rope being out of the shot. Rooke himself had not seen the trick.

A Colonel Barnard, chief of police of Calcutta, and an assistant took a camera to a performance of the trick. A rope was thrown into the air. A boy climbed up it, with a fakir in pursuit. Then both vanished. So did the image on Colonel Barnard's film.

It's little wonder that many doubt if the Indian rope trick exists at all. In 1954 a group of Indian stage magicians branded the trick a legend and nothing more. American mentalist the Amazing Kreskin studied the trick and came to the same conclusion. There is nonetheless strong reason to believe that there is or was a real rope trick. It may have been no more supernatural than a Western magician's illusions, but it was just as real.

The trick was not exclusively Indian. Ibn Batutu, an Arab from North Africa, saw the trick in Hangchow, China, in 1355. The rope trick has come to be strongly identified with the fakirs, India's religious ascetics who live by begging. The trick was performed to encourage donations, much as contemporary Hare Krishnas perform dance and music.

Such ancient Hindu texts as the *Vedanta Sutra* and the *Badrayana Vyas* mention the rope trick. A proverb holds that illusion and reality are as different "as the magician who in reality remains upon the earth is different from the magician who, with sword and shield, climbs up the string." This simile suggests that the rope trick was a conjuring illusion, and that this fact was appreciated by the educated.

Quite a few reputable Westerners, including William Beebe and Maxim Gorki, witnessed the rope trick during the 1800s. After 1900, reports dwindle to a handful. There are few if any authentic performances today (though stage magicians in India and elsewhere have devised their own versions of the trick). For that matter, one of many conflicting stories says that the trick was performed only by one long-dead fakir and that all subsequent performances are pale imitations of the real thing.

From time to time, Westerners have offered large rewards to anyone who would reveal the trick's secret or perform it under controlled circumstances. Lord Northbrook, viceroy of India, offered £10,000 in 1875. British magician John Nevil Maskelyne offered a stipend of £5,000 a year for any fakir who could perform the trick. The Magic Circle, a stage magicians' club, offered a $25,000 lump sum. Magician David Devant offered £5000 for a presentation of the standard version of the rope trick in England. Devant required that the performer work in the open, surrounded by spectators. He would throw the rope in the air, and a boy would climb to the top and vanish. "If the Magician cared to embellish his performance in accordance with some of the more highly-colored versions of this illusion, such as by himself climbing up the rope after the boy, cutting his assistant to pieces amid blood-curdling screams and sending the pieces of his body hurtling to earth, then, so much the better value we would be receiving for our five thousand pounds," Devant said. None of these offers had any takers.

There's more to the rope trick than you might surmise from cartoon depictions. The classic version has a fakir and several assistants. The principal assistant is always a small boy. At the beginning of the trick, the fakir sits on the ground playing a drum and flute. (The drum is a traditional element of Indian magic.) Nearby is a coil of rope and a large wicker basket. The fakir has a large curved knife. Incense or hashish burns in torches.

The pace of Indian magic is slower than that in the West. Minutes may pass with nothing happening. Eventually, the rope slowly uncoils and rises straight up in the air. The entire length of rope stands vertically. The top of the rope is said to be out of sight, according to the equivocal descriptions of the trick.

The fakir tells the boy to climb the rope. The boy is reluctant and argues with the fakir. The boy climbs the rope nonetheless until he too is out of sight. The boy laughs and taunts the fakir from his perch. The fakir angrily demands that the boy return. He refuses. The fakir puts his knife between his teeth and climbs up the rope himself.

Now both the fakir and the boy are invisible to the spectators. Their voices raised in argument are heard. The boy screams. Something falls from above, dropping near the base of the rope. It is the boy's severed hand.

Another scream is cut short. The boy's head falls to the ground. Other parts of the boy follow.

His clothing splattered with blood, the fakir climbs back down the rope with the blood-smeared knife in his teeth. The fakir or his assistants gather the boy's remains and put them in the basket. The fakir resumes beating his drum. The rope slowly descends, forming a coil at the fakir's feet. The basket rocks. A voice shouts from within. The boy, resurrected, steps out of the basket.

Rarely do two accounts of the trick agree on all particulars. The plot varies, and in some versions much Grand Guignol detail is omitted. Some reports say the trick was performed only at night. Others swear they saw it in daylight. At least some of the time the trick was performed in urban settings. In a village, it probably would not be too hard to suspend a supporting wire between houses. But others insist they saw it in an open field. The version Ibn Batutu saw in China used a leather thong in lieu of rope.

Audiences for the rope trick were probably less skeptical than contemporary audiences. The crowd often thought the tricks of the fakirs to be "real" magic (as did the audiences of medieval European magicians). Spectators were not necessarily trying to see how it was done.

It's one thing to levitate a rope onstage. All it takes is a thread attached to one end and an assistant up in the rafters. But the rope trick was done out in the open. If the description of the rope and climbers rising out of sight is interpreted to mean that the rope extended to a vanishing point at the zenith, then clearly the rope must have been fantastically long. The trick becomes altogether incredible.

Some of the attempts at a rational explanation for the trick defy belief themselves. Would-be explanations can be classed as physical or psychological.

Physical explanations usually postulate supporting wires or a stiff rope. Supporting wires seem to be ruled out if the trick was truly done in the open, during the daytime. The stiff rope idea has limitations, too. A metal-core rope stiff enough to climb could not be coiled. You'd need someone to push it up from a subterranean chamber. The most ingenious mechanical explanations suppose the rope was composed of linking segments that could somehow lock into rigidity when extended.

Limited versions of the rope trick have been performed with a stiff rope. In the mid-1950s, John Keel, an American journalist traveling in India, saw a street magician, Babu, demonstrating a rope trick at a Muslim festival in New Delhi. Keel bribed Babu for twenty-five rupees and learned his method.

Babu used a bamboo-reinforced rope. He sat on a raised platform with a high canvas backdrop. He allowed spectators to examine a ten-foot-long rope. Then he coiled it and placed it in a basket on the platform. As Babu tooted a gourd flute, the rope rose from the basket, completely rigid.

As any skeptical person would have guessed, it wasn't the same rope. The rope Babu passed for inspection was still in the basket. There was a pit beneath the platform, and an assistant in the pit thrust a rope-covered bamboo pole up through a hole in the platform and the bottom of the basket.

Babu remained on the ground. A boy in a large red hooded robe climbed to the top of the rope. Babu clapped his hands. The robe fell to the ground. The boy was gone. Then he reappeared in the crowd.

The boy's robe had a wire frame that collapsed like an umbrella. When the boy reached the top of the rope, he hooked the robe and frame onto the top of the rope. He unbuttoned the back of the robe and hopped over the canvas backdrop to the ground. Babu had a thread that triggered the frame to collapse on command.

Among the psychological explanations of the traditional rope trick is hypnosis. American psychologist V. E. Fisher claimed the trick was done with hypnosis in a 1932 text on abnormal psychology. Donovan Hilton Rawcliffe, a British investigator of the paranormal, endorsed that idea, arguing that the trick was often done for relatively small groups of royalty. It might have been possible to hypnotize the few witnesses. For demonstrations in front of large crowds, it would suffice to hypnotize a few suggestible members of the audience. The others would go away reporting the reactions of these persons and feel that they too had participated in something miraculous.

Clouds of smoke from burning incense and hashish are mentioned in many accounts. Maybe the performers drugged the audience with hashish smoke to make them more suggestible.

Finally, there are those who think the full-fledged rope trick is just a story kept alive by such petty imitations as Babu's. After vainly circulating handbills of his offer in India, Devant concluded that the trick is "altogether beyond the limitations of scientific illusion and therefore, humanly impossible. That no one has ever seen an Indian Rope Trick performed I do not for one moment assert. The evidence of its existence in some form is altogether too strong to dismiss the whole thing as a myth, but I believe that the trick is largely a tale that has grown in the telling and that those who have seen rope tricks in India are confusing many partial memories into one general and erroneous impression."

Wires and Hooks

There have been two believable exposés of the rope trick. In 1955 John Keel came across a guru who said he had performed the true rope trick years earlier. Sadhu Vadramakrishna told Keel that he had stopped performing the trick because it was a "false illusion." After Vadramakrishna revealed the secret, Keel attempted to demonstrate the trick on the grounds of the Ambassador Hotel in New Delhi. He failed miserably as a cloudburst upset his preparations.

In the December 1956 issue of *Tops,* a magicians' magazine, magician W. T. Lawhead claimed to have learned the secret from an unnamed high caste Brahman. ("He is of a wealthy East Indian family, was educated in America and England, and is one of the most influential personages in all India," Lawhead said.) The Brahman would not have known the secret himself but for subterfuge. When he was a child, his father gave him a birthday party. A fakir was hired to perform the trick as entertainment. The Brahman's sister slipped away during the performance. She got a pair of binoculars and observed from the house and was thereby able to see how it was done. Both Lawhead's informant and Vadramakrishna agree on the basics of the method.

The trick was done at dusk, according to Vadramakrishna. Bright torches illuminated the site, preventing spectators' eyes from adjusting to the dark. Anything more than a few feet in the air was invisible. Sometimes oily bonfires were used to produce a smokescreen as well.

The trick's mechanism was simple. A fine strong wire or thin horsehair rope was stretched in secrecy between two hills, trees, or houses. The trick could not be done entirely in the open; there had to be trees or something. But with a well-chosen site, such as a large grassy clearing bounded by a few tall trees, people would go away swearing it had been done "in the open." The wire had to be high enough to be invisible to the nightblind audience.

The end of the coiled rope (the rope that was going to rise) had a wooden ball serving as a weight. The ball had a few holes in it.

Another preparation was a fine thread with a small hook on one end. The fakir concealed the hook on his person, and the thread was draped over the horizontal supporting wire. The other end ran to an assistant. When this assistant pulled the thread, the hook would rise.

At the beginning of the performance, the fakir tossed the ball into the air a number of times. Each time, the ball and rope fell back to the earth. After the audience grew tired of watching the ball, the fakir casually attached the hook to the ball. Then he threw the ball up and the assistant reeled in the thread. This time the ball halted in midair.

The rope slowly extended to its full height. If the horizontal wire was fifty or sixty feet high, the upper end of the rope would be invisible at night.

The hook was designed to catch on the horizontal wire when the rope was extended. All the assistant could do to facilitate this was to jiggle the thread. Lawhead, who performed a stage rope trick based on the Brahman's description, modified the setup. Instead of using a ball, the end of the rope was frayed, and a hook was hidden in the frayed part. Lawhead used a four-pronged steel hook looking like four fishhooks set at right angles. He didn't use a thread. The horizontal wire was only twenty feet above the stage, and Lawhead threw the rope until it caught on one of the four prongs. This was strong enough to support the weight of a boy. Lawhead himself did not climb the rope.

In the traditional trick, as well, the boy climbed the rope, supported only by that hook. When he reached the top, he attached the ball to the horizontal wire with a sturdier hook. Then the rope was capable of supporting the fakir's weight.

Sometimes the boy tightrope-walked to one of the supporting trees or houses and climbed down. He then slipped into the basket unnoticed, or a similar-looking boy would be hidden in the basket from the beginning. In another version, the boy held tight to the fakir's chest and was concealed by his voluminous robes during the fakir's descent.

The fakir concealed parts of a slaughtered monkey in his clothing to toss down during the unseen argument. A monkey hand may not look exactly like a boy's, but no one was likely to examine it too closely. (Cavalier treatment of animals is common among India's street performers. Some snake charmers sew their cobras' mouths shut for safety. The snakes starve to death in a few days and have to be replaced constantly.)

The requisite degree of agility is probably what has killed the trick. Both the fakir and his assistant must be accomplished acrobats. Knowing how the trick is done is of little use unless they can climb a rope with ease and tightrope-walk. These skills, once passed from generation to generation among street performers, are dying out in contemporary India.

• 22 •

TONY ROBBINS'S FIREWALK

For $100, a guy named Anthony Robbins will teach you to walk barefoot on red-hot coals. More than fifteen thousand people have attended Robbins's "Fear into Power: The Firewalk Experience" seminars. Robbins has grossed over a million dollars teaching what, on the face of it, is not a very marketable skill. A scad of imitators put on their own firewalking seminars.

Robbins is a motivational speaker. The firewalk is a macguffin. "This seminar is not about firewalking," he says with Magrittian duplicity. "The firewalk is only a metaphor for what we think we cannot do. Once you've walked on fire, a lot of impossibilities become possibilities."

Robbins holds seminars in Marriotts and Holiday Inns — the old EST circuit — and he builds the fires on sidewalks or in parking lots in full public view. Police cordon off the inferno from curiosity seekers while an ambulance stands ready. Piles of logs burn until almost consumed. Then the coals are shoveled into a wheelbarrow and spread in even plots about three feet wide by ten feet long.

Robbins does not soft-pedal the risks but mentions them repeatedly during the evening. *The coals are red hot — hundreds of degrees! They could turn your feet into charred stumps! You could easily die!*

Robbins claims that he gives subliminal instructions that allow seminar attendees to do the impossible. He says the mind can rearrange the molecules of the feet somehow after it has been so taught in the seminar.

The track record of seminar attendees is very good. Most stride across the coals with little or no subsequent blistering. They walk quickly, to be sure, but it's not as if they do a broad jump across the bed of coals. Occasional persons are burnt. Robbins says he has been burnt twice. *Life* magazine published a color photo of the seared feet of its reporter Nancy Griffin.

What can Robbins say in a four-hour seminar that confers immunity to burning? According to people who have attended, the seminars go like this:

The energy level is not unlike that of a seminar for Amway products or Mary Kay cosmetics or Tupperware. The underlying assumption is that once you make it across those burning coals or once you sell enough Mary Kay cosmetics, you'll really get your life together. There are lists of important points or things to do that Robbins enumerates and repeats like the patient teacher of a slow child.

Robbins tells lots of jokes, and they all get big laughs. He comes onstage to the *Rocky* theme. It is only the first of several popular movie themes he will humorously weave into the proceedings.

Robbins mentions something called NLP, neurolinguistic programming. This he defines as a way of influencing the behavior of others through subtle cues. He has you lie on the floor, eyes closed, as the lights are lowered. You are told to imagine your childhood, when you were "comfortable, creative, confident, and curious."

At one point, you are instructed to face someone else in the audience and tell him your greatest fear, your goal for the night, and what is most beautiful about yourself. This and other cute icebreakers lend a Club Med ambiance to the proceedings.

You are counseled to do five things. Step on a wet piece of Astroturf before you step on the coals. Look upward, not at the coals. Hold one fist raised as you walk. Repeat "cool moss, cool moss." The instant you step off the coals, rinse your feet with water to remove any hot embers.

The fact that Robbins's firewalkers do not look at the coals is significant. The carnival sideshow stunt of walking on broken glass requires that the walker see where he is stepping. There, the bed of broken glass has been carefully prepared. Bottle shards are filed until quite smooth and then glued in place. During the performance, the glass walker breaks a few bottles for the audience and distributes the fragments along the outside of the glass bed. The performer makes sure that he steps only in the middle of the bed. Glass walkers also prepare their feet with alum solution and rosin.

A professional firewalker might be able to step around the hottest, biggest coals. That can't be how Robbins's skygazing walkers do it. They are given no chemicals for their feet, either.

A few people chicken out; their $100 is not refunded. The majority go through with it. Each walker must sign a release indemnifying Robbins before stepping onto the coals.

The secret Robbins *doesn't* tell you is that you can probably walk on red-hot coals without spending $100 for a seminar. Robbins didn't invent firewalking. People have been doing it in Fiji, Greece, India, and elsewhere for hundreds of years.

In the 1930s doctors with the University of London Council for Psychical Investigation observed Indian firewalkers under controlled circumstances and concluded that no tricks were involved. The firewalkers didn't put special chemicals or preparations on their feet, and the soles of their feet were not unusually calloused. Of course, the sole of the foot is a thick, relatively insensitive part of the skin.

Robbins's method is unconventional in one curious detail only. The studies with the Indian firewalkers in the 1930s suggested that moisture on the feet (as from Robbins's wet Astroturf) is bad. There is normally little adhesion between dry feet and coals. But moisture may cause embers to stick to the feet long enough to cause blisters.

It is the coals rather than the feet that must be prepared for Robbins's firewalks. To begin with, it helps that the walks are at night. Coals that would appear a dull cherry-red in sunlight seem to glow with hellish incandescence in the dark. They aren't as hot as they look.

At the right stage, coals are a light, crumbly substance that is largely air. They neither hold nor conduct much heat despite their high temperature. The *white*-hot sparks from a Fourth of July sparkler are usually not dangerous because the skin is exposed to a mere mote at a time. The principle — high temperature but little heat transfer — is the same with the coals.

Robbins's people stoke the fire until the logs disintegrate and smash the coals into small pieces with shovels. The smaller, lighter, and more uniform the pieces, the safer they are. The four-hour seminars may drag a bit toward the end, but it takes that long for the coals to reach the safe stage.

Walking on coals is like passing your hand through a candle flame. It seems dangerous, and if you're slow, you do get burned. But do it quickly and there's nothing to it.

· 23 ·

THE LEVITATING WOMAN

For years, magicians on TV have been telling you that you really don't want to know how it's done. *Of course* you want to know. For all the talk about the magicians' code, there is a weak link in the chain of secrecy. It is the companies that build illusion equipment — firms such as Louis Tannen (6 West 32nd Street, New York, New York 10001) and Abbott's Magic Novelty Company (Colon, Michigan 49040). This being a free marketplace, they are only too happy to sell you "workshop plans," exposing the illusions right down to the thread pitch of the screws. *Bigger Secrets* sent away for the plans of some of the biggies.

Like the trick where a person floats in midair. This is really several distinct illusions. In one version the woman is plainly visible at all times. In another, the woman is covered with a cloth and disappears in midair. There is also a "sword levitation," where a person is suspended on the point of a sword.

The original levitating woman illusion is known as Trilby's couch among professional magicians. It was created in the 1800s by a performer billed as Professor Herrmann. Two ordinary chairs and a plank are assembled into a makeshift couch. The subject lies down on the board. In Herrmann's act, the woman was supposed to be hypnotized; this fiction is often dispensed with today. One chair, then the other, is removed. The woman and the board remain suspended. Since everyone expects there to be unseen wires, the magician is obliged to take a large hoop and pass it around the woman. Depending on the method used and your powers of observation, you may or may not feel the wire theory has been quashed. The woman may rise on command or slowly tilt. Then the chairs are replaced, the woman and the board come to rest upon them, and the woman steps off.

Trilby's Couch and Variations

Trilby's couch uses not wires but a sturdy metal support, an arm that projects from the curtains or backdrop after the woman lies down. It is painted black or the color of the backdrop should it be partly glimpsed; anyway, the woman's body hides it. A notch in this arm grasps the board snugly. The magician or his assistant offstage makes sure the board fits into the notch properly. This action is performed under cover of adjusting the drape of the woman's dress for modesty's sake. (This is one of the few rational reasons for the sexism of stage magic — the male magician's subject is almost invariably female.)

The supporting arm is part of a machine that can lift or tilt the board as desired and is operated by an assistant behind the curtains. The chairs are removed, and the woman and plank are supported by the projecting arm. That much is simple enough.

There are three ways of handling the hoop demonstration. The cop-out is to pass the hoop over and under the woman. Any wires would probably be over the woman, of course. The hoop *isn't* passed over the woman's head down to her feet — which would be impossible with the machine arm at the side.

Or the magician can use a hoop with a break in it. Remember, the magician isn't levitating the hoop. He's holding it in his hands, and a hand has to be touching the hoop in at least one place at all times. The performer merely places his hand over the break when showing the hoop to the audience for the first time. It's possible to look like you're rotating the hoop when in fact the hand remains over the break. The magician later switches hands so that the break is away from the audience and the arm can pass through it. With misdirection, the actions are unnoticed.

187

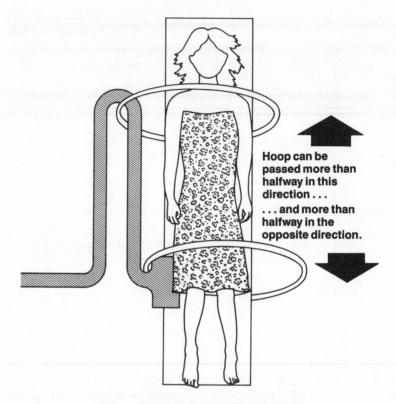

Hoop can be passed more than halfway in this direction . . .

. . . and more than halfway in the opposite direction.

The Gooseneck Support

The most ingenious method uses a gooseneck arm to hold the board. The hoop can't be passed all the way from head to foot, but it can go more than halfway from the head to the feet, then more than halfway from the feet to the head. Deftly done, it is quite convincing.

Details make this simple trick impressive. The magician makes a point of walking behind the plank before the support is in place. He knows that afterward, when the audience is trying to figure out how it was done, they will remember seeing the magician walk all the way behind the plank but probably won't recall just when he did it. That allays suspicion of a support. Professor Herrmann dropped the plank on the floor at the trick's conclusion to show it was just a piece of wood.

188

One flaw in Trilby's couch is that the woman can't move around much while suspended. Magicians since Herrmann have devised less stagy variations.

In one, the woman lies down on a regular-looking couch, and the magician covers her with a large silk. Momentarily she rises. Her form is visible underneath the cloth. Sometimes the magician maneuvers the suspended woman around a stage and out into the audience. Then — bang — he pulls away the cloth and the woman is gone.

In these vanishing-woman levitations, there is no woman — not after she lies down on the couch, anyway. The couch is a prop with a hidden compartment in the back large enough to conceal a person. While the magician spreads out the cloth with a flourish, the woman slips into the compartment, putting a balloon (hidden in the compartment) in her place on the couch. Or the couch may conceal a collapsible wire-frame dummy approximating the woman's proportions.

When a wire frame is used, it is manipulated by thin black wires connected to pulleys offstage. At the right moment, the wire dummy can be made to spring flat. The cloth is pulled away, and the "woman" has vanished.

In the balloon method, the "woman" is controlled by fine threads connected to the magician himself. The balloon dummy has two small hooks attached, sharp enough to penetrate the thin cloth when it is in place. The magician has two threads attached to buttons on his suit or elsewhere. The threads have loops on the ends. The magician makes sure that the loops catch on the hooks while he is arranging the cloth cover.

The thread is passed through the magician's fingers. By moving his hands slowly, he can make the "woman" rise. Moving his hands apart, in a horizontal plane, lifts the dummy; the audience assumes that only raising the hands could raise the woman.

There's no need to keep near the backdrop, as with other versions of the illusion. Given dim lighting and an ample cloth, the magician may levitate the dummy into the audience or over tables. Of course, the "woman" never strays far from the magician.

To end the trick, the magician bursts the balloon with a pin attached to a ring. The pop is covered by the ringing of a gong or a pistol shot. The balloon is black so the pieces aren't noticed.

Sword Levitation

The sword levitation is an entirely different illusion. The magician produces three swords. A spectator may be asked to examine one and testify that it is genuine. The three swords are arranged point up on a platform. A reclining person is lowered horizontally onto their points.

This seems illusion enough, but then the magician removes the sword under the legs. The subject remains suspended. Then the middle sword is removed, leaving the subject suspended horizontally on the point of one sword.

The two swords are replaced. The subject is lifted up and away from the swords, which crash down to the ground. Cosmetic variations of the sword levitation have subjects suspended on broomsticks or other unlikely supports.

Actually, one of the three swords is different from the other two. It is much heavier and has a sturdy projection from its handle. If an audience volunteer examines a sword, he must be given one of the regular ones.

The odd sword's projection fits snugly into an unseen hole in the platform that allows the sword to be fitted into the platform and remain rigidly vertical. A light cloth covering the platform keeps the audience from noticing the hole.

The person to be levitated wears a rigid brace in his outfit, a heavy metal bar running down his back and strapped securely to his torso. At the top of the bar is a socket that fits the tip of the strong sword. As the person is being lowered onto the tips of the swords, the magician makes sure that the tip of the strong sword goes into the socket. The bar protects him from the tips of the other swords, too.

The sword fits into the socket securely enough to hold the weight of a light person at a 90-degree angle. There is no direct support for the legs. The subject must be able to keep his legs rigid for the length of the performance.

· 24 ·

HEADLINE PREDICTION

*T*he prediction of newspaper head-
lines days in advance seems to be beyond the realm of stage magic.
Illusions defy the laws of space; headline prediction defies time itsel.
Magicians who predict headlines often claim ESP, and their audiences
often believe them. The same spectators would not believe in the
supernatural powers of a performer pulling a rabbit out of a hat.

That said, headline prediction is ill suited to the restrictions of night-
club or TV performance. It cannot be performed entirely in view of
the audience but has to be done as a publicity stunt.

The performer selects a person or group of persons to assist. These
assistants are pillars of the community and must not be suspected of
complicity with the performer. As the upstanding person(s) watches,
the performer seals the prediction of a future date's newspaper headline
in an envelope, box, chest, bottle, or other container. To keep things
on the up and up, the seal is secured by having someone write a
signature across the envelope flap. A wax seal or notary seal may be
used. The sealed prediction is entrusted to the solid citizen until the
day of the prediction. This person is not to let anyone touch the prediction until then. The prediction is locked in a safe deposit box, casino
vault, or the like.

These events are recounted to the audience on the day of the performance. The performer coaxes the local bigwig to affirm that the prediction has not been tampered with. The assistant produces the envelope or box and shows that the seal is intact. The prediction is opened. It is identical with the headline in that day's local paper.

The headline prediction stunt is a game of trust and betrayal. The audience sees but the last moments of the illusion. The credibility of the witness(es) who saw the prediction sealed is key. The audience must trust the account of how the prediction has been prepared, and they must believe that the prediction has not been tampered with. If not, there is no illusion. Yet someone is deceiving the audience somewhere, or it just wouldn't work.

Who Do You Trust?

It must be understood that the predictions themselves are valid. You might imagine that the performer prints up a fake or partially faked front page with his prediction as the headline. Not so.

The predicted headlines are real headlines about real events. The mentalist Dr. Jaks once correctly predicted a headline about a murder while playing a Las Vegas club. His publicity claims the Las Vegas cops detained him for questioning on the grounds that he must have been an accomplice. C'mon — police aren't *stupid;* they know a magic trick isn't real — but Jaks's predicted events are genuine. The magician may have someone else buy a paper on the way to the performance.

Other dubious conjectures are that the performer has friends at the newspaper who slant the headline to coincide with the prediction or that the performer is enough of a student of current events to guess future headlines with a modicum of accuracy.

What about the trustworthy person? He could be in cahoots with the performer. The assistant usually has some vested interest in seeing that the audience is entertained. Maybe there's no trick at all. The performer just gets the assistant to lie and say that he saw the performer seal the prediction days before. There are illusions as infuriatingly misleading as this. *Every* illusion is misleading, somehow.

If we can believe the account of how the prediction was prepared, however, the trustworthy person does not get to see the prediction at the time it is sealed. That suggests that the performer switches predictions. Either he gets into the safe or he makes the switch at the very last moment, as the predictions are being opened.

The secrets of headline prediction are to be found in manuscripts sold by magic suppliers. Two popular methods are "The Bally Prediction," credited to Wm. A. Stevenson (available from Abbott's Magic Novelty Company) and "Fogel's Headline Prediction" (sold by Louis Tannen). Both have some special features, but their basic outline is common to virtually all headline predictions.

The Bally method depends on the goodwill of a local newspaper editor. The magician contacts the editor of the newspaper and explains what he is about to do. The magician will send a prediction of a future headline to the editor in a letter. The editor is not to open the letter (which will be marked PREDICTION) but rather is to seal it between two pieces of cardboard and put it in a safe.

The magician actually mails two letters. Neither contains a prediction. (If the editor is curious and opens the letter, it wrecks everything.) One letter says PREDICTION as promised and is addressed to the editor in ink. The second letter is addressed to the magician in pencil. It is only lightly sealed. Both letters contain only a blank sheet of paper or a dummy prediction.

Several days later, when the magician receives the letter addressed to himself, he erases his address and writes in the address of the editor in ink. The magician lifts the flap carefully and discards the dummy prediction. This gives him a postmarked duplicate of the envelope the editor has.

On the day of the performance, the magician gets the newspaper and looks at the headline. He copies it on a piece of paper and inserts it in the duplicate postmarked envelope.

How to make the switch? The Bally manuscript describes two methods. Both use another, larger, trick envelope, which is constructed from two legal envelopes, big enough to hold a standard envelope with room to spare. The flap and address side of one legal envelope are cut out and pasted inside the other legal envelope, creating a legal envelope with two compartments. The smaller envelope, with the prediction, is slipped into the hidden compartment of this envelope. The big envelope can still be shown as an empty legal envelope.

By one method, the magician goes to the editor's office on the day of the performance. He asks the editor if he remembers the date the prediction letter was postmarked. Of course, the editor won't. So the magician asks the editor to remove the letter from the safe and look. This may put the editor on his guard, but he agrees. He takes the letter out of the cardboard to check. Then the magician casually suggests that it might be better if the letter is sealed in an envelope. That will help emphasize that the prediction letter has not been touched. Okay, says the editor. The magician holds out the double-compartment legal envelope so the editor can drop the prediction envelope into it. The magician makes sure to comment that he is not even touching the prediction. The prediction envelope, which of course contains only a dummy prediction, is sealed in the legal envelope, which also contains the headline the magician copied from that day's newspaper. Then the whole thing is sealed between two pieces of cardboard.

If the performer won't be able to see the editor until just before the show, he requests that the prediction letter be sealed in a legal envelope. Then the magician makes sure he runs into the editor backstage before the performance and asks him if he remembers the postmark date. After the editor opens the legal envelope to check, the magician supplies the doctored envelope to reseal it.

The magician need not touch the prediction even at the show. He asks the editor to verify that he has not touched the envelope since sending it. The editor truthfully affirms that he has not. The performer takes the legal envelope out of the cardboard, then tears the end off it. He carefully shakes the prepared prediction out into the hands of the editor, not touching it himself. (The dummy prediction the performer actually mailed remains in the other compartment of the legal envelope.) The editor reads the prediction while the performer shows the newspaper.

The basic scenario in headline predictions is always the same: a switch sometime after the paper has come out. A headline prediction described by Larry Becker in *Genii,* a magicians' magazine, is bolder yet. The headline prediction is the climax of a series of three predictions. The first two predictions, of a card and a geometrical drawing, are standard magic tricks whose workings are irrelevant here. The magician visits a trustworthy person well in advance of the performance. This person watches as the performer seals some predictions on 3-by-5 cards, along with the witness's signed affidavit, in an envelope.

194

During the performance, the envelope is opened. The cards, fastened with a paper clip, are read one by one. No one realizes it, but the magician put only two cards in the envelope — the predictions for the two self-working tricks. (The magician never said how many predictions he was making.) The third prediction is added after the envelope is opened. The magician writes that day's headline on an identical 3-by-5 card and places it inside a copy of the newspaper. The newspaper is on a table for comparison with the prediction. When the predictions are taken out, the first one is read by a spectator immediately. This throws the audience off their guard — clearly the magician has had no opportunity for funny business. Then the predictions are casually set down on top of the newspaper while the spectator goes about opening a box used in the card prediction. The magician picks up the newspaper so that the two cards from the envelope fall on the table, as does the headline card inside the newspaper. The second card and finally the third card, with the headline prediction, are read in turn.

Some performers use special gadgets to make the switch. Houdini used a sealed box with a special key. The box (supposed to contain the headline but actually empty) was entrusted to someone while Houdini kept the key. The day that the box was to be opened, Houdini wrote the headline, rolled it up, and put it in the key's hollow stem. The key was designed to shoot the headline into the box as it was being opened.

A modern variation of this is Fogel's Headline Prediction. The Fogel manuscript comes with a gimmicked hammer, a smallish, ordinary hammer, obviously an off-the-shelf item the Tannen people doctored for their purposes. A three-eighths-inch cylindrical hole is bored into the base of the handle. On the side of the handle is a slot exposing the hollow. A cylindrical wood plug resides in the hollow, kept in place by a screw that protrudes through the slot. Moving the head of the screw up and down in the slot moves the wood plug up and down.

The slot and screw are plainly visible unless you hold your hand over them — which is exactly what you do. The hollow in the handle will hold a rolled-up prediction securely. Pulling down on the head of the screw ejects it.

Fogel's method shares with Bally's the dummy prediction. In this case the dummy prediction is simply a piece of brown paper folded in half. This is sealed in an empty brown bottle such as that used for sweet German wines. Brown paper slips (identical to that used for the dummy prediction) are pasted vertically on the outside of the bottle. The bottle is sent or presented to a trustworthy person and sealed with wax, notary seals, and the like. It is placed in a small wooden box, and the top of the box is nailed on. The box may be locked in a safe deposit box, baked in a wedding cake, or sealed inside the Great Pyramid with Krazy Glue — it doesn't matter one iota. Skilled performers play up the picayune details of the sealing like clues in a John Dickson Carr mystery. The more the audience worries about how anyone could possibly unseal the prediction undetected, the less likely they are to suspect the switch taking place right in front of them.

The day of the opening, the performer reads the newspaper and slips a copy of the headline on *white* paper into the hollow of the hammer handle. In front of witnesses, the performer recovers and opens the box. All are invited to inspect the seals on the bottle. The "message" is visible in the neck of the bottle when it is tilted. Since no one saw you put the dummy prediction in the bottle, and since the bottle is brown, no one knows that the dummy prediction is on brown paper. White paper seen through brown glass looks brown.

The performer spreads a cloth on top of a board or some old newspapers and places the bottle in the center of the cloth. Two volunteers from the crowd hold the corners of the cloth. The performer remarks to them to be sure to move their hands under the cloth as the bottle shatters. "Watch your eyes," the performer adds just before he smashes the bottle.

The warning makes everyone flinch — and close their eyes for a split second as the bottle is smashed. That instant is all the performer needs. Just as the bottle smashes, he pulls down on the screw head and ejects the prepared headline. The headline, on white paper, stands out among the shards of brown glass. The dummy prediction on brown paper is not noticed, especially since the paper strips glued to the outside of the bottle are brown. (The brown paper strips do help prevent flying glass.)

The performer does not deign to touch the prepared prediction. He lets one of the spectators pick it up and read it.

· 25 ·

DOUG HENNING'S ZIGZAG WOMAN

*I*t is probably fair to say that more secrecy surrounds the zigzag woman than any of the manufactured illusions being presented today. I tried to uncover how it works for *Big Secrets* in 1982 and failed. None of the major magic suppliers sold workshop plans for it. Magicians wanting to learn how it works were required to buy the three-section cabinet. Catalogue prices range from $1,495 to $1,695 plus shipping, and per standard policy, you can't return it after you've learned about it. The illusion appears not to be patented, at least not under the name of inventor Robert Harbin, so no public record of its inner workings is available. Doug Henning required his assistants to sign a secrecy agreement forbidding disclosure of this illusion, among others.

The zigzag woman blows the regular sawing-a-woman-in-half illusion right out of the sky. The apparatus is a large, three-part rectangular cabinet on a wheeled base that is pushed out in full view of the audience. The cabinet's sections resemble three stacked boxes. A human form is painted on the front.

The front of the top box contains oval openings for a face and a hand. The middle section has a similar opening for a hand. In some models it also has a small rectangular door. The bottom section contains an opening for a foot.

Each of the three sections has a door on the side. The doors are opened, allowing a female subject to enter the cabinet, and then secured shut. The woman's face, both hands, and one foot show through the appropriate openings. Henning gives her a handkerchief to hold in each hand, and the silks dangle out the openings. He remarks on the color or style of the woman's shoes. The cabinet can be examined from various angles. It does not seem to have any connection to the backdrop. The wheels raise the entire apparatus a short distance from the floor, ruling out (?) a trap door to allow the woman to escape.

In a borrowed bit of business from standard sawing illusions, Henning brandishes two sheets of metal. The bladelike sheets are inserted between the top and middle and between the middle and bottom sections. The woman is cut in three.

Henning slides the center section of the cabinet to the left. The woman's midsection shears cleanly to the side. A tray with a diagonal support attached to the left side of the bottom section props up the center.

Your natural reaction is to check the openings. The face is still the face of the woman who entered the cabinet — a living, breathing, moving face and not a fake. The face can talk and answer questions. If it is *not* the woman who went into the cabinet, it is her identical twin sister.

Identification of the other anatomical features is less absolute. You couldn't swear in court that you recognized the hands and foot as belonging to the original woman and no one else, but you are given no reason to believe that another woman or women are involved. The hand in the top section still grasps the handkerchief and moves it. So does the hand in the middle compartment. The foot is a moving foot (the toes wiggle) wearing the same shoes. When the cabinet has the small rectangular door in the middle section, the door is opened to expose a swatch of the woman's dress.

Ultimately, of course, the sections are squared up and the woman steps out unharmed. "Be the first in your area to 'knock them for a loop,'" blusters the description of the zigzag cabinet in the Louis Tannen catalogue. "Take it from us, if you're looking for the perfect illusion to start you off in the presentation of illusions, THIS IS IT!!!"

Red Herrings

Regular sawing illusions use partial mannequins or a second woman. The feet you see sticking from the cabinet are either fake or another woman's. There seems no doubt that the foot in the zigzag woman cabinet is real, however.

There is the dwarfs-and-amputees theory. It has been seriously suggested that a pair of three-foot-tall women are used. The bottom section is mildly suspicious. It's about half the height of the entire cabinet. A very short person could fit in there. Maybe a not-so-short person could crouch down in the bottom section.

But the woman who enters (and leaves) the cabinet is of approximately average height. It's clearly her face you see when the cabinet is divided.

All right, allow that the face is that of the original woman. She could be lying on an unseen plank projected from the backdrop, facing squarely forward. That would be uncomfortable, but possible. The foot in the bottom section would be from another woman. No one really knows whose foot it is. There is opportunity for a quick switch as the cabinet is rotated or as the magician passes in front of the cabinet.

Audience members knowing a little about magic might suspect that the woman's missing center section is concealed by a diagonal mirror. One old illusion was a living head resting on a triangular table. Mirrors between the table's legs reflected the sides of a folding screen. The audience thought it could see under the table, to the screen backdrop. Actually, the person's body was in the triangular nook between the mirrors and the screen.

A sort of zigzag illusion could use a diagonal mirror in the "empty" midsection, running from front left to back right. The mirror would reflect whatever was offstage right 90 degrees to the audience — probably a curtain or screen matching the backdrop. The audience would think it was seeing through the midsection. (The edges of the mirror, always a giveaway, could be concealed by the cabinet's edge ornamentation.)

The woman would be scarcely cramped by the mirror. For the "detached" hand, she would merely reach out to the side under cover of the mirror. The other hand, face, and foot would also be legitimate.

The handkerchief dangling from the hand in the top section would cast a reflection in the mirror, but it would not be visible to the audience. The mirror would have to slide into place as the center section is pushed out.

Neither the mirror nor the multiple women theories fit the Harbin-Henning trick, however. Tannen's catalogue copy says: "This illusion can be done under any and all conditions. . . . IT IS COMPLETELY ANGLE PROOF!!" The performer can and does put his hand or head in the space left by the midsection. He can stand behind the cabinet and be seen through the space. The empty cabinet is not a mirror.

The entire cabinet, divided, can be turned around. Nothing projects from the back. Other people onstage (audience volunteers or a TV show's host) claim that they can't see how the trick is done.

A safe assumption about any good illusion is that it has an optimal design. No simple modification ought to make it better; if it did, they would have made it that way. Taking that into account, several features of the zigzag woman stand out.

1. There must be a good reason why the four openings aren't any larger. The trick would be better yet if we saw more of the woman. Why not take the front of the cabinet off and let us see the whole woman? There must be something in there we're not supposed to see.

2. As far as I can tell, the woman is always the performer's assistant. On some Doug Henning TV performances, it's a celebrity guest star. The woman is *never* an audience volunteer. It seems that the woman has to know how the trick works and cooperate.

3. The division of the cabinet is peculiar. A three-section cabinet could be divided into even thirds. Instead, the bottom section is large and the middle is small. I got a press release photograph of the zigzag woman illusion and measured the proportions. The relative heights are about 45% (bottom, not including wheeled platform), 20% (middle), and 35% (top).

The Girl Without a Middle

Henning and others perform an illusion that seems to be a distant cousin to the zigzag woman. It has long been known as the girl without a middle. Henning seems to avoid doing both illusions in the same performance.

Abbott Magic sells workshop plans of the girl without a middle. This illusion uses a different type of cabinet, one equipped with doors in the front that open out to reveal the cabinet interior. A woman enters the cabinet from the front. Handcuffs and shackles secure her arms and legs in the cabinet. The various doors are closed. With all doors closed, no part of her body is visible.

Two metal blades are fitted into the cabinet from the side. The blades divide the woman at neck and thigh levels. First the door concealing the head and then the doors covering the legs are opened. The head and legs are still in place. But when the middle doors are opened, the cabinet is seen to be empty.

To further establish that the woman has no middle, the magician opens the back of the cabinet. The back of the middle section is on a horizontal hinge that opens away from the audience. The magician can peer through the hole from behind, and you see him plainly. There are no mirrors or false backs. Then the doors are closed, the blades are removed, and the woman steps out of the cabinet unharmed.

In 1983 Harry Blackstone, Jr., performed this illusion on an experimental 3-D TV broadcast on Channel 11 in New York. You had to wear special glasses. To prove the woman had no middle, Blackstone's assistants stabbed the empty space with swords, Dr. Tongue style. The 3-D effect was sorely lacking.

The-girl-without-a-middle illusion sounds better than it looks. It is designed for use onstage, where the audience is some distance away. It doesn't play so well on television, 3-D or otherwise, where tight camera shots are expected, for the woman's head is a fake.

Anyone standing off to the side can see what happens. As the woman gets into the cabinet, her head fits into a hollow in a false back to the head compartment. The false back is on a swivel. The other side of the concavity is a convex fake head. As soon as the door to the head compartment is closed, the woman swings the fake head around so it

201

faces the front and covers her face. She can use her hands (the hand-cuffs are large enough to slip off). The fake head has to be custom-molded to match the features of the subject.

The leg shackles attach around the knees. The woman adopts a sitting position. Her lower legs, still in the chamber, will be visible when the lower doors are opened. The legs bend naturally at the knee, the joint concealed by the shackles. Fake thighs make it look like the woman is standing. As the back to the middle section is opened, the woman is sitting on a secret seat that juts out below the hinge of the back. The back section is reclosed so that the woman will not be visible when the front doors are opened.

The top blade divides the fake head from the missing body. The lower blade goes just over the lap of the sitting woman. When the doors are opened, the body is indeed missing. The head does not move but the feet do. The magician must take care that no audience members are far enough to either side to see the woman sitting behind the cabinet. Ornamental wings on the corners of the cabinet help to restrict the view. The woman grabs a bar on the back of the middle section of the cabinet and hangs on as the magician opens out the back. The audience never suspects that the woman is hanging behind and underneath the back panel that the magician, as effortlessly as possible, opens for a moment or two. As the doors are closed and the blades removed, the woman returns to her original position in the cabinet.

Despite surface similarities, the girl without a middle can't be very similar to the zigzag woman, for the zigzag woman can blink her eyes and move her mouth as she talks.

For a long time, I was all but convinced that the woman had to be in the top compartment only. I was a guest on a TV show where the producer wanted to discuss this illusion. I told him that I had been unable to find out how it was done, though I suspected that the woman was in the upper box. As it happened, the producer had some excellent footage of the zigzag illusion, taken from a variety of camera angles. We watched it over and over and decided that the woman could not possibly fit in the top compartment — it wasn't deep enough.

The code of secrecy surrounding the zigzag woman has recently eased. The Louis Tannen company now offers a workshop plan for it. I also found someone who had been associated with the company that makes Henning's equipment — and who sneaked inside the cabinet.

An Optical Illusion

What do you find if you peek inside the zigzag cabinet? The answer is *nothing*. Each of the three boxes is completely empty. The zigzag illusion vanishes right before your eyes. There are no mirrors (I still hadn't completely written that off), no mechanical, electrical, or optical devices. You can skim the illusion blueprints for some time before you have any idea what's going on.

The blueprints don't show how the woman fits into the cabinet, and the manuscript has but a note on how the thing actually works. The plans are the handiwork of Paul Osborne, not inventor Harbin. Harbin is evidently dead, as Osborne speaks of him in the past tense. Osborne says that his plan incorporates certain features that other manufacturers have added to the illusion over the years.

Let's start with a few fine points, for the zigzag illusion is an orchestration of details. The cutouts for the hands are backed with black elastic material. The hands pass through a slit in the material. That way, the spectators cannot see the wrist and arm (which would not be in the expected positions). The hand actually protrudes from the cabinet. That leaves no doubt that it is a living human hand.

Minor problem areas are the tops and bottoms of the boxes. There are no interior partitions to the cabinet, of course. The top box has no bottom, the bottom box has no top, and the middle box has neither. You would expect to be able to see down into the middle box when it is pushed over. Since the blades do not cover the full widths of the boxes, it would also be possible to see up into the top box and down into the bottom box as well. (The tray covers the bottom of the middle box.)

To prevent peeking, three rollers are attached to the cabinet. These work like horizontal window shades. As the middle box slides left, three strips of black fabric roll out to cover the open areas.

I was completely wrong about the woman being in the upper compartment. The depth of all three compartments is about 15 inches. It would be like hiding in a picnic basket.

In a word, the secret of the zigzag woman is *fudging*. Nothing is quite as it seems. There is no one secret compartment or trap door. The woman hides in the aggregate misperception of the cabinet's

203

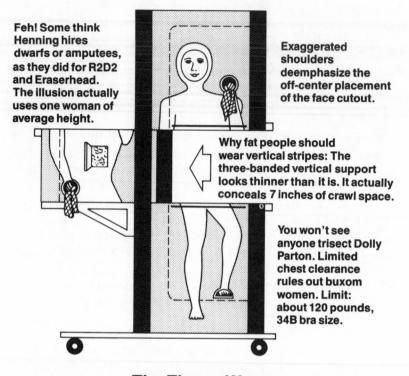

Feh! Some think Henning hires dwarfs or amputees, as they did for R2D2 and Eraserhead. The illusion actually uses one woman of average height.

Exaggerated shoulders deemphasize the off-center placement of the face cutout.

Why fat people should wear vertical stripes: The three-banded vertical support looks thinner than it is. It actually conceals 7 inches of crawl space.

You won't see anyone trisect Dolly Parton. Limited chest clearance rules out buxom women. Limit: about 120 pounds, 34B bra size.

The Zigzag Woman,

dimensions. Optical illusion is piled on top of optical illusion, yielding just enough crawl space for a slender, limber woman.

Think of the familiar optical illusions: the two lines that seem of different lengths but are the same or the bulging lines that are straight and parallel. You can't put your finger on one detail of the diagrams and say, here is the optical illusion. The illusion lies in the totality of the diagram. The same thing might be said of the zigzag woman.

The head, both hands, and the foot are all real. You can reach in and touch them; they are not mirror images. All are part of the same woman. Only the view of the woman's midsection through the optional door in the middle section is fake. All you see is the woman's dress showing through. That's all that's in there — foam rubber covered with material matching the woman's outfit.

204

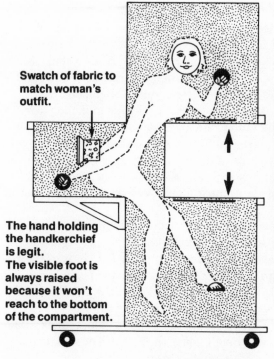

Swatch of fabric to match woman's outfit.

Brain-dead Miss America smile conceals the uncomfortable posture: The woman's neck and upper torso are craned 90 degrees to face forward.

Metal blades. The handles are much wider than the blades or the painted strips around the slots. The woman's position is *less* comfortable when the three compartments are squared up than when they are zigzagged.

The hand holding the handkerchief is legit.
The visible foot is always raised because it won't reach to the bottom of the compartment.

Inside and Out

The woman inside is bent at the hips. Her neck is twisted almost 90 degrees to face straight forward (this is uncomfortable). Her breasts are just inside the top compartment. The side of the top blade presses against her ribs. Her hips are in the lower part of the middle compartment. The side of the lower blade touches her thighs.

How can the woman fit such a tight squeeze? There are a number of tricks involved. None is sufficient by itself, but they add up to the illusion as we know it.

The person to be zigzagged has to be thin and short. Osborne's manuscript says the subject must be under 120 pounds and about 5'4".

The crude representation of the woman's figure on the front of the cabinet is crucial to the trick. It gives a false impression of the woman's posture inside the cabinet. In Osborne's blueprint the design is simple and geometric. Shoulders are emphasized. The head (with the oval cut out for the woman's face) is well to the left of center. This arrangement is minimized by the wide shoulders. The cutout for the hand on the right balances the composition.

The painted woman's waist is thin and centered on the cabinet front, with plenty of space to either side. When the middle section slides over, even a few inches, the design looks out of alignment.

The hand cutout in the middle section is always on the left side. In the bottom section, the cutout for the foot is raised about 6 inches from the bottom. The painting of the figure justifies this by showing the woman's left foot (on the audience's right) as slightly bent at the knee. In fact, the foot has to be raised because it won't reach all the way to the floor of the compartment. A footstep may be built in the cabinet.

The metal "blades" are not as they appear, either. The audience sees the slots for the blades passing through the painted figure on the front of the cabinet. The top slot slices through the chest of the silhouette, and the bottom one severs the legs from the pelvis. They see the magician insert blades matching the slots in the cabinet and assume that they are trisecting the real woman inside.

The blades and slots are not as wide as the audience thinks. The handles for the blades are much wider than the blades, particularly on the left side. The slots are painted black on the cabinet, and the black paint extends far beyond the slots. According to our informant, the insertion of the blades is the most uncomfortable part of the illusion for the person inside. There is more room once the middle section is moved over.

One consistent feature of the zigzag cabinet's paint job is the trim on either side of the cabinet. The left and right sides are painted in a contrasting (usually darker) color. The strip of dark color is 3 inches wide on each side, according to Osborne's plans. On the left, a strong metal bar is centered in this painted region. This bar attaches the top box to the bottom. When the middle box slides over, it must support the weight of the top box.

Everyone is suspicious of that dark strip at first. The middle box slides behind the strip. That means you can't see any overlap the magician leaves behind it. But the strip is only 3 inches wide. That's not wide enough for the woman to squeeze in to.

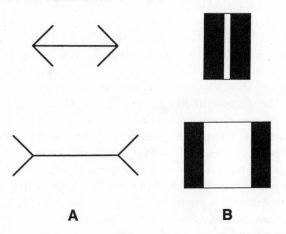

A   **B**

The right strip of the middle box is *not* pushed over so that it coincides with the support strip. It doesn't even touch the support strip. There is about an inch of the lighter-colored face of the middle box visible between the two strips, even when the box is pushed over fully.

That means there is about a 7-inch overlap — the support strip (3 inches), the sliver of the lighter-colored region (1 inch), and the dark strip on the middle box's right side.

An optical illusion minimizes the overlap. Look at figure *a*, where two lines with arrow shapes on their ends are compared. The lines are the same length, but the top one looks shorter. The eye tends to subtract the length of the arrows at the top and add their length at the bottom.

Figure *b* is a similar illusion. The width of the three-banded rectangle at the top is the same as that of the middle white band at the bottom. Since the eye tends to add on the two black bands at the bottom, the bottom white rectangle seems larger than it is.

The zigzag cabinet's paint job incorporates an optical illusion identical to the top of *b*. Spectators are impressed, at least subconsciously, by the thinness of the 1-inch light region. The mind tends not to add up the three bands of contrasting colors and realize that between them there is a significant overlap — 7 inches' worth. Even the total width seems shorter than it is, as in the top examples in *a* and *b*.

The front of the middle box has a sliding panel secured by tracks. It's this panel, mostly, that you see as the front of the middle box. The painted design of the woman's midsection and the cutout for her hand are in this panel. Behind this thin panel is the "real" front of the middle box.

The woman enters the cabinet through the three-section door in the front. The door is on hinges and opens out naturally. Both the sliding panel and the real front of the middle box have matching hinges. To open the door, the panel must be positioned so that its hinge is directly over the hinge in the front of the middle box.

The sliding panel is about 6 inches narrower than the middle box; there is room for it to slide 3 inches to the left from its initial position. While the middle box is pushed as a whole to the left, the sliding panel moves the 3 extra inches to the left. The middle section of the front design looks all the more out of alignment.

How is this possible with the cutout? Although the cutout the audience sees (in the sliding panel) is circular, it goes over an oblong cutout in the real front of the box. There is black elastic backing behind the entire oblong cutout. As the cutout in the sliding panel shifts, so does the hand. The foam rubber fake of the woman's midsection is handled similarly.

· 26 ·

DAVID COPPERFIELD'S STATUE OF LIBERTY DISAPPEARANCE

On April 8, 1983, CBS broadcast a special in which illusionist David Copperfield made the 225-ton Statue of Liberty vanish from New York Harbor. Miss Liberty's disappearance was billed as "the illusion of the century." Copperfield's performance was a disarming and mystifying experience for millions of television viewers.

The illusion does not — cannot — fully live up to its premise. There are physical and psychological laws to be reckoned with. And everyone knows the Statue of Liberty isn't going anywhere.

It makes no difference that you can't see the vanished statue. You *know* it's still there, somehow. No matter how superb the illusion may be otherwise, no one is going to suspend disbelief and think it really did disappear. Or are they?

The disappearance took place at night. There were two audiences for the illusion: the television audience and a live audience on Liberty Island. The latter folks were "drawn from all walks of life" (there was a priest). The spectators included Michelle Lee and William B. Williams.

The live audience sat in chairs. They had a somewhat restricted view of the statue and its surroundings. Copperfield had constructed a proscenium arch between the audience and the statue. Two wide towers supported a curtain between them which could be closed to conceal the statue. The audience saw the statue only through the proscenium. So did the TV cameras.

A circle of lights on the ground around the base illuminated the statue. There were searchlights, too. A helicopter hovered around the site to take pictures for TV. Copperfield also had a "radar" screen showing a blip that supposedly marked the statue.

This was Copperfield's agenda: You'd see the statue. The curtains would close. The curtains would *stay* closed for some time. Then the curtains would open and the statue would be gone. Copperfield would reverse the same steps to bring it back.

Copperfield editorialized for the TV audience on the sheer impossiblity of it all: "If it were possible to lower [the statue] into the ground with elevators, it would take fifteen minutes." A flotilla of helicopters would be required to lift the statue, Copperfield claimed. He mentioned getting special permission from the U.S. Government. This made you wonder just how much fiddling with national monuments James Watts's Department of the Interior would stand for. Would they let someone dismantle the statue if he promised to put it back together?

Three Kodak flash cameras (Eastman Kodak was a sponsor) were positioned to take instant pictures of the statue automatically. Several provocatively clad models stood nearby in the TV camera shot. These cameras at least shot the statue from around the curtains. Copperfield emphasized that he had no control over the flash cameras once they started clicking away. A picture taken before the disappearance showed the statue plainly enough, with a model in the foreground.

The curtains closed. Copperfield launched into a lengthy soliloquy. "Freedom is the true magic," he said. "It's beyond the power of any magician." He talked about how his mother had been an immigrant to America. You know a magician is stalling when he talks about his mother. The telecast broke for a commercial while the curtains were closed.

It must be emphasized that there were no TV pictures of the statue as it was dematerializing behind that curtain. The TV audience saw nothing that was hidden from the live audience, and the live audience saw nothing but two towers and a curtain between them.

Finally they came back from the commercial break and the curtains parted. There was nothing there — nothing visible, at any rate.

The TV cameras showed the circular ring of lights. The searchlights swept back and forth, revealing nothing. It looked as though they had created some sort of artificial fog to make the searchlight beams visible. There were a lot of helicopter shots that left you unsure of what you were seeing or from what angle. But neither the statue nor a suspicious silhouette was visible.

Once the statue had diappeared, Copperfield showed that the blip had vanished from the radar screen. He went over to one of the automatic cameras. It had cranked out a pile of photos, and Copperfield leafed through them. The earliest pictures showed the statue. Later pictures showed only the models — nothing where the statue should have been. There were no transitional pictures showing any funny business going on. First the statue was there, then it wasn't there.

Copperfield had an hour to fill. (Much of the special was small-scale magic requiring considerably more dexterity and psychological manipulation than the Statue of Liberty trick.) It seems reasonable that he might have wanted to draw out the disappearance part of the illusion for effect. He'd probably want to be a lot quicker in bringing the statue back, though, I thought, for the reappearance is anticlimactic. It wasn't faster.

The curtains closed again. Copperfield waxed patriotic, telling the audience to think of the word "freedom" — "freedom, and how easily it can be lost." After another interval, the curtains were opened to reveal the statue restored to its rightful place.

Speculation and Hearsay

I took the ferry to Liberty Island to search for any spoor of the trick's workings. There is no permanent outdoor seating on the island, so the chairs must have been set up for the illusion. It was nonetheless easy to locate the area where the audience and proscenium arch must have been.

The Statue of Liberty is on the east end of a roughly oval island. Liberty Island is small, and much of it is given over to tourist facilities and administration buildings. There is only one large open area on the island, a grassy mall extending west from the statue. The day I went, this area was occupied by rubble from the restoration of the statue. The areas on either side of this mall are wooded with large trees that did not seem to have been disturbed recently. On the seaward side of the statue, there just isn't room for an audience.

There is an information booth right as you come off the boat to Liberty Island. I asked the guy manning it if he knew how they made the statue disappear. He said it was a television trick. I said I had figured that out. Did he know any details? He said he heard that they cut away to a model of the statue and the real statue didn't move. It didn't sound as though he knew a whole lot about the matter, but take that as hearsay: "They cut away to a model of the statue."

The Statue of Liberty does not glow in the dark. Suppose they just cut the lights off. How visible would it be against the night sky?

There is a lot of scattered artificial light in the New York area. From Battery Park, at the tip of Manhattan, the statue *is* faintly visible at night, even with the lights turned off. I don't see how the statue could fail to be visible under similar circumstances to Copperfield's audience right on Liberty Island and several hundred feet from the statue. The faint outline of the unlighted statue might not show up on television, but it would have to be visible to the live audience. They interviewed the priest on camera, and he said he didn't have any idea how the trick was done.

The Statue of Liberty has a green patina. Green reflects light better than black. What if Copperfield somehow changed the color of the statue? What if he painted it black, or what if he had a big black bag hidden in the torch or crown and pulled it down over the statue?

It would probably still be visible in silhouette. Even the sky in the New York area is faintly lighted at night. If it were a cloudy or hazy night, the silhouette would be prominent.

A Giant Lazy Susan

According to *Bigger Secrets'* informants, who include a person directly connected with the production, the disappearance was done like this.

The easiest part of the trick to explain is the radar screen. The blip looked too perfect, as though it was part of a video game animation. That's what it was.

The trick was in that proscenium arch and in an unnoticed (by TV viewers) platform on which the chairs were set. Both were part of a gigantic motorized lazy Susan. While the curtains were closed, the

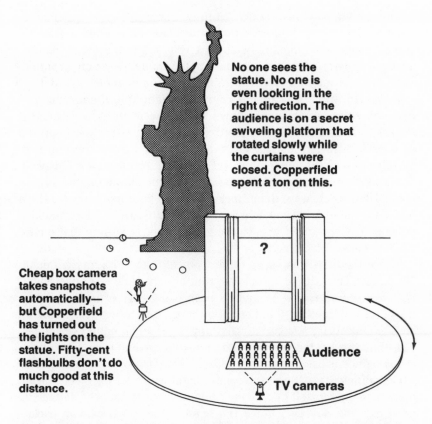

No one sees the statue. No one is even looking in the right direction. The audience is on a secret swiveling platform that rotated slowly while the curtains were closed. Copperfield spent a ton on this.

?

Cheap box camera takes snapshots automatically— but Copperfield has turned out the lights on the statue. Fifty-cent flashbulbs don't do much good at this distance.

Audience

TV cameras

entire audience, along with the arch, were turned mechanically — very, very slowly — to the side. Both the motion and the cumulative shift were imperceptible to the audience. When the curtains were opened again, the audience was looking to the side of the statue, which was actually behind one of the towers.

The towers were so brightly lighted that the audience was night-blind. Even if a bit of the statue — now dark — was within some viewers' field of vision, it would not have been noticed.

There were two rings of lights: the real ones around the statue and a duplicate set somewhere else. While the statue "vanished," the original set was turned off. The TV people cut to shots of the duplicate site. Viewers at home saw searchlights probing the empty space in the center of the duplicate ring of lights.

The camera ploy was so silly it's funny. Come on — how much light is a Kodak flash bulb supposed to put out? The statue is 305 feet high, and the cameras seemed to be at least 100 feet from its base. As any amateur photographer knows, a flash bulb would have no effect at that distance. You might as well take a flash picture of Halley's comet.

Even with the flash cameras pointed straight at it, there is no way the dark statue could have shown up in the pictures. The nearby models, standing just a few feet from the flash, were necessary to demonstrate that the cameras were working, so the cameras churned out pictures of the models instead of totally blank photos. In each picture you could see a blank space where the statue ought to have been. The models were the primary source of light in the shots. They provided enough reflected light so that the shutter would close quickly. Otherwise, Copperfield could have gotten time exposures that might have revealed the statue.

These methods raise some philosophical issues, I suppose, about TV magic. The cuts to a duplicate ring of lights and the faked radar blip are camera tricks. Magicians have been leery of using camera tricks (or any method that could not be used in a live performance) on TV. Obviously, you can do anything at all on an edited videotape. The thinking has been that magic loses its credibility on TV unless the audience is assured of an undoctored version of what went on.

Copperfield has a long-term commitment with CBS for specials, and he tries to top himself in each one. But after you've made a jet vanish, what can you do next? Once you bend the rules on camera tricks, there is no turning back. The problem of surpassing past feats — of ultimately trying to do something so impossible that the illusion is defeated by its own implausibility — is not new to magic. Harry Houdini crossed that same fine line in the 1920s with an elephant's disappearance. As a review of Houdini's put it: "Two assistants wheeled a raised platform out onto the stage and spun it around to show all four sides. Curtains hanging from a framework on the platform could be opened and closed. An elephant lumbered up onto the platform, the curtains were instantly reopened, the elephant had completely vanished, and *eight* assistants pushed the platform off-stage."

The Statue of Liberty was show number five. Copperfield's sixth CBS special had him levitating across the Grand Canyon, the wire gleaming in the desert sun if you looked carefully.

· 27 ·

AMUSEMENT PARKS

*T*he demented thirteen-year-old in all of us knows that the whole point of amusement parks is watching other people freak out. But nothing threatens your smug, detached feeling of superiority more than being scared out of your wits. Face facts. One in fifteen thousand persons who go into an amusement park leaves in an ambulance. And the most popular attractions are often "mystery" rides, where you don't find out what you're getting into until it's too late. We went through some of America's dire amusements, touching, prodding, leaning over the railing, and pressing nose against glass.

Haunted Mansion

Disneyland/Walt Disney World
Anaheim, California/Lake Buena Vista, Florida

The Haunted Mansion is a showplace of spookhouse special effects. Many are found in similar rides elsewhere. From the outside, the mansion is a three-story French Colonial affar. People are admitted in groups of about fifty at a time. You walk from an entrance foyer into an octagonal room with large portraits on the wall. When the entire group is inside, the door closes flush with the adjoining walls.

A strangely familiar voice welcomes you to the Haunted Mansion. The voice is that of Paul Frees, who did Boris Badenov in the Rocky and Bullwinkle cartoons. (Frees is also the narrator of the Abraham Lincoln animatron show at Disneyland.) Frees milks lines like "Every room has wall-to-wall creeps and hot and cold running chills" for all they're worth. The floor of the octagonal room slowly sinks to simulate a stretching room. Then a door opens and everyone walks out into a hallway.

The rotating busts. The first interesting effect is at the end of this hall. Two somber-faced busts of a funny pale orangish color are set into the wall. One of the busts has a neck slightly thicker than its head and a Moe Howard haircut. From a distance the heads look like simple decor, but as you come closer, you notice out of the corner of your eye that they seem to follow you. When you move to the right, the heads turn to the right. If you move your head back and forth, the heads rotate in perfect step. It's one thing to have a mechanical head rigged up to swivel, but the busts seem to know when you're looking at them. Some think they're holograms. They're not.

The secret? Reach over and touch the heads. They're hollow — inverted like a death mask. The noses, rather than being the part closest to you, are the part farthest, and so on.

The illumination comes from behind the translucent masks, so you don't see any telltale shadows. You normally don't expect to see anything so bizarre as an inside-out face, so you interpret them as normal, three-dimensional faces. This confuses the perspective. Instead of realizing that you are seeing different views of an inside-out face, you perceive a solid face rotating.

Once you know that the heads are inside out, you can usually see them as they really are. It helps to duck and look at them from a low angle. The (convex) 3-D effect is surprisingly prominent even in photographs.

The talking heads. Part of the Haunted Mansion is a real ride, a train of tunnel-of-love cars that go past fabricated scenes. Among the exhibits are spectacularly realistic animated heads. The first is a woman's head in a crystal ball. She is saying something, though I couldn't make out what. Later there is a gallery of singing statues. They are busts of men, character-actor types, mugging as you pass.

The heads are cadaverous white. The facial expressions change, the mouths contort, the lips move as they speak. The illusion of a real, living head is much stronger than with the two rotating, inverted heads. Nonetheless, you gather that they are not real heads with the bodies concealed. Even Disneyland wouldn't hire someone to grimace all day.

That there aren't human actors inside the heads is demonstrated by a final, tiny animated head as you leave the Haunted Mansion on a moving walkway. This is a female head about four inches long on a doll's body. Perched on a tombstone, it is wearing a white wedding gown and holding a bouquet of dead-looking flowers. This head spouts some kind of good-bye message in a half-intelligible voice.

The animated heads are simply movies. Actors were hired to mug for the camera with their heads immobile, and a short black-and-white film was shot for each head. The films are played in endless loops, projected on an essentially formless white head. I think there's a suggestion of a nose, but that's it. You see this formless head if you shine a flashlight on the heads or photograph them with a flash.

I snapped a flash picture of the last head as I passed it. When the picture was developed, it showed a head with much-faded features on the doll's body.

This effect seems to be too costly for most other amusement parks. Few organizations other than Disney have the resources to produce short movies just for a haunted house ride.

Cabaret du Néant. The Haunted Mansion has a ballroom with an assortment of animated ghosts eating at a table or dancing. The ghosts are a pale greenish color. You can see furniture and other objects through them, and one ghost floats high above the table. Two paintings on the wall periodically come to life as one figure draws a gun and shoots at the man in the adjacent painting. The ghosts' motion is more animatronish than human.

This effect dates back to the 1890s, at least. It was used in a sideshow presented in Paris and New York called the Cabaret du Néant, or Tavern of the Dead, and is still known by that name.

The secret is a large pane of invisible glass. In the Haunted Mansion version, you observe the ghosts from a moving train about fifteen feet above the floor of the ballroom. Directly below the train is a chamber containing animated robots. This chamber adjoins the visible part of the ballroom. There is also a chamber above the train cars; it contains the animatrons for the ghosts above eye level (the floating woman and the dueling paintings). The invisible glass runs from the floor up to the ceiling. There is a giveaway: if you look closely, you can see a fake spider on the glass pane.

The part of the chamber you see contains only the furniture. The animatrons, out of sight, are illuminated with a greenish light. The ghosts are the reflections of these animatrons on the secret glass pane. The viewing angle and the relative positions of the animatrons and the furniture are such that the ghosts appear to be seated, superimposed on a painting, and so on.

The reflections need not be of mechanical dummies. In the original Cabaret du Néant, the ghosts were reflections of human actors who were likewise out of the audience's view.

Cheesecloth ghosts. Not all the ghosts are reflections. At one point in the Haunted Mansion, swarms of indistinct ghosts rise from a graveyard. They are the same greenish color as the ballroom ghosts, but they involve a different m.o. These ghosts are rounded Arp forms with no internal detail. They look gauzy.

That's how they are made: A projector shines ghostly images on suspended sheets of a cheesecloth-like fabric. The fabric is a dark color so it won't be noticed where it's not directly illuminated. Victorian mediums pulled this same trick to impress clients at séances.

Hitchhiking ghosts. The climax of the Haunted Mansion comes at the end of the train ride. Frees's voice warns, "Beware of hitchhiking ghosts." You coast past a diorama with three animatron ghosts thumbing for a ride. The cars turn a corner and you pass a gallery of mirrors. In the mirrors you see a reflection of yourself, your car, and a green ghost apparently seated next to you. Everyone turns their head to see if the ghost is really in the car next to them. It isn't; it's just in the reflection.

The ghost is always in the center of the two-person car. When two people are seated normally, the ghost appears to be between them. If you sit in the middle, the ghost face is superimposed on your face. The hitchhiking ghosts are a two-way-mirror effect. They are projected from behind the mirror so as to merge with the normal reflected image.

The only original twist is getting the ghosts to move with the moving cars. The projectors must be synchronized to move with the cars on a parallel track behind the mirrors.

Club 33

Disneyland
Anaheim, California

Club 33 is Disneyland's secret club, the only place in the park where alcoholic beverages are served. It is so secret that many Disneyland employees don't know it's there, at 33 Rue Royale in New Orleans Square, near the Pirates of the Caribbean and just to the right of the Blue Bayou restaurant. It is identified only by the number "33" on an ornate oval plaque near the door.

To get in, you must be a member or a guest of a member. You talk into an intercom, and a buzzer beckons you in instant-teller style. An elevator takes you to the second-floor club. Membership is expensive (said to be about $10,000); there is a long waiting list. My informant says that membership is limited to about a thousand — few indeed, considering how infrequently one would go to Disneyland. Club 33 is open even when Disneyland isn't. During the winter, members are escorted from the park's front gate.

Beyond the door it is nothing like Disneyland, save in attention to detail and obsessive cleanliness. The staff wear blue tuxedos with a "33" logo. The menu has entrées such as Steak Diane for a fixed price of about $25. Waiters put ice cubes in your glasses one by one. When you get up from the table (there is a good view of the fireworks), you return to find a new napkin, freshly folded. There is a full wine list. When my informant ordered Riesling, they took away the wine glasses used with the entrée and served it in proper Riesling glasses. At each table is a matchbook engraved with the name of the guest. A Trophy Room displays Mrs. Disney's butterfly collection. The women's room has wicker toilets.

The story is that Disney had intended to live here and entertain dignitaries, so an apartment was built on the third floor. But Disney died before it was completed, and it was made into a private club. The third floor is used for Disney organization offices.

Club 33 is wired for sound: Tiny microphones are hidden in the chandeliers. My informant asked a waiter about this and was told that Disney had planned to eavesdrop on diners' conversations. The waiter also pointed out a china closet built to accommodate a hidden camera. (Security is a big concern at Disneyland. The Magic Kingdom has its own secret police, some of them dressed in cartoon character outfits.)

Yeah, you could say Disney got a little quirky in his old age. He apparently planned to talk to people through the moosehead in the Trophy Room. *It* has a hidden speaker.

Test of Strength

Various parks

Amusement parks, carnivals, and Popeye cartoons have a game called the "test of strength" or "high striker." A bell is mounted on top of a tall pole. The player strikes a lever device at the foot of the pole with a mallet. This sends a weight sliding up a wire attached to the pole. The pole is calibrated with point values or invidious comments on the player's grit (e.g., "Mama's boy"). You usually have to ring the bell three times (out of three tries) to win a prize.

Many of these games are fixed. If you stand aside and watch for a while, you may find that many persons can ring the bell once or twice, but no one ever seems to do it the three times required for the prize. The secret is in the wire supporting the sliding weight. This wire runs from the bottom of the pole to the bell, then passes through a loop or pulley and becomes one of the guy wires supporting the pole.

This wire is normally a bit slack, which means that the weight sways as it rises up the wire, hitting the pole and losing its momentum. No matter how fast the weight is traveling initially, it is almost impossible for it to make it up to the bell on a slack wire.

To make the game look easy, the concessionaire or a confederate leans against the faked guy wire. When the wire is taut, the weight rises much more easily. Often the proprietor will let players ring the bell on their first two attempts and then step free of the wire to sabotage their third.

Hell Hole

Astroland
Coney Island, New York

The really scary ride at Coney Island is the Hell Hole. Nothing on the outside gives any clue to what the ride is — other than the muffled screams, which make it sound like a miniature torture chamber. Its reputation as a superscary mystery ride gets a lot of kids to drag unwitting parents into it. The kids think it's loads of fun and the parents throw up.

The ride's façade is a multicolored tableau with monsters. "Abandon all hope you who enter here," the inscription says. Other signs cover all the legal bases. "Persons with heart condition, pregnancy, or children under 5 yrs. old not allowed on ride," one says. "This is not a dark ride. No refunds," another reads. "Beware of attack dogs" suggests unpleasant scenarios itself.

The Hell Hole organization does not scruple to pander to your voyeurism. A sign announces that a ticket gains you admittance to the ride itself *or* the observation deck. There is a circular stadium around the ride for such curiosity seekers.

Entering the Hell Hole, you ascend a rickety metal catwalk. An interior mural has a surprisingly risqué picture of a man holding the nipple of a nude fat woman's breast. An attendant admits you to the Hell Hole proper, a cylindrical room about twelve feet in diameter. The walls are wood; the floor is metal. Above you are the seats for people who are just watching. A roof encloses the cylindrical room and seats, but the construction admits ample daylight. There is a light above you for night use.

After a small number of customers are inside, an attendant appears in the voyeurs' section and switches the ride on. The room starts rotating about its center vertical axis. As it spins faster and faster, everyone is pressed flat against the walls.

What makes this different from other rides is that it *keeps* going faster. The forces in the Hell Hole are greater than on any roller coaster I have been on by a considerable margin. The faces of your fellow passengers are pulled back like Eva Gabor's second facelift. The room spins so fast that you have trouble breathing; it takes a conscious effort to expand your chest against the centrifugal force. The effect is distinctly uncomfortable enough to set you pondering about the essential sadomasochism of amusement parks. As the force multiplies, your head is jammed into the ridges of the wood plank wall. Your head is twisted to the side to lower its artificial center of gravity . . .

Then the floor drops away beneath your feet. It is difficult to turn your head to see how far the drop is, but I estimate from the outside dimensions of the building that it's about ten feet. The force is so great that you remain glued to the wall.

Gradually the rotation slows, which causes you to slide down the wall to the floor again. For the dénouement, the floor rises back up to its original position, pushing you along with it. The door opens and you are free to stagger back down the stairs. One of the passengers wanted to know what would happen if you threw up on the ride.

There is a wimped-down version of the Hell Hole at the Six Flags Great Adventure Park near Jackson, New Jersey. Called the Rotor Ride, it goes *much* slower — not fast enough to keep you pinned to the wall. The floor drops about a foot.

Aladdin's Magic Cave Playland

Ocean City, New Jersey

Aladdin's Magic Cave is a puzzling ride at the Playland amusement park on the boardwalk in Ocean City, New Jersey. The exterior is a papier-mâché mountain decorated with fake palm trees, a knife-wielding mannequin, and flashing red lights. It looks like a spookhouse ride with a Middle Eastern theme. What the ride actually is is not revealed.

Customers are led into the "cave" in groups of a half dozen or so. Passing through a green door, you find yourself in a claustrophobic chamber perhaps six feet wide by ten feet long by ten feet high. You stand on a bridge that you enter by a gate. The top of the bridge is at about waist level on an adult. Once everyone is on the bridge, the attendant closes the gate, leaves through the door, and locks it behind herself.

At first I thought the chamber was a passageway into a maze of some kind (it seemed too small to be the whole ride). The room is illuminated by an orange fluorescent light bulb. The wall of the chamber is spray-painted green and black with demonic eyes à la Kenny Scharf.

The bridge starts to sway, rotating back and forth on its long horizontal axis. Each swing arcs higher than before. Before long, the thing is doing a 180-degree arc and passengers are digging their nails into the wood railing. Finally, the swing does a complete loop-the-loop. Only centrifugal force seems to keep the customers from falling out when the swing is upside down. The effect is dizzying and unreal.

The ride is short. The swings die down, the attendant opens the door, and the passengers get out. Many leave dizzy, thinking they have survived a wild, possibly dangerous ride.

Yet something doesn't jell. You get the impression that the Magic Cave isn't what it seems. It took me a while to figure out what the tipoff was. It was the wind — rather, the lack of it. You feel a breeze against your face as the bridge rotates, but it's too weak for the speed at which the platform is moving.

Aladdin's Cave turns out to be a latter-day incarnation of a ride once called the Haunted Swing. It sounds like the cave is a cheap knockoff of the swing.

According to *The Great American Amusement Parks: A Pictorial History* by Gary Kyriazi, the Haunted Swing was a popular ride at Dreamland, Coney Island, in the early part of the century. Other Haunted Swings were built in Atlantic City and at the Midwinter Fair near San Francisco. The Coney Island ride was very successful for a couple of seasons and then was dismantled, for repeat business was poor. (There does not seem to be any such ride currently in operation at Coney Island.)

Customers entered through a door to a small room furnished as a living room. It had a chair, a cabinet, lamps, and pictures on the wall in contrast to the stark Aladdin's Cave. Suspended in the middle of the room was a large swing that almost filled the room. The swing was suspended from a large bent metal pipe running horizontally from one wall to the opposite wall, about ten feet above the floor. The room had an unusually high ceiling.

All the customers got in the swing and were firmly strapped in place.

Then the attendants left, and the swing began to rotate much as the Aladdin's Cave ride did. With the Haunted Swing, the axis of the rotation was far above the riders' heads rather than at waist level. The dimensions of the room were such that it looked as though the swing was going to crash into the ceiling when it made complete turns.

The secret of the Haunted Swing is that it's the *room*, not the swing, that is gyrating wildly. The room is a shell free to rotate about the big pipe (or about the axis of the bridge in Aladdin's Cave). Attendants give the swing a slight push to start it going before they leave. While the swing rocks gently, the room is rotated back and forth with inceasing arc. "The illusion was so perfect that the passengers would grab onto each other in fright, even though they were informed of the trick before they entered, for safety's sake," wrote Kyriazi of the Coney Island swing.

The operation of the original Haunted Swing was all manual. "The operatives do this without special machinery, taking hold of the sides and corners of the box or 'room,' " reported a turn-of-the-century exposé in *Scientific American*. I couldn't tell if the Aladdin's Cave was motorized or manual. I saw only one attendant, the woman who let us in.

The omission of the homey mise en scène in Aladdin's Cave is disappointing. In the original Haunted Swing, everything in the room was glued in place. Carefully crafted details, like a vase containing water, an open book, a baby carriage, and a kerosene lamp (actually electric) reinforced the conviction that the room wasn't moving.

· 28 ·

BACKWARD MESSAGES IN RECORDS

*T*here really are backward messages on rock albums. And the controversy over "backward masking" and "porn rock" has inspired a whole new spate of messages. There may have been more genuine backward messages in the past few years than ever before.

The backward message controversy is usually traced to the 1960s and John Lennon's avant-garde sound mixing on such tracks as "Revolution 9" on the Beatles' *White Album*. Lennon probably wasn't trying to conceal a message so much as create an interesting sound.

The matter might have ended there had it not been for the Paul McCartney death rumor of 1969. College kids tried playing Beatles records forward, backward, and at various speeds to find "clues" to McCartney's fate. In the process they found snippets of speech from Lennon's experiments. Even after McCartney was found safe and sound in Scotland, some rock listeners continued to look for hidden messages.

Somehow, fundamentalist Christian groups became convinced (ca. 1982) that the alleged messages were commercials for devil worship. Not a single indisputable satanic message has turned up, but there were scattered attempts to ban or label certain albums. In 1986 one fundamentalist group announced that the theme song for the old *Mr. Ed* TV show contains the word "Satan" when played backward.)

Ironically, the publicity accorded nonexistent messages has inspired several artists — among them porn rock hearing witness Frank Zappa — to hide real background messages in their music. It's easy to do.

The performer speaks or sings the message normally, then reverses the tape, which is mixed into the soundtrack. This is all accomplished simply enough at any recording studio.

What's not so simple is playing it back. Most home record, cassette, and compact disk players won't play backward. You can turn a record backward with a pencil eraser, but it's not good for the needle or the turntable. The only way to reproduce the message with full fidelity is to use a professional-quality reel-to-reel tape player and splice the tape in backward.

We used the facilities of KLOS radio in Los Angeles to reverse some recent records containing true backward messages.

"Secret Messages"

Electric Light Orchestra, Secret Messages

ELO's *Eldorado* album was among those alleged to contain satanic backward masked messages. A patient listening to *Eldorado* played backward reveals no such messages. You hear only what you ought to hear — the reversed lyrics of the songs, which sound nothing like the "messages" claimed to be there. In the wake of such allegations, ELO did put an (innocuous) backward message on their *Face the Music* album. Perhaps they thought this would show how silly the allegations were. Instead, the backward-masking people seized on this as proof that the other "messages" were real. In the latest volley, ELO has named an album after the controversy.

In Britain (where the backward-masking issue is viewed as an American eccentricity), the cover of *Secret Messages* has a mock warning to youth about the hidden message. Word of the album's impending release in the United States caused enough of a furor to chill CBS Records into deleting the cover blurb.

The reversed message is easy to find. It's at the very beginning of the first song, which is itself called "Secret Messages." You can hear reversed speech when you play the record normally. A voice intones "secret messages" — forward — in the middle of the reversed speech, lest anyone dare be so unhip as to not know what's going on.

We transferred a new copy of *Secret Messages* to reel-to-reel tapes and played it backward. The backward message goes: *"Welcome to the big show./Welcome to the big show."*

That's it.

"Ya Hozna"

Frank Zappa, Them or Us

"Ya Hozna," a six-minute composition on the first record of the *Them or Us* double album, is *entirely* backward. The album's inner cover, which includes lyrics for the other songs, says, "backwards vocal — you figure it out" of this cut. It credits Frank and Moon Zappa, George Duke, and Napoleon Murphy Brock as vocalists.

Played forward, "Ya Hozna" sounds like a record played backward — reasonably so. The vocals are prominent and unintelligible. Moon Zappa's voice is curiously recognizable, even in reverse. It is hard to tell whether the music was recorded forward or backward.

When "Ya Hozna" is played in reverse, you discover that the music is virtually a palindrome — it sounds about the same forward and backward. The voices are all backward. In some cases they have been modified electronically. Many of the words are muffled. Even after repeated careful listening on both stereo tracks, it is difficult to make out many of the lyrics. It doesn't help that the words seem to be stream-of-consciousness nonsense. Some of the unintelligible stuff sounds like opera.

Starting at the beginning of the reversed tape — the end of the forward tape — the clearer vocals go like this: *"I am the heaven, I am the water."* This is in a hymnlike register. *"You're a lonely little girl./ But your mommy and your daddy hold you."* A singsong synthesizer voice.

The most interesting part of the lyrics is an intermittently orgasmic rap in Moon Zappa's Valley Girl voice. There are three short monologues:

> *I'm like green!*
> *I'm like squat!*
> *I'm like soul!*
> *Repeat, like soul!*
> *I'm like pull, push,*
> *Okay, like slow, slow.*
>
> *You're never too old*
> *Like slow, like slow, like slow*
> *Okay, I like it.*
>
> *All right, faster, faster,*
> *Go, do it, do it twice,*
> *Yeah, that feels good,*
> *I'm looking great.*
> *Yeah, fer shure!*
> *Like, no way!*

"No Anchovies, Please"

J. Geils Band, Love Stinks

"No Anchovies, Please" is a novelty song, really a narration with sound effects, about a woman who is kidnapped after eating anchovies. She is taken to a "foreign-speaking" country. The sound effect of the foreign tongue seems reversed. When you do play it in reverse, it becomes: *"It doesn't take a genius to know the difference between chicken shit and chicken salad."*

"Darling Nikki"

Prince, Purple Rain

"Darling Nikki," cited as porn rock before Congress, is about a dominatrix in a hotel lobby masturbating with a magazine. In part, the complaint was that the album cover (flowers, and Prince on a motorcycle) wasn't explicit enough to warn kids of the suggestive lyrics. Senator Paula Hawkins apparently was not aware of a backward message hidden in "Darling Nikki." The last thirty-five seconds of the song is gibberish. The music changes abruptly and becomes a repeated glottal sound. Then a two-syllable sound is repeated twice, something like "heaven, heaven." Unintelligible speech follows. At the end is a sound reminiscent of rain or bacon frying, and wind sounds.

Played backward, the message becomes:

Hello, how are you?
I'm fine 'cause I know that the Lord is coming soon.
Coming, coming soon.

It is clearly Prince and the Revolution singing this. The words are clear but the intonation is funny — they linger on some words. Perhaps this is to make the reversed message you hear playing the record normally less conspicuous.

This is a weird reversal of the supposed secret message menace. Raunchy forward lyrics conceal a religious secret message.

"Judas Kiss"

Petra, More Power to You

Petra is an obscure group that sings religious songs to a rock beat. As further proof that things have gone full circle, the backward-masking controversy prompted Petra to include a wholesome backward message on their *More Power to You* album. It is in the transition between two songs, just before "Judas Kiss." Clearly audible gibberish reverses to this (the husky voice a cross between George Beverly Shea and Dee Snider): *"What are you looking for the Devil for, when you ought to be looking for the Lord?"*

231

BRANDO TALKS

You've heard the stories about Brando in Tetiaroa. He plays chess, gains weight, and turns down scripts. Another way Marlon Brando occupies his time in Polynesia is with amateur radio. After a 1985 visit, director Roger Vadim revealed that Brando talks to ham operators all around the world using a secret alias.

Wouldn't ham operators recognize Brando's voice? Maybe not. Shortwave transmission can distort voices.

Tetiaroa is a coconut-clad atoll of the Society Islands, a twenty-minute plane ride north of Tahiti. Virgins used to be sent to Tetiaroa for ritual fattening before marriage. The first European to set foot on the island is believed to be Captain Bligh, who went there hunting *Bounty* deserters in 1789. The royal Pomare family gave the island to a British dentist, Dr. W. J. Williams, in 1904 in payment for their dental bills. The dentist's stepdaughter sold the island to Brando in 1966.

Brando had ambitious plans for Tetiaroa. He wanted to make it an ecological showplace. He was going to harvest nutrients from sea water and generate electricity from the sun and the wind. There would be an artists' and intellectuals' colony open to geniuses the world over. There would also be a self-contained village of Polynesians using eighteenth-century technology.

"Most of Marlon's ambitions for his island paradise have foundered in impotence," his former wife Anna Kashfi Brando wrote in *Brando for Breakfast*. "Perhaps ashamed of the lack of achievement, Marlon reacts defensively. When a reporter waded ashore on the private atoll to investigate the project's progress and, if possible, to obtain an interview, he was greeted with Marlon's fury: 'I'm going to give you to the count of three to get out, and then I'm going to punch you right in the face.' "

Brando reportedly lives on Tetiaroa all of his free time. He walks on the beach naked and sometimes sleeps under the stars. He built Tetiaroa Village, a small resort of bungalows and thatched huts, since destroyed by hurricane. A profusely illustrated brochure reveals that the village offered wind-surfing, outboard canoeing, excursions to uninhabited islets, French and Tahitian cuisine, and a well-stocked bar. Many of the women in the brochure are bare-breasted.

Okay, so you want to talk to Brando. There aren't that many ham operators out in the middle of the Pacific — not who speak English and sound something like Brando, anyway. The bearing for Tetiaroa (the antenna direction, measured in degrees clockwise from due north) is about 241 from the East Coast of the United States, about 209 from the West Coast. With most antennas, you need only be within about 10 degrees of the signal's true direction. Since he's in French Polynesia, Brando's call letters will start with F08. Tahiti is two hours behind the West Coast. Assuming Brando keeps normal hours — there's not much nightlife on Tetiaroa — and assuming that he favors the evening hours for his hamming, when signal propagation is best, the prime hours for contacting Brando ought to be around 8 P.M. to midnight French Polynesia time, or midnight to 4 A.M. in mid-America.

Brando might not sound like Brando. Single-side band and close talk microphones alter voices. The radio hobbyists I consulted felt that Brando's voice would not threaten his anonymity. The poor fidelity, plus the fact that most hams aren't expecting to hear Brando, makes the chances of recognizing the voice pretty small.

I asked several radio hobbyists if they knew anything of Brando's doings. Dave Ingram, a columnist for *CQ* magazine, checked his log of contacts and found that he had spoken with an amateur in French

Polynesia with call letters F08GJ. The amateur's name: *Martin Brandeaux.*

It seems as though it would be too great a coincidence for there to be another operator in French Polynesia with a name that similar. Ingram said that "only a couple" of amateurs with the French Polynesia prefix are active on the ham bands.

Brandeaux gave Ingram this address: c/o Radio Club of Tahiti, BP 5006 Pirae, Tahiti, French Polynesia. Our polite inquiry to this address, asking if he was indeed the movie star Marlon Brando, brought no reply.

· 30 ·

MOVIES

Disney's Lemming Snuff Film

In the pathetic lemming scene of *White Wilderness* (Disney, 1958), hundreds of the Arctic rodents dutifully toss themselves over a cliff into certain death in the icy Arctic waters. One of Disney's classic True Life Adventure nature films, *White Wilderness* purports to be a cinema verité look at the life of the Arctic. But lemmings *don't* commit mass suicide. As far as zoologists can tell, it's a myth. How did the Disney people document it on film?

According to a 1983 investigation by Canadian Broadcasting Corporation producer Brian Vallee, *White Wilderness*'s lemming scene was sheer fabrication. Vallee says the lemmings were pushed and, uh, thrown off the cliff.

White Wilderness's voice-over implies that lemmings take the plunge every seven to ten years to alleviate overpopulation. It's no picnic in the lemmings' "weird world of frozen chaos." "The lemmings quite literally eat themselves out of house and home," explains narrator Winston Hibbler as the lemmings pig out on the tundra. "With things as crowded as this, someone has to make room for somebody somehow. And so, Nature herself takes a hand."

Crazed rodents assemble for the mass migration. "A kind of compulsion seizes each tiny rodent and, carried along by an unreasoning

235

hysteria, each falls into step for a march that will take them to a strange destiny." The narration says that once they get the urge to move, the lemmings are oblivious to their fate. They are shown crossing a tiny stream. They will even swim lakes in their desperation. A few fall victim to birds and an ermine.

Hibbler plays up the psychological angle: "They've become victims of an obsession — a one-track thought: Move on! Move on!" A trumpet of doom sounds.

Finally, the fey pack approaches the Arctic Ocean. "They reach the final precipice. This is the last chance to turn back." Lump in throat, Hibbler blurts, "Yet over they go, casting themselves out bodily into space." The mixed-up rodents think this is "just another lake"!

The camera angle is fantastic. Lemmings are seen leaping into the sea from an airy vantage point far above. They remain in razor-sharp focus as they plunge into oblivion. You don't have to be a cinematographer to guess that this shot took a little advance preparation.

The final shot shows a leaden sea awash with dying lemmings. "Gradually strength wanes . . . determination ebbs away . . . and the Arctic Sea is dotted with tiny bobbing bodies."

Of course, certain scenes in nature films are staged as a matter of expediency and economics. On occasion, that means sacrificing an animal to show the natural cycle of predation. What has raised a few eyebrows about *White Wilderness* is the mass imperilment of animals to depict a mythical event.

According to Vallee, the lemming footage was filmed in Alberta — a landlocked province — and not on location in the lemmings' natural habitat. Lemmings do not congregate in that area, so the Disney people bought lemmings from Inuit children in Manitoba.

Once they got the lemmings to Alberta, they placed them on a giant turntable piled with snow. Carefully edited footage of the rodents' travails on the spinning turntable became the film's migration segment. Then, Vallee claims, they recaptured the lemmings and took them to a cliff over a river. When the well-adjusted lemmings wouldn't jump, the Disney people gave Nature a hand.

Allen Smithee

"Allen Smithee" is a pseudonym directors or others use when a movie turns out so bad that they don't want their name on it. (Union rules require that the director receive screen credit, so they need *some* name.) Among major films, *Death of a Gunfighter* (Universal, 1969) was directed by an Allen Smithee, and *Student Bodies* (Paramount, 1981) was produced by an Allen Smithee.

Who are these guys really? *Death of a Gunfighter*'s Allen Smithee has been unmasked as two respected directors, Robert Totten and Don Siegel. Totten, the original director, got into a fight with lead actor Richard Widmark (playing what one critic called a "singularly thankless role"). The studio brought in Siegel to replace Totten. Ironically, the *New York Times* had good words for the director: "Mr. Smithee has an adroit facility for scanning faces and extracting sharp background detail."

Student Bodies' Smithee was Michael Ritchie. The film was supposed to be a funny takeoff on adolescent splatter films. Vincent Canby felt that " 'Student Bodies' just slowly topples over as you watch it, like a stand-up comedian in the act of falling." Ritchie even took the precaution of naming the production company Allen Smithee Classic Films.

Gunga Din's *Ghost*

The ghost of Rudyard Kipling haunts George Stevens's *Gunga Din* (RKO Pictures, 1939) when it is shown on television. The film concludes with a scene in which the main characters pay their respects to the dead Gunga Din (Sam Jaffe). Colonel Weed (Montagu Love) reads the title poem over the body. You notice that something's funny from the way the camera shot is composed — the colonel, the only person in the shot, is strangely off center. If you look closely, you may notice an eerie blob to the side of the colonel.

The blob is all that's left of Rudyard Kipling. The film originally had Kipling (author of the poem the movie was, very loosely, based upon) as a minor character. But audiences didn't recognize the character, and the studio decided to erase him from the film — *not* edit out the scenes he was in, but erase him out of the very frames in which he appeared.

Rental videocassettes of *Gunga Din* contain the original version, Kipling and all. The Kipling character (who is not credited) appears only near the end. A short scene in Colonel Weed's tent shows Kipling in a cap, glasses, and mustache, looking unnervingly like Michael Palin. Kipling is scribbling the poem on a notepad. Several passages are struck out. Kipling gazes reflectively into the camera. Then the colonel takes a look at the poem. The dialogue in this scene does not ring with historical authenticity:

> Colonel: Very good, my boy, very good.
> Kipling: Thank you, colonel.
> Colonel: Not half bad.
> Kipling: Thank you, colonel.

The colonel suggests taking a look at the men. They go out and stand beside the three main characters and the dead Gunga Din. As the colonel appoints Gunga Din a posthumous colonel, Kipling steps into the scene. The colonel starts to say something about Gunga Din, and his voice falters. He turns to Kipling and asks him for the poem. The colonel then reads the poem. While he is reading, the shot shows the colonel and Kipling, the latter with a basset hound expression. The colonel and the soldiers wear military whites in the funeral scene. Kipling looks woefully out of place in his suit and tie, as if a studio executive had strayed into the shot.

Subliminal Shots

Film critics have long suspected that Alfred Hitchcock and other directors included secret images in their films to make them scarier. "Subliminal" shots are held to be tantalizingly brief images not consciously perceived or remembered by the viewer. They are supposed to be perceived on a subconscious level only and to establish a mood — usually suspense or horror.

There are no cinematic secrets in the VCR's brave new world. Now anyone with a videocassette recorder can step through such films frame by frame and see just what secret images may be hidden there. We rented cassettes of films alleged to contain subliminal shots and did just that.

The length of a brief shot may be measured by the number of frames of film it occupies. The minimum is a single frame. There are 24 frames per second in a movie, so a single-frame shot would be on the screen for just 1/24 second.

Examining a movie on videotape complicates things slightly because videotape contains 30 frames a second. In order to convert a movie to videotape, 6 "extra" frames per second are needed. What they do is to repeat every fourth frame of the movie. A movie that runs frame 1, frame 2, frame 3, frame 4, becomes a videotape that runs frame 1, frame 2, frame 3, frame 4, and frame 4 again. The pairs of identical frames can be identified in the videotape. For the following movies, we'll give the number of frames in the film (this being closer to the original editor's and director's intentions), even though the information came from videotape.

Spellbound

Alfred Hitchcock
Selznick International, 1945

Spellbound is claimed to have a subliminal flash of red — in an otherwise black-and-white movie.

The story's Dr. Murchison (Leo G. Carroll), director of a psychiatric hospital, is being forced out of his job after a nervous collapse. Near the film's end, Dr. Peterson (Ingrid Bergman) discovers that Murchison has murdered his supposed successor, Dr. Edwardes. She confronts Murchison late at night in his study. He pulls a gun from his desk and takes aim at her. The camera shows the room from Murchison's point of view, the gun looming in the foreground. (Hitchcock used a gigantic fake hand to achieve focus of both foreground and background.) Peterson edges toward the door as she tries to talk Murchison out of shooting. She leaves safely to call the police. Then the camera shows the gun turn toward the audience — that is, toward Murchison. It fires with an explosion of light.

A flash of red is barely detectable if you know to look for it. Most viewers don't see it. No one expects there to be color in a black-and-white film. Even if you think you catch a hint of the color, you're likely to think it your imagination.

Stepping through the sequence reveals three red frames. The first is filled with the radiating explosion, the second shows the explosion slightly subsided, and the third shows the smoking gun. About a dozen normal black-and-white frames of the smoking gun follow. All told, the red flash is on the movie screen for three times 1/24, or 1/8 second.

The color in the red frames looks unnatural. The explosion is white turning reddish yellow at the fringes. The room behind the gun is suffused with red, too, rather than its natural color. The red frames were hand-tinted on each print of the film, according to the studio.

Psycho

Alfred Hitchcock
Paramount, 1960

Two impressions nearly everyone has about *Psycho* are that the shower scene includes explicit, very brief shots of Janet Leigh's breasts that must have been scandalous at the time; and that it shows very gruesome, brief shots of Leigh being knifed. Both ideas are usually denied in discussions of the film. In a feature on a Hitchcock film festival, the *New York Times* said that when *Psycho* was released in 1960, "many people thought it was excessively violent and objected especially to the scene in which Janet Leigh is brutally stabbed to death in a shower. The scene, Hitchcock once said, took seven days to shoot, and involved 70 camera setups for what wound up being 45 seconds of film. Despite the violence, the knife never touches the body on the screen — the effect was created in the editing."

Clearly, the short scene was filmed and edited with unusual care. Many accounts mention that Hitchcock's wife, Alma, noticed that Leigh gulped at the end of the murder scene, when she was supposed to be dead. This amounted to just a few frames, but it was removed at the last minute. According to John Russell Taylor's biography, *Hitch*, some people even swear that the film switches into color during the shower scene, as in *Spellbound*. Hitchcock chose to film in black and white (unusual, by 1960, for a major film) to "avoid a wash of technicolor blood," claims Taylor.

Single-framing through the murder scene in the shower shows it to be generally understated. Breasts are visible in a short sequence, but only from an angle. (The body shots are not of Leigh, but of a model Hitchcock hired. Leigh did the face shots only.) The goriest shot is of the knife slightly penetrating the abdomen below the navel. Not a single frame is in color.

More interesting is an alleged "single-frame shot" some film critics have claimed to find in Tony Perkins's last scene. In *The Art of Alfred Hitchcock: Fifty Years of His Motion Pictures,* Donald Spoto states that the skull of Bates's mother is flashed over Bates's head.

Norman Bates (Perkins) is a serial murderer who runs a motel. Unhinged by the death of his mother, he keeps her preserved body in his house. Bates kills Leigh's character, stuffs her body in the trunk of her car, and heaves the car into a swamp behind the motel. The supposed subliminal shot comes at the very end, after Bates has been arrested. A cop takes Bates a blanket, and another cop (a young Ted Knight) locks his cell. Bates has now assumed the personality of his dead mother. He thinks to himself, his thoughts audible in his mother's voice, that he/she wouldn't even harm a fly. The camera comes in on Bates's grinning face. The scene switches to a shot of Leigh's car being hoisted out of the swamp. Then, "The End."

The shot of Bates in his detention cell gradually fades into the shot of the car being dredged from the mud. The transitional frames are double exposures. So far, nothing unusual. Single-stepping through the transition frames reveals a superimposed *third* image.

The third image is never the dominant one, but it is plainly visible in individual frames. It seems to be the mummified head of Bates's mother. An earlier scene showed the corpse's head with prominent teeth and hollow eye sockets. In the transition frames, the teeth are superimposed on Perkins's closed, grinning mouth. A ragged, dark shadow under Perkins's eyes seems to result from the shadows in the corpse's eye sockets. Another shadow on Perkins's forehead suggests the pulled-back hair of the corpse.

The image of the mother's head is at least slightly visible for about

51 frames of the film (64 frames of the videotape.) That means it is on the screen for about 2 seconds. However, the image is relatively prominent for only about 18 frames of the movie, or 2/3 second.

The mother's head is less noticeable than that suggests. Since the shot of Perkins is also fading into the shot of the car, you aren't quite sure what you're seeing. The corpse head is not likely to be noticed by someone not looking for it.

It's debatable whether Hitchcock thought the superimposed corpse image would make the shot scarier or whether he included it as an inside joke. It is possible that Hitchcock was influenced by the furor over subliminal images in films dating from 1956. In that year marketing researcher James Vicary tried flashing brief commercials for popcorn and Coca-Cola during movies and claimed success in creating demand at the refreshment counters. A couple of exploitation films were released in 1958 and 1959 using fleeting shots of skulls and other scary stuff to frighten the audience at appropriate points. *Psycho* was released in 1960. It's said that Hitchcock wanted to make *Psycho* because so many bad horror films were enjoying box office success.

Twilight Zone — The Movie

John Landis, Steven Spielberg, Joe Dante, and George Miller
Warner Brothers, 1983

Some people are convinced that they see John Lithgow's eyes pop out of his head in the *Twilight Zone* movie. This fleeting sequence is in the final segment, directed by George Miller. It is a remake of an old *Twilight Zone* TV episode that starred William Shatner. In the movie version, John Lithgow is a man who sees a monster on the wing of a commercial airliner. He tries to alert the other passengers and crew and is thought to be crazy.

Very fast cuts between Lithgow and the monster outside prevent you from getting much of a look at the monster until the end. The effect in question occurs just once, after Lithgow has taken a sedative and is trying to sleep. A knocking sound disturbs him. He opens the window shade. The monster is outside, looking in.

A shot of the monster runs for about 17 frames. Then it cuts to Lithgow's face for 10 frames. The monster reappears for 42 frames. Then there is a 5-frame shot of Lithgow's head incorporating the eye-popping subliminal.

The first 3 frames of the 5 show a slightly wild-eyed Lithgow. The fourth frame shows bulging eyes. The left eye is larger, glazed, and pointing to the right, somewhat like the monster's left eye. The final, fifth frame is the most extreme. It shows an egg-sized left eye and a bulging but smaller right eye. This 5-frame sequence is on the screen for 1/5 second, but the most distorted image is only visible for 1/24 second. Blink at the wrong time, and you miss it. But if you watch the shot carefully at normal speed, the sequence is detectable. Lithgow's eyes seem to inflate with an accelerated, cartoon-like quality.

Video for Wham!'s "I'm Your Man"
Columbia/CBS Records, 1985

Parental heat has cooled down music videos. Witness the gauzy "pink balloon" of the Tubes' "She's a Beauty" video, covering what was a giant, Philip Rothian breast in the days when MTV was young. Wham!'s "I'm Your Man" video, which started playing at the top of MTV's rotation schedule in December 1985, mixes sex and music with a subliminal message.

Most of the black-and-white clip is performance footage of Wham! and shots of dancing fans. Cut into the video are countdown numbers — the descending sequence of numbers that flashes by before the titles on prints of old movies.

"NINE" and "SIX" are usually written out so that they can't be confused even if the film is threaded into the projector upside down or backward. A normal countdown goes: 10, NINE, 8, 7, SIX, 5, 4, 3, 2, 1. The "I'm Your Man" video does not show a full 10–1 countdown, just fragments. The numbers run by faster than in an actual film countdown.

Three times you see "SIX" followed immediately by "NINE." Then it cuts to a couple kissing. That seemingly alludes to the sexual position (9 comes before 6 in a real countdown).

In the last countdown sequence, "SEX" replaces "SIX." In freeze-frame, the word is as clear as any word can be. It's *not* some blur you can interpret any way you want like Wilson Bryan Key's ubiquitous SEXs. Three frames of the video contain the word SEX. That means it's on the screen for 1/10 second — about as long as a blink of the eye. The SEX is further concealed from the conscious mind by the fact that the frames appear only after you have seen and gotten used to the SIX in the countdown.

Those who believe in the power of subliminal advertising would claim that the SEX makes people who see the video go out and buy the record as sublimation for their sexual desires. There is little if any evidence that subliminal ads work, though. A number of TV and radio stations experimented with subliminal messages in the 1950s and soon abandoned the idea. WAAF radio in Chicago tried to sell subliminal ads in 1957 at $1,000 for four hundred spots. In January 1958, the Canadian Broadcasting Corporation flashed the message "telephone now" during TV programming to see what effect it would have (viewers were warned of the subliminal but not told its content). The experiment flopped. People wrote CBC telling of sudden urges to change the channel, go to the bathroom, or get a beer.